Jen—
I'm passing along a read that found its way near and dear to my heart—seemed so fitting with life changes, turning 40, and mostly exploring and loving what we create!

I just want to thank you for jumping in without a second that and allowing me to get away, feel rejuvenated and find some peace!

I'm truly grateful and in awe of so many amazing people!!

♡ Kristen

MILE MARKERS

MILE MARKERS

THE 26.2 MOST IMPORTANT REASONS WHY WOMEN RUN

KRISTIN ARMSTRONG

Contributing Editor, **RUNNER'S WORLD**®

RODALE®

© 2011 by Kristin Armstrong

Rodale books may be purchased for business or promotional use or for special sales. For information, please write to:
Special Markets Department, Rodale, Inc., 733 Third Avenue, New York, NY 10017

Printed in the United States of America

Rodale Inc. makes every effort to use acid-free ♾, recycled paper ♻.
Portions of this book were previously published in August 2004 edition of *Runner's World*; June 2009 edition of *Runner's World*; and February 2007 edition of *Runner's World*.

Book design by Christina Gaugler

Library of Congress Cataloging-in-Publication Data

Armstrong, Kristin.
  Mile markers : the 26.2 most important reasons why women run /
Kristin Armstrong.
     p.   cm.
  ISBN 978-1-60961-106-4 (hardback)
  1. Women runners—Anecdotes.   2. Running for women—Anecdotes.
3. Marathon running.   I. Title.
  GV1061.10.W66A76 2011
  796.42082—dc22   2010050646

Distributed to the trade by Macmillan

  4 6 8 10 9 7 5   hardcover

RODALE

We inspire and enable people to improve their lives and the world around them
www.rodalebooks.com

*For my brother, Jon—who loves me enough to
trade some of his sleep for my happiness.*

For my parents—the best cheering section around.

*For my Sweat Sisters—I could not mark any miles without
you: Paige, Katie, Cassie, Hoochie, KT, Courtney, Jena, Ellen,
Amy, Amy, Dawn, Robyn, Dinah, Melissa, Alice, Jamie,
Terra, Nancy, Ashley, Jenni, Sara, Debra, Karen.*

*For my Sweat Brothers—I am a stronger woman for knowing
you: Scratch, Michael, Robert, and Gilbert.*

*For my children, the finest motivation I have ever known—
Luke, Isabelle, and Grace.*

Contents

1: WARMUP   1

2: BEGINNINGS   5

3: FRIENDSHIP   13

4: HEALING   31

5: PLAY   41

6: MOTHERS   53

7: KIDS   69

8: ENDURANCE   85

9: BODY   99

10: FREEDOM   111

11: IDENTITY   119

12: CONFIDENCE   127

13: FEAR   137

14: BURDENS   151

15: PEACE   161

16: PURPOSE   167

17: PASSION   175

18: HILLS   185

19: CLARITY   195

20: THE WALL   205

21: BALANCE   213

22: LOVE/HATE   223

23: RACE DAY   233

24: PACE   247

25: ROADBLOCKS   255

26: GRATITUDE   265

26.2: EPILOGUE   275

ACKNOWLEDGMENTS   277

ABOUT THE AUTHOR   279

1 WARMUP

In our high-speed-access, digital world, I am more like a paper calendar with a pink cover. I would rather write on paper, with ink. I would rather go see somebody than call them, let alone e-mail or text them. Today's humor is conveyed with "lol" and "☺" but I like to be able to recognize someone's laugh from across a room. I like licked mail, stationery with my name on it, and knowing someone's handwriting at a glance. I think it's important to be able to spell without spell-checker. You could say that in many ways I am an old-fashioned gal. So when my boss at *Runner's World* magazine approached me back in 2006 about writing a blog for the *RW* Web site, I was not entirely comfortable. Make a connection, over cyberspace, with strangers? What if I only know how to write on paper? I only know how to write the way I talk.

I agreed to try, but I didn't know how to start. I decided to call it *Mile Markers,* because it would be about more than running—it would be about marking miles on the road of life.

I did what I usually do in a pinch or whenever I'm nervous: I asked my mother, Ethel, how to begin. She said simply to begin the way you begin anything: by remembering your manners. So introductions are in order. My name is Kristin Cate Richard Armstrong. *Kristin Cate* was hard for my little brother to say, so he called me Kiki, which stuck with me through college and beyond, until my wasband, Lance, a man of few words, shortened it to Kik (sounds like *keek,* not *kick*).

Lance and I have three kids: Luke, who is 11, and twin daughters, Grace and Isabelle, who are 9. Having three school-age children means I am usually busy on the mommy-clock, trying to fit my other-aspects-of-self around them. This means when I am not with my kids, I am usually running or writing, two of my passions. I am a contributing editor at *Runner's World* and the author of six books, and I have done freelance work for magazines like *O, Glamour, Parents,* and lots of faith-based publications. I give speeches sometimes, too, which usually makes me so nervous that I sweat more than when I'm running and my spit turns to pancake batter when I step up to the mic. I guess I do it because I love words and how they resonate with and connect people. The feeling of translating an emotion or experience into language that makes it communal, when people nod and smile and say uh-huh, is my writing equivalent of a PR (Personal Record). It keeps me hungry, seeking, training.

I have run six marathons, including two Bostons, and one ultramarathon on trails (50 kilometers). I am not particularly fast or talented as a runner. I don't talk much about split times, the newest nutritional theories for runners, best training programs for varying distances, or how it feels to win my age-group. But here is what I do know, and maybe you can relate: I *love* running. Give me a slow, plodding, painful run. Give me a zippy, light-on-my-feet, springy morning. Give me a downpour. Give me a beast of a hill. Give me a fartlek. (I can't believe I just said that.) Give me a godforsaken track workout if you must. But whatever you do, *give me my run*. I cannot pinpoint the exact moment when running transitioned from a jiggly, postpartum "have to" to a "can't wait to." But it did. And when it did, something happened for me as an athlete, as a woman, as a mom, as a friend, and as a writer—all at once.

This book is the history of that journey. It is an adaptation of previous *Mile Markers* blog entries, arranged thematically according to a list of subjects that my heart returns to again and again. These are the topics I think about on pensive, solitary runs. They are the things my friends and I dish about over miles in the early morning hours. These are the things I care enough about that I will overcome my shyness on paper or in front of a microphone and be authentic and vulnerable in front of total strangers. I chose broad themes because although I'm sharing my stories with you, this book is about our collective journey as runners and as women. This history belongs to all of us.

So to understand me and what's behind the pages of this book, first of all you have to understand why I run. That's the hardest and easiest question. It's like asking why we love who we love. We love them because of all the precious moments we have spent together, because of all the intimate ways they understand us, the subtle acts of kindness and grace they offer us, the way they accept us—good and bad—the way they offer us insight when we are stuck in a bad place, the way they keep us humble and make us feel great all at the same time, the way their presence is our insurance that we will never be numb . . . because we are at ease in their company, because we love them even when we don't like them, because we like ourselves better when we're with them, because they lead us to our truest selves. Because we can't imagine not.

If running were a person, that paragraph would be my love letter. Running has taken me in and continues to comfort, heal, and challenge me in all kinds of magical ways. I am not a good runner because I am me; I am a good me because I am a runner. There is nothing impersonal about anything when I relate it to running. Running is connected to my family, my parenting, my spiritual life, my fitness, my friendships, my health, my sanity, my peace. I can clear my head and solve problems when I run, or make peace with not knowing. I can find beauty, or at least redemption, no matter what.

Getting to know someone on a long run is more intimate and fulfilling than conversations anywhere else. Let's consider this book a nice long run together, and this is our warmup. We are just starting out, a little stiff, a little slow, just trying to even out our breathing and find the pace that suits us both.

I look forward to sharing the road—and marking the miles—with you.

2 BEGINNINGS

I love new beginnings.

I love clean slates, late-in-life romances, before-and-after photos, second chances, springing forward and falling back on the clock, birthdays, newborn babies, New Year's Eve, weddings, starting lines, fresh school supplies, accepted apologies, renewed vows, and journals full of blank pages. I love the hopefulness upon embarking. I love the thought of not knowing how things will turn out but the willingness to invest anyway . . . both the prudent, slow investment and the cowabunga off the cliff. I love new beginnings for myself, but perhaps even more, I love watching someone experience her own. I love new runners—the exuberance and the defeat, the look of wonder on their faces as they cross the finish line. I know what they're thinking, because I thought the same thing. These are the questions that change every finish line into a starting line: *Is this really me? Did I do this? Am I really . . . all this?*

The answer is yes. I am all this. You are all this. Best of all, we are all this. We get to give our best, our all, leave nothing out on the course. And if we blow it, we can always wait for fresh legs and try again.

MILE MARKERS

There are certain moments in a lifetime that leave a mark.

We are all on a journey, connected perhaps by our preferred mode of travel: running. But running is, by nature, fast. Sometimes, as in a race, it's nice when the mile markers tick by quickly, when we are on pace and pushing toward a goal. In life, however, I believe it's best to slow down and acknowledge the mile markers as they come. We are often in such a rush that we blow past them, barely noting them in our hurry to get to "next." Or we give them the equivalent of a button-push on our watch, taking splits.

On Monday my son, Luke, turned 10. *Double digits, big time, decadeville, halfway to 20—you know it, baby*. I have a small idea of what turning 10 means to Luke. I know he likes his stature in double digits. I know he understands that more freedom and more responsibility come with age, and he is appropriately excited—and nervous. Mostly he is happy to be celebrated, and we are marking his passage with great gusto.

As for me, I am pausing at this mile marker. More than collecting a split time. More than slapping the sign on my way. I am stopped here, stretching. As of Monday, I have been a mother for 10 years. When I try to think about my life before Luke, I can barely remember it. And not because it wasn't a good life, because it was surely very good. I know I was happy and busy and living well. But life after Luke shines for me, sparkles so brightly that my past life is only dim by contrast.

Every mile marker can be met with some measure of trepidation, in a race or in life. Am I on target? Do I have what it takes to finish strong? Am I taking care to stay nourished so I can endure? Is my training proving to be sufficient? Am I prepared for the hills? It is impossible to fathom the full distance, so we make our way to the next mile marker, and the next, checking in with ourselves as we go.

That's what I did on Monday. Luke and I stood at the kitchen counter and looked at his baby book before we left for school. Every child loves the story of the day he entered the world, and I indulged us both with recounting his. I saw the photos of his tiny, curled hands and the way he fit perfectly into the crook of my arm. In every photo I am staring at him, marveling, mystified, utterly and irrevocably in love. At this mile marker, as I check in with myself, I realize with deeper conviction than ever before that the decisions that amount to fully and presently raising a child are impossible to regret. I do not grieve time, talent, or energy I could have spent otherwise. I do not grieve the acquisitions or experiences that have been sacrificed or sidelined along the way. And even if I mess up parenting in countless ways on a regular basis, it is an effort worthy of the best I have to give.

Each of us has this gift, this amazing opportunity to check in at our mile markers and make sure we are still running the course we set out to run. Make it a point to notice, and either adjust or celebrate, where you are today.

BOOKMARKS

When the kids and I deplaned in Austin earlier this week, crossing the jet bridge into the airport felt like opening an oven door to check on cookies. The blast of heat was at once utterly relentless and familiar. *Welcome home.* I always joke that the only thing warmer than the weather in Texas is the people, and that still stands. Seeing our friends again is like pancakes for breakfast: sweet and filling.

We stayed up too late that night with the time difference, the stack of mail, the suitcases, the toys we hadn't seen in 2 months, my brother, Jon, (aka Unkie) coming to spend the night, the hamster back from the neighbors. Even so, I woke up just before my alarm. It was still dark outside. There were small girl bodies tangled in the sheets, so I crept quietly around my bedroom using the light from my phone as a lantern. I dressed quickly, slammed a half cup of coffee, and walked out the front door. I sat on my front steps to put on my shoes and socks, remembering how humid and tropical the air feels here. I felt a mist of sweat forming on my face before I even stood up. My friend Paige pulled up, stumbling sleepily out of her car and locking it with the familiar beeps of her keys. We hugged, walked a few paces, and fell into step as our jog worked its way into a run.

I wanted to hear all about her summer, not in the way we caught up over phone or e-mail, but the real stories, the kind that take time to tell. I am turning into my mother, the way she says, "Tell me everything. And start at the beginning." I sent Paige "bookmarks" this summer, placeholders for conversations I wanted to have later—things like photocopies of interesting pages of a book I was reading or a copy of a page from my journal, with scribbly notes and fragments of thoughts in handwriting that only someone who loves you can decipher. We might be all caught up by late October. Maybe.

From a distance we saw another pack of runners, silhouettes of varying heights and strides that were all delightfully recognizable. After shrieks and waves (Southern for "hello"), we stopped, exchanged sweaty hugs, and stood talking in the middle of the road like that was a perfectly normal thing to do at 6 a.m., because for us, it was. We decided to trek home together.

I entered my house with rivulets of sweat streaming down my stomach, my arms, my legs, and the sides of my face. My entire household was asleep, silent. There was no coffee cup indicating

Jon had surfaced. I crept back into my room, peeled off my drenched attire, rinsed off, put my pajamas back on, and found my former spot in the twisted jumble of Grace and Bella in my bed. They were breathing deeply, sound asleep, and yet they closed back around me, reabsorbing me into snuggle formation the way footprints sink and disappear into wet sand. Within seconds, I was back asleep.

The next few weeks have the potential to burst forth, spawning chaos. School starts, activities resume, fall sports begin, homework escalates, friends want to reconnect and make plans, acquaintances get very chatty, editors have deadlines. It's going to be important to find quiet spaces, pockets of time in the dark, if necessary, to ensure that I am sufficiently filled to transcend the chaos and linger in a state of grace.

RESET RUN

I had my kids with me until Christmas afternoon, so if it seems I went under the radar over the holidays, it was purely intentional. I soaked in and savored every moment. We went ice-skating on the deck at Whole Foods, saw lights in our pajamas, went to movies, brought treats to the families staying at the Ronald McDonald House, baked cookies, had family and friends over for dinner, and paid no attention to the clock—staying up late and snoozing without setting the alarm. The best part about winter break is the break. I love the respite from schedules. I get so tired of being the clock-watcher, hurry-upper, activity-shuffler; it's a treat to just be together and let time flow.

At our running group session before Christmas, Cassie told us to meet at the track and that it was okay to bring little people. My kids know Cassie is tough, so they were up, dressed, fed with oatmeal and scrambled eggs, armed with full water bottles, and ready to roll on time. Cassie doesn't have kids of her own (yet), but she handles kids as though she has a full house at home. She somehow managed to keep the mommies on track with warmups, drills, and a tough workout and simultaneously put the kids through the paces. They did a warmup lap, drills, 400-meter timed laps, core work, stretching, and a cooldown. I cannot tell you what a delight it was to get a great workout, watch my kids wear themselves out and have fun, and skip the babysitter. We were all pleasantly pooped when we piled back into the car. I want to encourage you to gather your friends, family, and the entire brood of kids and make your workout a collaborative effort. The only thing better than getting and staying fit is doing it together.

After I dropped the kids off at Lance's on Christmas, I went on what I now officially call my reset run. It is how I transition between mom time and me time, and it works like a charm. The first few years after our divorce, the holiday transition was bumpy and I was sad, and my run helped me work through that. Now I have a brief wave of letdown, more a sigh than a cry, and I can move through it without getting stuck for long. My reset run still serves its purpose, clearing my head and my heart, refreshing me.

I left the next day to visit my grandparents, who now live in an assisted living residence in Phoenix. Seeing my grandmother in a wheelchair—a woman who was once the matriarch of the holiday season, moving through the kitchen with efficiency and skill, feeding everyone in her midst—was hard. She now needs people to help her dress and undress, use the facilities, and wheel her to a dining hall filled with people who stare blankly and barely speak. She told me it was hell getting old, and we cracked up.

The idea of a reset run as means of transition between one year and the next sounds appealing, so I am planning one for the morning of January 1st. I have to do some thinking before I hit the pavement that day. I want to spend some time and consider the things I want to leave behind, so I can tread lightly this year, as well as the things I want to run toward. I want to leave behind things like any form of lingering guilt, any resentments, any relationships that weigh me down, any worries that hold me back, any old definitions of myself that I've outgrown, any fears that limit my view.

And I want to run ahead, into beautiful things like freedom, friendship, contentment, joy, love, and understanding.

3 FRIENDSHIP

To discuss running, out loud or on paper, without delving into the subject of friendship would be like talking about the beach without the ocean, the night sky without the stars, or a mom's car without the crumbs and reeking, balled-up socks on the floor. You just can't. It wouldn't do. This subject makes me stop for a second and collect myself. I have to take a deep breath and think about where to begin. I have to adjust my stance just to support the weight of the topic. If it weren't for my friends, I would not even be a runner. When we all first met, they were *runners,* and I jogged sometimes. Maybe I originally laced up and paced up as a way to spend more time in their company. Or maybe they knew I needed to run before I understood it for myself. I am not sure. But I can tell you this: My friendships are sacred to me. *Sacred.* When it comes to these friends, I will fight for them, give everything I've got for them. I will chase them down, I will wait up, I will show up, I will shut up, I will put up with it all. I will gladly take a hefty chunk of their burden and carry it as my own, and I will willingly hand over a piece of mine, knowing they will carry it expertly, tenderly.

There is a quotation by Isak Dinesen that I love: "The cure for anything is salt water—sweat, tears, or the sea." My girlfriends are my sweat sisters. Since our first mile together, whatever hill we have faced we have climbed together. I would not consider facing any challenge without them. We train each other in ordinary times, and we surround one another like a moving fortress when a crisis hits. We share humor like a cold germ and contagiously crack up to the point of soundless laughter and roadside hyperventilation. We have woken sleeping neighborhoods with our storytelling. We have seen each other's strengths and weaknesses, and we know when to push and when to protect. When something needs to be said, we have earned the right to say it and have built the courage to hear it. When the ache of disappointment or loss is greater than words, we run quietly side by side and wait for God.

BUDDY SYSTEM

Twitchy: That was the best word to describe Paige after she put her watch in her numbered gear bag and checked it in. My friend, running partner, and veteran of 15 marathons has never gone on any run, let alone the Boston Marathon, without her watch.

But we had other things in mind for this day. Making it to Boston was cause for celebration and reflection, not measurement— chronological or personal. Ditching the watch symbolized our commitment to remain in the moment.

How often in life do we place undue emphasis on our performance and fail to appreciate the pleasure of our accomplishment? It's like praying for a miracle and then forgetting to say thank you when it arrives. It takes a specific effort to break that cycle, but we wanted to give it a try.

At the Chicago Marathon, where we qualified for Boston (and I set a PR of 3:35), Paige and I wore pace bands listing split times and "prayer intentions"—the name of a person to honor on each of the 26 miles. In Boston, our bands were time free; they listed "praise miles"—26 things to be grateful for. No requests this time, just thanks.

We began the downhill start with my friend Scott Dunlap. Scott is a 2:54 marathoner and Paige can run 3:15, so I consoled myself knowing that these speedsters had to be sticking by me for my wit, charm, and conversation, however limited. (As I said, it was a day to celebrate gifts, not focus on shortcomings.) We were in the second of the two start waves, so none of the official race clocks along the course applied to us, and we ran in blissful ignorance and liberation. In the early miles, we ran for the gifts of life, love, health, prayer, family, and protection.

Many times during the journey from Hopkinton to downtown Boston, people ran up beside me and flashed their pace bands—with prayer intentions beside the splits. It felt so good to see that something personal had resonated with likeminded souls. Runners are an inherently spiritual crew, having firsthand experience with the concept that the spirit is willing, but the flesh is weak. Going physically beyond yourself helps you understand that there is something bigger and mightier than you.

On Boston's infamous hills, we gave thanks for the gifts of pain, humility, and provision. The appropriateness of these seemingly random words became evident as the soles of my feet alternated between aching and numb and my legs cramped and complained. I took salt pills and ibuprofen like my kids pop Pez candy.

Meanwhile, Scott was taking photos, doubling back for beer, and enjoying what was apparently a walk in the park for him. Paige had enough spunk to maintain a continuous sideshow. I think she high-fived every outstretched hand and said a personal thank-you to everyone who shouted, "Go, Paige!" Before long, I regained my enthusiasm. I slapped hands, rejoined the beauty of the moment, and—dare I say it—had fun. Just as some of the best laughs come in the midst of a meltdown, fun is that much more memorable when in the company of pain.

At Heartbreak Hill I got a rowdy, over-the-shoulder shout from Paige—"C'mon, girl! Been there, done that!"—and we were up and over without incident. I realized that enduring heartbreak of any kind without her would be unacceptable, and it made me well up with emotion of such PMS proportions that I had a hard time catching my breath on the descent. There is something to be said for people you can talk with about any-thing, for any length of time, under any circumstance, or with whom you can remain in shoe-slapping silence and still enjoy each other's company.

And so mile 21, the friendship mile, was a particularly gracious one. Then came praise for the gifts of freedom, forgive-ness, and peace. Paige, Scott, and I grabbed hands as we crossed the finish line together under a digital display of 4:15. I was off my normal finish time, but I enjoyed every minute (well, almost) of it. We headed to our hotel's bar for a cold beer and a decadent plate of french fries.

I called my parents to verify my survival, and my Internet-savvy mother said, "You ran a 3:44:35, sweetheart. I'm so proud of you." "Huh?!" I had forgotten that our start time was a half hour after the first wave—and official course clocks—started. Time really does fly when you're having fun.

SOUL TRAIN

I popped out of bed Thursday morning before my 5 a.m. alarm ever sounded. I pulled on running clothes, fed the dogs, called Jon to make sure he was out of bed to cover my absence, made a cup of coffee and a slice of toast, found my shoes (one was in the dog crate, natch). Jon pulled up, and I slid out the door; high-fived my sweet, sleepy brother on my way down the front steps; and shuffled off down the road to Courtney's house. She lives around the corner from me, not far, but up a slight hill that always takes my breath away as I command my body to arise and shine. My breathing evens out as I reach her driveway, just like clockwork. Paige and Katie took a snooze pass, so it was just us.

As usual with our early morning sisterhood, we talk about everything under the sun. Our conversation dips and dives like hummingbirds; one second we land on shallow topics, the next something sweetly intimate, flitting from one to the next with ease and grace. We never talk like this at parties, restaurants, school gatherings, community functions, football practice, or play dates. The blanket of darkness adds a shroud of privacy, the pounding footfalls a buffer. If you saw us passing each other as we do sometimes with just a hasty nod or a wave out a car window, you might never guess the depth of our friendships. We don't even have to bother with small talk anymore. Our pack has made peace with the silence of good company. These are the people I want to grow old with, puffing out miles side by side. In honor of us, I take calcium and glucosamine and do yoga.

At running group this week, Cassie gave us the choice between a fartlek or a train; we picked train. There are many names for this workout, but none of them suffice. Some call it Indian File, but this is no longer PC. (I suppose it could be called Native American File?) My daughter Grace does this in PE, and she calls it Switcharoo. Basically it is a fartlek, but you are in a group, running single file, and the last runner in the lineup (the caboose) sprints to the front of the line, followed immediately by the next person, and the next, in a constant stream of passing. The trick is that you have to stay together and communicate; the faster runners can't set a pace that breaks the train, and the slower runners can't ruin the juju. The workout has to benefit everyone.

We finished 5 miles in a time far faster than I could ever run that distance on my own. We must have looked powerful (or insane), because people gave us wide berth on the trail as we flew by. As we sprinted and sputtered around the 5-mile loop, it occurred to me that this workout is a perfect illustration of true friendship. When you are lucky enough to have it, you learn that laughing and suffering are not mutually exclusive. You experience the transcendent shift from *I can't* to *but we can*. When it's right, it simultaneously challenges us and never leaves us behind.

That's one train I don't want to miss.

LOST WITHOUT HER

Katie and I debated racing a 10-miler Sunday morning, but after a couple of glasses of white wine, we honored our indecision and formed a new plan. Paige was already signed up, so she was in with both feet. Katie and I met early and did a hilly detox run, finishing up just in time to see the lead car and the two race leaders coming up a street in my 'hood. Then we sprinted to my house to pick up my dog Mercy, who was so excited to be included in our cheerleading scheme that I practically water-skied behind her once she spied the runners on the course. In classic dog fashion, she wanted to take off with the pack. It is not easy to deter more than 115 pounds of determined canine.

There was not much fan support for this race—most everyone we knew was running in it—so Katie and I were, shall I say, conspicuous: two sweaty, screaming, leaping fools being tugged by a Swiss mountain dog through the hills of central Austin. Quite a picture. Katie was a true cheerleader. (I wasn't. I was the girl who, as the new kid in my Minnesota high school, thought

I was ready for tryouts . . . only to learn that the simple moves I proudly thought I had mastered would actually be done on ice skates—yep, hockey. Whoops. Yes, I quit, immediately.) I encouraged her to dust off her Herkie technique, but she claimed possible hamstring injury, so we stuck to our screaming.

We first spotted Paige, dressed in pink, hauling up Pecos. We were definitely "those people." We yelled, we jumped, we practically Herkied, as other runners craned their necks to see who was eliciting such a shameless display of emotion. Either that or they pitied her for hanging around with the wrong crowd . . . but we didn't care.

Then we threaded through a back route. Mercy flew at the helm, careened around corners, and plowed down a steep hill (I had visions of my sweet skiing move, "the pizza") until we caught the pack again on the backside of the neighborhood loop, on Scenic Drive. Scenic is a staple in every Austin runner's training diet. We suffer through it over and over until we know it intimately, alternating between disdain and respect, depending on our mood and where we are in our training program. Katie and I tried to keep Mercy to the side as we hustled over to the steepest section of the hill. By then Katie had fully resurrected her inner cheerleader. She was smiling, telling people how great they looked, how fast they were. She has such a beautiful smile that they had to believe her. Either that or she was a nice distraction from the misery of the hill.

We continued hollering at unsuspecting strangers. Cassie, our coach, zipped by, and we started screaming her mantra, "UP AND OVER!!!" It felt so good to yell at her for a change. She wasn't even racing, and she was still a blur. Soon enough we caught a glimpse of Paige, and her face broke into a big grin. Likely she was shocked that I knew how to get from over there to over here.

If you don't know this about me, I may as well confess that I am abysmal, utterly hopeless, when it comes to directions. It does not matter a bit if I have been someplace one *hundred* times before; I am lost. When leaving for home from a destination, I have no clue if I should go right or left out of the driveway. Truthfully, I have to make an L with my left hand to be certain which side is really left. Once, on a beach trip, I got completely turned around while on a rare solo run, and when I finally showed up, my friends were huddled together in search-party planning mode. I felt like Norman from *On Golden Pond*, teary and disoriented and very happy to be home. When I come out of a movie or the mall, I am always convinced that my car has been stolen because it never seems to be where I left it. This is really not a good way to live, but it's all I know. And lest you think me foolish, I was in honors chemistry! President of the National Honor Society, for Pete's sake! It's just a bothersome quirk in my DNA.

Paige loves me anyway, and I think she must have once swallowed a GPS chip, because she is never lost. I call her often, lost and in a panic, trying to describe my location using a unique Kristin-style narrative that never, ever includes things like "east of . . ." My plight might sound like "Hey, it's me. I'm at a light and I don't know which way to turn. There's this store on my side [i.e., of the car, aka left] that's in an olive-green-colored little house, kind of cute, with white trim . . . the grass needs to be watered . . . and oh yeah, I'm trying to get to my hair cut . . . um . . . so . . ." And somehow, after many years of living in Austin and many years of putting up with me, she directs me where I need to go. I'm not sure where I'd be without her, literally.

So, as I was saying, Paige was probably shocked to see us again, but we were hard to miss as the only fans on this stretch. "GO GIRL. YOU LOOK GREAT. YOU CAN DO IT. YOU ARE FLYING. THIS HILL IS NOTHING TO YOU. EAT IT FOR BREAKFAST. WE LOVE YOU." It was exhausting—for me and Katie. Paige just laughed and flashed us her skort and took off like the hill suddenly got flat.

Katie and I waited for a few more friends before we parted ways to go clean up for church. I cannot tell you how much fun we had and how special it was to support the person who is always supporting us. Paige is our guide, our mentor, our motivator, our map, and our timekeeper. She leaves at least 20 minutes on the table when she runs a marathon with us. She's the one with enough air to tell funny stories on the plodding, endless miles. She's the one high-fiving all the spectators and thanking all the policemen on our winded behalf. She's the one with enough extra energy to tote us around when we start lagging behind. So to be there for her today, to support her race at her pace, was sheer delight.

Some days it's good to run. Some days it's even better to be a fan.

WATER WEIGHT

This week has been a series of challenges. Luke had a weird bug bite that developed a staph infection, then Bella got a virus, then Grace had some allergic reaction that caused her eyes to puff and swell shut like Hilary Swank's in *Million Dollar Baby*. Multiple trips to the pediatrician and one business trip thrown in for measure and I am one tired mommy. And also a grateful one. It takes a combined effort of my supportive ex, my parents, and my brother to deal with travel, three sick children, and five pets. I am lucky.

I got back in town on Friday in time to pick the girls up from school. After another trip to the pediatrician with Luke and dinner with my aunt and uncle, who are visiting, I got the kids tucked in and fell straight into bed. I had Hilary Swank (Grace) with me so I could check on her swollen eyes and watch for fever. When the alarm went off at 5:15 a.m., the buzzer sounding with the backdrop of steady rain, I was not amused.

We were set to run 13.1 miles at 6 a.m., at race pace, with no water or food stops. I was so dehydrated from the airplane that my mouth felt like wool. Of course I opted for coffee over water—probably not wise, but I felt it was my only option considering the circumstances. The toaster waffle I grabbed on my way out the door was still cold in the middle. I couldn't wear my new shoes (which, by the way, are a half size bigger than my last pair, and if this keeps up I will be changing sports to cross-country skiing by next winter) because I couldn't bear to soak them on our first date. I didn't think I needed gloves. I was wrong.

What began as a steady patter progressed to an angry downpour, punctuated by lightning for emphasis (on our stupidity), by the time I got to the parking lot by Randall's supermarket. Courtney was already lobbying for a group treadmill adventure at her gym nearby. She was full of all kinds of promises— smoothies, reality TV, warm towels, music, her good mood— but it was not to be. Paige pulled up and hopped out, all skippy-happy like it was 70 and balmy and we were headed to a massage appointment, not 13 miles at race pace in a freezing thunderstorm in the dark. Courtney tried her pitch about the treadmills, only to be met with Paige's emphatic "I ain't runnin' no 13 miles on no treadmill." End of story. We were off.

The rain was steady and manageable until about mile 7. (Texas weather is unbelievable. It was 76 the day before, 52 when we started running, and 41 when we finished.) At about mile 8 the storm really started to rage. The wind was whipping, damp, and bone cold; the lightning and thunder were constant; the sky never got much lighter; and the rain came down like a waterfall. We ran in the middle of the road on less populated streets to avoid the bog on either side. By mile 9 we were nearly blinded by the sheets of rain, we couldn't hear each other over the din of drops hitting asphalt, we were sloshing through midcalf-deep puddles, and there was a current on street corners.

Our feet were frozen, and our waterlogged shoes felt like they weighed 5 pounds apiece. (Mine are still sitting outside, fermenting.) At one point I thought I might have hit my elbow because I felt tingly in my hand . . . until I realized I was just numb from the elbows down. We ran well, though I have no idea how. Martha, our resident GPS guru, said we ran an 8:23 pace. We didn't make it 13 miles, because the lightning was so bad we feared we wouldn't make it home alive to make pancakes for our peeps. Instead we ran almost 11. But I still felt like we were on an episode of *Survivor,* kicking some major b-u-t-t. (I am a mom; I spell all naughty words. Wait, Luke can read . . .)

When we were almost finished, running upstream to get back to the Randall's parking lot, Jennifer and I tried talking through clenched, frozen jaws. (I am not certain if my lockjaw came from determination or frost.)

J: Don't you love it when it just sucks like this?

K: Hmmmph.

J: When the conditions are just awful and it hurts.

K: Hmmmph.

J: It really makes me feel alive to feel this bad.

K: Hmmm. [*Sniff! Nosewipe on shirt sleeve.*]

J: Like God will just wash me off and start me over.

K: YES!

I did feel alive. I learned a few things, too. I learned that treadmills aren't necessarily a bad option. That my waterproof jacket is not waterproof. That a hat is priceless. That I should always take off every bit of mascara before bed. That my friends are complete studs. (And the fact that I can hang with them means that I could be studly by virtue of their good company.) That when your skin is frozen red and you hop into a hot shower, it burns. That chocolate chip pancakes, eaten with warm, bed-headed, cuddly, and syrup-sticky children, are absolutely delicious. And that miserable conditions, weathered with the right people, can be divine.

BEYOND COMPARE

Yesterday we met at 6 a.m. at "the rock." The rock is the usual congregating point for runners in Austin, a stretching area under the MoPac bridge. We did an 18-mile loop that included a good portion of the new marathon course. Our group runs are as social as a cocktail party in motion. We split up in groups of two or three that alternate throughout the run so we can get caught up with everyone, taking turns at the front or lagging behind, depending on hills, topics, mood, and motivation. Time with these women is always one of the highlights of my week.

I noticed during our conversations yesterday that we are totally free to talk about our lives, the good and the bad, without judgment. As far as I can tell, no woman feels compelled to talk herself up or down; there is no need to puff ourselves up or to take ourselves down a notch with the useless self-deprecating remarks that are often typical in other social arenas. A running group can be such a unique and supportive group of friends. One woman may be grieving a miscarriage or venting about sour office politics, while another is thrilled about a new client, date, adoption, or upcoming trip. But no one, and I mean no one, steals anyone's joy or minimizes anyone's pain. And this is within a diverse group of women who would have every possibility to be competitive: partners in law firms, business owners, and authors; married, wish-they-were-married, and wish-they-weren't-married; mothers and wish-they-were-mothers; healthy and injured; financially successful and struggling to make ends meet. Some of us huff and puff up the hills, and others are 3-0-something marathoners.

My point is this: I wish women could be more like this in other areas of life. I wish we could always support each other without comparing. I wish we could always allow others to be sad without trying to fix it. I wish we could always be happy for someone else without seeing the holes in our own lives. I wish we could always share in another's gratitude for good fortune instead of poisoning it with our own regret. I wish we could always laugh together without our mirth coming at the expense of someone else. I wish we could always lift each other up without having to be on top. I wish we could always applaud others' gifts without pining. I wish we could always freely celebrate our own gifts without feeling the need to play small.

Until then, I will appreciate my running friends for being consistently and undeniably real. Thank you, ladies. I love you.

THE FORCE IS WITH US

I felt like a time traveler yesterday—like I stepped out and back into my everyday routine, had a great adventure, and no one was the wiser.

I flew on a Sunday-evening flight to New York to be a guest Monday morning on the *Today* show, then turned around and flew home in time to get my kids from Paige after school. The subject of the segment was a roundtable discussion about the values of female friendship. I was sitting in a circle with Naomi Wolf, Rene Syler, Dr. Judith Sills, and hosts Hoda Kotb and Ann Curry. With so many intelligent, powerful, eloquent, and educated women, it felt like a loving and lively Ping-Pong game. I'm frankly surprised I got any word in edgewise. I sure had fun. Because female friendship is one of my all-time favorite topics.

They asked me to come on the show because of my work in *Runner's World* and my emphasis on friendship as it relates to running. The basis of the show was a recent study that came out of UCLA. I checked it out and found it to be very interesting. Here are a couple of highlights.

The study was done by Laura Cousino Klein, PhD, and was originally conducted to test the body's response to stress. The authors discovered that females have a very different physical reaction to stress than males do. In a stressful situation, our brains release oxytocin into the bloodstream, which apparently buffers the typical fight-or-flight stress response. Oxytocin somehow encourages us to take care of children and gather with other women, which then produces more oxytocin, and this has a calming effect. No wonder we scramble to find our girlfriends whenever the *&^% hits the fan! It's biological. I am quite happy to know this. I happen to think oxytocin and wine go nicely together. Perhaps I'll let Dr. Klein know . . .

The study goes on to say that women who have close ties with other women have lower blood pressure, heart rates, and cholesterol levels. How about that?

Women who maintain close and consistent relationships with girlfriends over a 9-year period cut their health risk by 60 percent! By contrast, women who do not maintain close female relationships have health risks similar to those caused by smoking or carrying extra weight.

Okay, wow. So if these facts are true for regularly fabulous female relationships, can you *imagine* what the studies would look like for close and long-lasting female friendships between runners?! Take the added health benefits and likely subtract smoking and too many extra pounds (I mean, we run, after all), and maybe we will live as long and as wisely as Yoda. The Force is with us, ladies!

The bothersome news is that the study showed that when women become overly busy with the demands of work and family, the first thing most of us let go of is maintaining our friendships. I hear this all the time, the bane of busyness! My opinion is that good girlfriends bolster and honor all other relationships and every task on our to-do lists. Therefore, we are actually harming ourselves and all our other priorities when we let our friendships slide, because then other relationships (those with our spouses, children, parents, siblings, coworkers, etc.) are forced to take on weight that was never intended for them.

The point I brought up on the show (the only one I could squeeze in—ha!) was that every single one of us makes time for what is mandatory. The problem lies in thinking that friendship is a luxury, when instead it is essential for optimal health and happiness in all areas of life. This is precisely why I meet my friends at 5 a.m. to run: because if it got shuffled to later in the day, it might get swallowed by other demands, and I cannot risk that. I have to make that time. It is mandatory for me.

How lucky are we then, to run with our friends? For runners, running is mandatory. It keeps us healthy; it keeps us sane. We are simply going to run; no matter what, we will make time for running. Our friends feel the same way—so we are doing something we are ultimately going to do anyway, but we have the pleasure and the good fortune to be able to do it together.

SPEED QUEENS

Paige is the kind of friend who emanates energy. When she enters a scene, the overall volume rises, and you can almost feel the molecules pinging around her, especially if she has had caffeine. She is confident enough to be kooky and humble enough to be real. In keeping with her festive spirit, on my birthday she put 35 balloons in my front yard and a latte on my doorstep—all before 6:30 a.m. Her 40th birthday came a mere 6 days after my 35th, and as her best friend, I wondered how to celebrate the celebrator.

A traditional gift like a vacation, fancy dinner, shopping spree, or mani-pedi would not suffice. Paige's favorite things, aside from her faith and her family, are running and horseback riding. I opted for running (more in my comfort zone) and signed us up— along with 15 of our friends—for the Keep Austin Weird 5-K on August 29, Paige's birthday, without telling her.

The fact that we have that many friends who would race wearing feather boas in 100-degree heat is quite amazing. But it shouldn't surprise me. There's a closeness about people who run together. We become better friends, better athletes, and better women by the company we keep. As our mileage logs grow, so does our ability to speak the truth to each other, not hesitating when someone is limboing her potential rather than pole-vaulting it. We expect the best for and from each other yet on any given day feel comfortable enough just as we are. With no makeup, no status, and no BS allowed, running purifies friendships. We all have a tendency to put a pretty face toward the world yet lose patience and get edgy with the people we love most: spouses and little people. Running friendships offer a safe zone where we can relax, recharge, and take our best back home where it belongs, making us stronger mothers, wives, and girlfriends, as well as runners.

About an hour before the 7 p.m. start of our race, our clan parked down the street from Paige's house to "get weird" out of sight. She thought we were going out for a stuffy dinner, and her husband, Jamil, played along. Our shirts said "Speed Queen" on the front and "Rage with Paige 2006" on the back. Clad in tiaras and tutus, we rang her doorbell. She was silent for a moment as she took in the scene before her, adjusting to the change in plans the way a 3-year-old reacts to a detour to the ice cream parlor. A grin cracked across her face and she darted up the stairs, returning in less than 5 minutes in her running clothes, which we accessorized with a pearl necklace, boa, and crown.

We fit right in. There were people wearing bathing suits and inner tubes, superhero costumes, stilts, and cowboy boots, and one guy had a doll stuffed upside down in a BabyBjörn. Austin is a weird place, after all.

We crossed the finish line en masse, arms linked, singing an unruly round of "Happy Birthday." Soaked in sweat, we went out for margaritas, Mexican food, and cake. It was the perfect way to celebrate our friend as well as the women we all are and the women we are becoming. We celebrate our years, and our friendships, the best way we know how: We run straight into them.

4 HEALING

I cannot approach the topic of healing without my heart turning toward my friend Dano. I met him last year when I joined a totally new training group to learn how to become a trail runner. Dano was one of my new friends. He showed me how to navigate the twists and turns of a new sport. He was patient and brutally funny. Hours passed by while training for my first ultra in his good company. I had big ideas about running beside him on even more epic adventures. Little did we know how truly epic his own adventure would become.

Months after my race in Huntsville, Texas, Dano's health began to deteriorate. His illness was first diagnosed as chronic fatigue or a blood infection, but we later learned that he has ALS, or Lou Gehrig's disease. The man who flew over mountains all over the world now has a serious peak to climb. I have spent some time at his bedside over the course of recent months, and though seated, I somehow still find myself training beside him. I copied down this passage, which he wrote in one of his photo books from an expedition to Machu Picchu.

I am a seeker. I am a wanderer. I am who I am. Nothing more. Nothing less.

Life is a series of great paradoxes. To find ourselves, we get lost. To gain, we lose. To know the light, we plunge into the dark. To succeed, we fail. Opposites seem forever linked. Without one, we cannot define the other.

Blessings to all who share these mountains, who share journeys—both guide and traveler. Blessings to all of those who seek, knowing they may never find. May you breathe in every moment and with it know that you are truly loved.

—Dano Keitz

I don't know personally what it is like to be seriously ill, but I have deeply loved a few who do. I do understand what it is to be broken. And perhaps, in some instances, the only way to truly heal is to radically come apart.

CALLED TO ACTION

There is an underlying purpose and meaning behind my training, always. It isn't about the next race or the next workout. It's about fitness and fortitude for the next test around the corner that I cannot see. Everyone faces challenging experiences, whether we want to acknowledge that inevitability or not—the doctor calls to say he needs to discuss the test results in person, or a police officer has news at the front door, or you find a lump in your breast, or you lose your job, or your child is diagnosed with something, or your spouse walks out the door. When my next moment comes, I want to be strong and centered enough to handle it with some measure of grace. But perhaps even more importantly, I want to be fast enough to be first on the scene when a loved one needs me, and I want to be fit enough to help carry the load for as long as it takes to reach the other side.

At the races that I run, I see excerpts from people's lives, glimpses of their hearts, often the essence of their existence printed, taped, pinned, or scrawled on the backs of their T-shirts. I read mottos, scripture verses, slogans, quotes, hopes, and tributes: RUNNING FOR DONNA. IN HONOR OF MY DAD. FREE TIBET. CURE CANCER. END ABUSE. JESUS LOVES YOU. WE MISS YOU, WALTER. I get so caught up in these words—so busy reading, imagining, and often asking questions about the people and the circumstances—that I sometimes miss mile markers and aid stations.

Some of the messages on race Ts are incredibly personal. They touch on topics that may never come up in a conversation at work or in the car-pool line, but on race day they are worn as a banner. It seems that when people are ready and willing to lay it all out on the line, they want the moment to count deeply. They want people to understand the magnitude of meaning behind the effort.

When people are hurting, we want to reach out, help, solve, assist, support, love, and comfort. Yet our desires are often thwarted by futility. We can't cure cancer. We can't heal a child. For as much as we wish we could, we can't always make things okay. And this is where a runner's heart beats loud and true. Runners are doers by nature—we're not people content to sit back and let life happen passively. We want to move, act, contribute, stand for something. So that's what my friends Ellen and Paige did at the Austin Marathon in February.

We know a woman named Desiree whose non-Hodgkin's lymphoma had recently returned. This time it was stage IV and in her bone marrow. She has a husband and children who are 6, 8, and 11. Some of her close friends helped by taking care of the kids, dropping off dinners, and driving Desiree to the hospital for her treatment sessions. But what about those of us who weren't in Desiree's inner circle? What about those of us who have run with her and have been inspired by her bold, bald head, her fitness, her determination, her humility, and her grace?

Ellen took action by sending an e-mail that shared Desiree's story and requested that everyone who was able to please send $26.20 to help pay for medical expenses and a meal delivery service for Desiree's family. For the race Ellen wore a yellow LIVESTRONG shirt and pinned 60 paper hearts to it—one for each person who had donated to Desiree's cause.

On race day, my children and I looked for Ellen on the course. It was hard to miss her. She looked like a floating Valentine, covered in fluttering paper hearts inscribed with names. Ellen used her endurance to help someone else endure. After the race, she attached the paper hearts to the ribbon of her race medal and gave it to Desiree, who is now in remission and awaiting a bone-marrow transplant.

Paige ran the same race wearing a T-shirt emblazoned with "BeyondBatten.org" on behalf of some friends who have a 6-year-old daughter with Batten disease. This rare, incurable disease causes blindness and mental disorders, and children with the disease usually die before they reach their teenage years. What can you possibly say to comfort parents who are living with the knowledge that they are losing their child? When words are insufficient, people who run make an offering of miles.

I have also felt this way about the power of miles, as when Paige and I made "prayer bands" instead of pace bands in a couple of our marathons, dedicating each mile to a particular person. Running for someone else makes me less willing to give up and more able to withstand the pain and the fatigue, knowing that someone else is drawing power from my effort. I look at it as an opportunity to carry a portion of someone else's burden, to cover some ground on that person's behalf, to try to lighten the load by shouldering some of it on my own back. That's endurance. That's what moves me to move.

RETRACING MY STEPS

There are certain places and eras of my past that I can access physically.

I haven't invented a time machine, though that would be pretty cool, particularly if I could go back to the mideighties and stop myself from using Sun-In on my hair, which necessitated a lifetime commitment to artificial highlights. Maybe this has just been 25 years of corrective color? I digress.

What I mean is that by placing my feet one after the other and traveling on exactly the same familiar path, I can go there in my head and heart. And that is what I have been doing all week. I took a trip to Santa Barbara, California, and keeping with the theme of roots (ha, enough), mine are here. We moved so many times throughout my childhood that our yearly trip to SB became my touchstone. This place is my heaven on earth, and it never changes. Santa Barbara is similar to the south of France, an interesting pocket of the world nestled quietly between mountains and the sea. I like to think that for me to be in my sweet spot, God has to confine me, much the way parents put a toddler in a playpen. God hems me in between the barriers of rock and water and I seem to do just fine. Better than fine.

All my major life moments seem to stem from or return to this place. I have played here, thought things through here, fallen in love here, fallen apart here. When I watch my children build sandcastles here, I sometimes have trouble catching my breath, utterly overcome by the collision of my past and my future. Naturally, I learned to love running here as well. I have a couple of routes here that are so travel worn in the map of my being, I could probably run them in pitch darkness. Perhaps I could run them by scent alone. Something about SB and the nose; this place smells delicious. If I could bottle this essence and sell it, I could maybe afford a place here after all. It's a combination of gardenia, beach, eucalyptus, pine, and something I can't figure out (which is why I haven't bottled it yet).

On one particular path, I spend all my time looking at the ocean on the way out and meditate over the mountains on my way home. This is the same path I ran the morning of my wedding, the same path I walked when I was lumbering and pregnant, the same path I ran with Paige on our trip here last September and we played a version of This Is Your Life. The path here never changes for me, but it's interesting to note the changes in the runner. Sometimes it's easier to notice change when it's set against a backdrop of sameness. The most notable change of this visit is that my runs here have been less a time of training or processing (thoughts, ideas, issues, relationships) and more a time of clarity. I leave this rental house and return to it sweaty and clean, with no major conclusions about life other than it is damn good.

I haven't worn a watch, while running or otherwise. I run as far as I feel like it, and then I turn around, in classic Forrest Gump style. The funny thing about running here is that no matter what direction I'm going, I am always coming home.

Just as I pick up shells when I walk on the beach, I store these memories in my mind, and when I need to escape or find my way, I run these steps by heart. I share this with you because it's beautiful to me and because I want to remind you to seek your own favorite routes, the paths that take you back to yourself.

THREE-LEGGED RACE

My brother, Jon, is getting stronger after his sledding accident, and meanwhile I am getting punier. It is cedar season in Austin (when allergy levels go off the charts), and so I am plagued by red, itchy eyes, an endlessly runny nose, and headaches and chills. It has not helped my running much. To be perfectly honest, I should tell you that I was dead last at running group today. It was all I could do to just complete the workout. Cassie didn't even ask me about my splits. I think I am tired through and through. Running feels like shuffling, but I refuse to give up. If Jon can walk the driveway, I can run it. The 3M Half Marathon is in 2 weeks, and I want to be strong. Meanwhile, my friends are patient.

I got an e-mail this week from my friend Mary Ellen. She was sharing a quotation from Frederica Mathewes-Green's work *The Illumined Heart.*

In communities, at work, but particularly in families, people are put together in something like a three-legged race. God means us to cross the finish line together, and all the other people tied together with us play some part in our progress. They are oftentimes to rouse our stubborn sins to the surface, where we can deal with them and overcome them. Bundled together in families, a giant seven- or nine- or fifteen-legged pack, we seem to make very poor progress indeed and fall to the ground in bickering heaps with some regularity. But God has put us together—has appointed each person in your bundle specifically for you, and you for them. And so, "little children, let us love one another" with might and main, and keep hopping together toward the finish line.

How fine is that?! I love the image. Whoever we are bundled with right now—our families, our friends, our running partners (even those of us in last place), our communities, our coworkers—let's be loving and patient with each other. A three-legged race involves lots of leaning, stumbling, encouragement, and laughter.

But we aren't getting anyplace if we don't do it together.

PINK HEART

When you have a tight-knit group of friends, you all end up being emotional voodoo dolls for one another. If someone else is hurting or grieving, it is impossible not to feel the sting or share the hazy cloud cover of melancholy. Maybe it's the transitive property of friendship (I loved math): If A is affected by B, and B is affected by C, then A and C have an effect on each other. And so it happens that Jennifer's best friend has a sister who is dying of cancer, and so even though I don't know the sister, my mind keeps returning to their family. I am like a rubbernecker on the highway; I keep turning my thoughts at obscure angles, incredulous and gawking. Maybe because she is exactly our age, with little children. Maybe because Jennifer's friend is such a sweetheart that I know her sister must be, too. Maybe because Jennifer's ache is so profound for her friend that it is contagious, like pinkeye, but for the heart. Or maybe because if it's really true that prayer divides a burden, then all of us are carrying a few more rocks than usual in our pack this week.

When we ran this weekend, Jennifer explained how they all hung out together on a trip last December, having fun and ringing in the festivities and possibilities of the new year. And now, a mere 7 months later, one of the three of them is dying. This blows my mind. The very idea fragments my brain into a million bits, and then just as suddenly, like watching a movie in rewind, the pieces all suck back into place at warp speed . . . and there it is. Clarity.

Clarity comes to me like this: I need to be living my life in such a way that if I knew my expiration date, I would continue living just as I am. I wouldn't want to have some grand epiphany, an impetus to change everything, or a sudden desire to travel the world and leave my normal life behind. I want my normal life to sparkle with the allure of the ordinary and speak to me, just the way it is. Or if there are some changes to be made, I want to be motivated to incorporate them as I go along. If I travel and explore, I want it to be because my heart is ticking, not because my clock is. I want to be brave enough to say the important things like "I'm sorry; please forgive me" and "I love you; please help me love you well." I want my heart to be tidy.

Why is it, then, knowing what we know and thinking deeply the way we do, that we all need a wake-up call (either our own or the sound of someone else's) over the loudspeaker of life?

As we finished the last 30 minutes of our 2-hour Saturday morning run, we talked about things like this, about how our mortality can be motivating or morbid, liberating or immobilizing. We talked about how we could all love better than we do, extending grace and generously offering what we have to share. And finally, when our words ran out (and our breath, too, as we crested a hill close to home), we just prayed. We prayed for our sick friend and her family. We prayed in gratitude for our health and the health of our families. We prayed for insight into living well—today.

We all know that life is fragile. I bet everyone knows someone who is ill or has been in a serious accident, or if not, all we have to do is read the newspaper to know that tragic events are unfolding all around us all the time. I pass squirrels lying prone on the side of the road and explain to my children that just like God plans everyone's birthday, He also plans everyone's homecoming. It's up to us to make the most of every day in between.

Let's run well, my friends.

5 PLAY

I can be pretty serious about taking myself seriously. I accept responsibility with somber reverence, stuffing the weight of the world into my pack and shrugging my shoulders into the straps. What can I say? When I care about something, I don't want to blow it. Whether it's raising my kids, meeting a work deadline, paying a bill on time, training for a race, or being there for a family member or friend, I am a girl who gets up in the morning with the intention of being better than I was the day before. But it's not easy to keep all the balls in the air, to juggle this master schedule called Aspects of My Life. I drop balls. They go thudding and bouncing and rolling away, and I skid and scramble to collect them and start over again, breathless.

There are three things in my life that have saved me from myself, from turning into the most regimented, boring, git-'er-done kind of gal. They are my children, my friends, and running. Why? *Because they remind me to play.* When I chase my giggling girls or shoot hoops with my son, when I try to retell a story to a girlfriend and laugh so hard that I cry, when I lace up my shoes and run through freshly cut, damp grass that sticks to my calves—I am ageless. My pack of responsibilities grows lighter and more manageable. I can reclaim my joy in the simplest tasks or most mundane moments. I can see possibility, create space, and shift my perspective.

If we aren't intentional about being unintentional, we can forget how to play. After all, running isn't just running. It's also frolicking, meandering, prancing, cavorting, sashaying, parading, scampering, loping, bounding, soaring, scurrying, dashing, sprinting, strutting, flying, leaping, skipping, kicking up our heels, and letting down our hair.

PLAY DATE AT THE PARK

Cassie must have known I needed a contrast to the rough race last weekend. She planned our last running group at Butler Park, by Palmer Auditorium. Butler Park makes tiny Austin feel more like Chicago on a summer day. The city skyline is the backdrop behind rolling green, grassy hills, the river, bike paths, and a fountain that shoots water up from holes all over the ground. There is no basin to the fountain, just sidewalk. It's like the one in Aspen, if you have seen that one. On any given sunny day in Austin, the fountain is filled with children squealing and playing in the spray. Families picnic around the perimeter, runners stretch and start or end their workouts, dogs lounge on blankets, kids ride bikes and scooters and skates. It's the perfect new addition to our family-oriented, outdoor-loving city.

We did a warmup on the trail along the river, followed by drills up the big, grassy hill at the center of the park beside the fountain. We jogged backward up and down the hill, did sashays, lunges, high-knees, and butt-kicks, and all the while my legs were groaning but my heart was smiling. It was a perfect, crisp, sunny morning. I was surrounded by my friends, laughing, breathless, and telling stories, comparing our race tales from the weekend before. I felt suddenly, achingly, profoundly *lucky*.

Cassie had us do all kinds of exercises on the stone ledges that surround the fountain. We did several series of pushups, dips, hop-ups, step-ups, kick-backs, and wide-stance frog-jumps. As I worked I watched a little toddler run in and out of the water, ditching wet layers of clothing until he was down to a puffy, soggy diaper. Eventually that came off, too, and he giggled and raced around naked. The water comes up in spurts, so kids are always surprised by it, sending every age-group into happy hysterics. Cassie pushed us in each circuit to the point of fatigue before we ran on our leaden legs around the park. *Back to the stone ledge, work, run, repeat.* The exercises and the laps eventually wore us into silence, but there is community even in quiet when you are with the right people.

Finally it was time to cool down. Our cooldown was to run the series of grassy hills, up and over each one in the area, twice. Now it was my turn to feel like the uninhibited toddler in the fountain, or at least like the childhood Kristin on the playground—the girl with braids and freckles and glasses sliding down her nose who thought she could one day maybe pick up enough speed to fly. There is something about the smell of grass and the stampede of friends' footsteps that takes me right back to when the word *exercise* was foreign to me. All I knew was play. And when this happens to you again as an adult, it is a holy feeling, erupting like a giggle. It's a feeling you want to bottle and save and sniff and dab behind your ears and on your wrists when you feel grumpy and old and responsible.

I guess part of me still wants to fly.

CHEERS

This past weekend I had the honor of being part of the gift for my grandmother's 90th birthday. All she wanted was for her entire family to be together, and we made it happen. We spent the day in North Park, in Pittsburgh; the kids fished and played, and we had a picnic. Watching my children play with my cousin's children, with Grandma Millie looking on and smiling . . . it was pure delight. Millie is happy and healthy, still living unassisted in her same house, no walker, no cane, no handicap bars in the bathroom, no nothing. Her bedroom and bathroom are on the second floor, and she has 32 steps from the front porch down to the street. If she isn't inspiration to stay fit and live well, what is?

This morning I met with my trail group at 5:30 for another flashlight run. Our trail coach Robert planned a looped route for us on trails we have already traversed in daylight, but of course it looks and feels completely different in the dark. He plotted our course with strategically placed dangling light sticks and sent us on our way. For my first lap I tried to keep up with the group, ever fearful of being alone, but as usual I realized that I had to set my own pace, especially if I wanted to stay upright and uninjured. I could feel my pulse, and my breathing was raspy as I started my second loop. The only sounds were my feet and my breath; the only lights were the round glow of my flashlight and the random sparkle of glow sticks in the distance.

There is something exhilarating and empowering about running alone in the dark. It's very taboo and unsafe for a woman to be alone, wandering about in the forest in the unlit hours of early morning. Like my parents used to tell me, nothing good happens out there after midnight. But taking a flashlight and hauling ass over rocks and roots is like snubbing your nose at fear and gender mandates and going for it anyway. Although I admit that on what was supposed to be my final cool-down lap, I heard a rustling sound in the trees off to my left and took off like a rabbit, with little regard for foot placement or glow sticks—I just fled. Fear still haunts me even in my moments of relative freedom. It was very kind of Robert to tie some flags on a low-hanging limb with a broken branch protruding at eyeball level.

I burst in the door and into my kitchen, where my brother already had the kids up and dressed, in preselected school-picture-day outfits. I must have had a look on my face that reminded Jon of when we were kids, because he smiled over his coffee cup and asked me how my play date was. I laughed and told him it was perfect. He thinks all grown-ups need more play dates. I agree.

How else can we manage all we have to do and still maintain our energy level and sense of perspective and humor? Last week I had two speaking engagements, a trip with my three kids, and final edits on my manuscript proofs. This week I fly out to Minneapolis for the Twin Cities Marathon—I am speaking and running the 10-Miler. I should be depleted, but I am energized. My friend Scott Dunlap, a trail runner, ultra runner, and fellow blogger, summed it up perfectly in a recent e-mail. He closed with this little beauty, which I plan to file away: "I know I should be exhausted these days, but I'm drinking from the cup of life until it spills down my cheeks. Wouldn't want it any other way . . ."

I have one word to say to that: *Cheers.*

HANGING UP THE CLOAK

Our Internet service here has been down all week, which has put me by turns irritatingly and blissfully MIA from the world, depending on my mood. Some writing deadlines (those requiring some online research, anyway) have been simmering on the back burner while the kids and I play. Luke finished his final week of sailing camp and announced that it is his favorite thing. There was an awards/closing ceremony yesterday, and the little bugger got Top Skipper, so I guess sailing likes him, too. Being a bit (ha, understatement) of a chicken about open water, I admire this passion from the sand. From my time spent at the yacht club watching or waiting for Luke, I can gather that, like running, sailing is a culture as much as it is a sport. As a parent, watching a child discover a passion is just as sweet as (perhaps sweeter than?) finding one for yourself.

I ran a half marathon in Sonoma last weekend, for fun and to cover it for an issue of *Runner's World*. Any race where your medal is a wine coaster, and where you are handed a wine glass and ushered into wine-tasting tents immediately after you pass the finish line—well, let's just say it was right up my alley. I loved it. I came home happy and dehydrated—and sporting a blood blister on the bottom of my foot the size of a silver dollar. I have never gotten one of those before. I think it was running on uneven pavement that did it; I am not sure. The wine probably helped dull the pain as I hobbled through the airport on my return trip later that afternoon.

Two days later I went on a trail run. The blister seemed okay until the downhill, when it started bothering me again. It only bothered me until I tripped and sailed over some roots and a rock, scraping up my left side—then the blister wasn't as noticeable. Now I have road rash (trail rash?) that looks vaguely like hamburger on my left elbow and left calf. It leaves little blood splotches on my sheets and reminds me of being married to a cyclist. The girls wanted to see where I fell, so I took them hiking on the same trail. I was happy to see that they love hiking as much as I do. Best of all, they have a natural sense of direction that I don't have, so they could remember which way we came from, and we were in and out without having to double back and redirect, which I do all the time.

Another adventure this week involved one of those goofy bike-cars that seat four people. Tourists rent them here and cruise along the bike path by the beach. My kids have been pointing at them and begging me for 2 months now to rent one, and I finally caved, resigning myself to looking like a major dork and likely capsizing the oversize thing off a curb, owing to my stellar cycling skills. We rode along the beach, crossed over and followed the path by the zoo and the bird sanctuary, everyone taking turns being my copilot. I had only sporadic pedaling help, so I got an unexpected workout, lugging three kids plus my own body weight. I am not sure who had more fun, the kids or me.

I took the kids to see a free jazz concert in a park last night, and we showed up with our backpacks and snacks and blanket. One of the officials took a look at my scrapes and asked me, "How'd you manage that?" One of my brood replied, "Mommy is a runner." And that explanation sufficed. The man smiled and said, "Nice." He looked like a runner, too. I may not look so great right now, but I can't remember the last time I felt as free and as happy as I do this summer.

The heart resonates in present and playful moments, in a spontaneous hug, a laugh, a communal activity, or a shared delight. It's the simplest notion in the world, *being* with loved ones as opposed to doing something on their behalf. Even if the weight of our responsibilities remains the same, cultivating the ability to be in the moment is a gift—to ourselves and to those we love.

THREE BLIND MICE

I think I could probably climb Mt. Kilimanjaro if I thought we were just going for a hike.

I'm not sure what it is with me, but when I have no objectives and no expectations, I seem to do much better in life. For example, this Saturday morning I met Paige and Courtney for a run at 6. I had no plan in mind, no idea if we were running 5 miles or 15 miles or anything in between. I didn't avoid margaritas, hydrate properly, or load up on carbs the night before. I didn't set my alarm extra early to ensure plenty of preparation time in the morning. I just rolled out of bed, shoveled in a toaster waffle on my way out the door, sat on my front steps to put my shoes on, and walked over to Courtney's.

When I got there, she was lying down on her sloping driveway.

"Whassup?" I said.

"Mornin'," she said. "This angle feels really good."

So I joined her, sprawled out in her driveway. We would have been roadkill if her husband were backing out on his way to work, but luckily, her husband was sleeping. She was right, it felt really good. I'm not sure if it was the cool hard surface, the angle of the slope, or the fact that we were just chilling out.

Paige pulled up, hopped out of her car, and said hi, thinking absolutely nothing of our supine status. She undid her ponytail to show off her cute new haircut. (We would never know the style of anyone's hair otherwise; all we know are sweaty clumps of ponytail.) Courtney and I complimented her do and stood up slowly, lamenting the blood now pooled in our feet, and we got started.

Time passed in a complete blur. We talked, caught up, cracked up, toured cute neighborhoods in South Austin, looked at houses, complimented people's gardens, detoured down memory lane, paid homage to meaningful spots around town, shared corresponding stories, got Gatorade, shared some powdered doughnuts at a 7-Eleven (dee-licious!!!), and eventually wound our way back to Courtney's house.

We ran for 2 hours.

You know the feeling when you see a great movie . . . you leave the theater kind of disoriented and wobbly, the light has extra glare, and you feel like you have been in a wonderful time warp? I love that! That is exactly how I felt as I walked home afterward. I was hungry and happy, having just spent 2 hours in a way that somehow felt like 10 minutes.

If I had planned a long run of 2 hours, come home early the night before, rested well, hydrated properly, considered possible routes to accomplish our intended mileage, woke up early, packed Gu—all the things I would normally do—I am not sure I could have had a better morning. Maybe this casual pace works best for me. Maybe I can go farther and enjoy more fully when I just go and let go, leaving the planner in me at home in bed.

After all, she needs her rest.

SALAD GIRL

There is something to be said about completing the last long run before a marathon:

Ahhhhhh.

You know how they tell you before you start nursing a baby that you should chafe your own nipples in preparation? (Where on earth did I read that?!) Well, I have had a similar feeling that God has been trying to toughen me up. First there was a long run with intestinal issues. Then last week was the tsunami run. This week was 22.2 miles in the cold, windy, constant drizzle. I am not sure what marathon day will look like, or if God is training me for something that has nothing at all to do with running, but I do feel the wimp in me starting to pack her things.

Midway through our rainy run, when we stopped in at the Quickie Mart for a food and potty break, I noticed in the bathroom mirror that the peach fuzz on my face was covered in a dewy combo of sweat and rain mist. I wasn't really aware that I had hair on my face, so this was not a pleasant revelation. Near the cash register there was a yellow plastic "slippery when wet" sign with the stick figure wiping out. I threatened to carry it with me, but since my hands were numb, I thought better of my feeble humor. Instead I dutifully paid for my brown sugar Pop-Tart and orange Gatorade and wished we were done. Paige chimed in that we only had "an hour and a half or so to go!" She got some menacing glares for that one. Melissa said, "Well, think of it this way: We are closer to coffee than we were when we started." I pointed out that I live very close to Starbucks, so this statement was inaccurate. With that, Melissa ushered me back out into the damp, gray muck of a morning, and I tried to coax my legs back into a rhythm reminiscent of running. The final few miles are a choppy blur. We finished with the now customary leg soak in my frigid pool; this time Paige ran straight in, shoes and all (we were frozen and soaked anyway). It was so cold in there that it reminded me of New Year's morning in Minnesota, when folks do the crazy Polar Splash into an ice-covered lake. It is impossible not to scream and pant *Oh, oh, OH!* (think Lamaze) upon entry. We stood in bitter, blue-lipped silence until Paige started singing a song from *Grease*. We all joined in (I think every woman our age knows every word), and it helped pass time in Arctic submersion. If my neighbors had any question that I was nuts, this rainy, mid-January, fully clothed karaoke swim party pretty much sealed that verdict. No more wine bottles in the recycle bin for me for a while, not until things die down.

Then, after taking a scalding shower and putting my pajamas back on, I had to have Maudie's breakfast tacos: egg, potato, and cheese, with salsa. I picked them up in pajamas, Ugg boots, and a coat, then ate them in my car in 2 seconds flat.

Speaking of food, I have weaned myself completely off gels, and my stomach is much more polite to me these days. Cassie told me that Fig Newtons were possibly not the wisest choice, since high-fiber fruits are not always runner-friendly. So now my snack of choice is a Pop-Tart Go-Tart (in the shape of a bar) or my ever-trusty peanut butter sandwich. I had one shoved in the back pocket of my jog bra, along with some Motrin pills, in case of emergency. I made the mistake of leaning back against my car seat when I drove to meet up with everyone and heard the telltale squish of my lower lumbar sandwich support. I didn't care too much back at mile 19, when we stopped in at Jester Hall at UT for some water and I shoveled the flattened peanut butter and Motrin sandwich into my mouth with total abandon. I did not offer anyone a bite, not that they would have wanted one. If my mother saw the decline of my manners while running, she would be appalled. She and I once went to Whole Foods for breakfast after I did a long run, and I noticed her staring at me while I inhaled two slices of breakfast pizza. "What?!" I snapped at her. "Nothing," she said. But I could tell she was horrified. I am sure I was talking with my mouth full and eating as much and as fast as a frat boy in the college cafeteria. Gross.

One of my finest postrun culinary experiences was in San Francisco with Paige. We did this epic run back in 2003 through the city, through Chinatown, by the Marina, under the Golden Gate Bridge to slap the bronze hands (check this out if you have never done it), along some crazy cable-car-incline-streets that were so steep we were barely moving, and back to our hotel. It was about 15 miles, which at the time was the farthest I had ever run in my entire life. Going on vacation with Paige is like being a kid again, and she wanted to go to Alcatraz "right away." So we left our tangled hair unwashed, threw on clothes, cabbed to the wharf, and grabbed a huge sack of greasy burgers and fries from In-N-Out Burger. And real Cokes. I will never forget sitting on the ferry in the bay, next to my best friend, with remnants of sweaty salt crust along my jawline, shoveling big burger bites and fingers full of greasy, ketchupy fries into my mouth and talking the whole time, alternating bursts of chewing and caffeine/endorphin-stoked chatter.

Prior to becoming a runner, I was a salad girl. That was not as much fun.

6 MOTHERS

I have two favorite quotations about motherhood, both uttered by absolutely brilliant, elegant women. One is from Jacqueline Kennedy Onassis: "If you bungle the raising of your children, I don't think that whatever else you do well matters much." And the other is from Katharine Hepburn: "Love has nothing to do with what you are expecting to get, only with what you are expected to give . . . which is everything."

I write often and with great reverence and fondness about and for mothers—by which I mean everyone who mothers. Being a mother is the biggest undertaking I have ever assumed, with the least amount of preparation. There has been nothing close to the desire I have in my heart to do this thing well. I have never been as determined, as devoted, as intentional—or as tired. One of the main things I have learned about motherhood is that I can't do this gig on my own. I need my friends. I need to make and honor time for myself, and I need to make and honor time with them. No matter how tired I am, I will get up at 5 a.m. just for the chance to catch some miles in their good company before my family has a chance to miss me. When I return to the fold, sweaty and breathless, I am restored. I am a better woman and therefore able to be a better mother. I am ready for whatever the day holds, which, when you are a mom, can be anything. I can pour myself out all day long, filling everyone's cups, because my pitcher has already been filled. When I am in community with mothers who run, I am home. This chapter, and my heart, are for you.

RIGHT HERE

My Mother's Day started with breakfast in bed (cinnamon toaster waffles, a cup of coffee, and the newspaper) and a stack of gifts. Some were the cute handmade booklets and coupons from school ("I love my mom because . . .") and some were thoughtfully chosen items from around our house, wrapped in many layers of Christmas wrapping paper and hermetically sealed with duct tape. Speaking of, I want to seal these ages in duct tape—I love 9, 7, and 7. They are innocent enough that nothing is impossible and wise enough to be sarcastic. I am in heaven.

These last few weeks of school seem to take on a life of their own, picking up speed and rolling toward us like the giant rock chasing Indy in *Raiders of the Lost Ark*. It seems I need to be up at school for more hours than I'm in my office (an exaggeration, but still); everything is packaged as a celebration, so it's amped up to all-new levels, and everyone is exhausted at night but no one wants to go to sleep. We are all ready for summer. No schedules and no homework is starting to sound pretty good to all of us. Seasons of the year are like this, the start and end of the school year, and just before the holidays. These are the times when it feels like everyone around us has picked up the pace as if we were doing a fartlek. Last week was a series of things; each day my schedule perched precariously on the item preceding it like a Jenga game. A workout, a deadline, a meeting, a radio interview, a mother's day tea. If one thing was off, everything else toppled.

On Thursday morning I considered not going to yoga because my day had no breathing room. Huh? I had specifically scheduled "breathing room," literally, and now I was going to cancel it so I could have more time to hurry? Was I insane? I chastised myself for my stupidity, slid into class, unfurled my mat, plunked down on it, and tried to relax. (Okay, scheduled time to relax: 1, 2, 3, chill! This works about as well as telling yourself when you are plagued by insomnia to *sleep—now!*) I am sure my aura was dingy and pockmarked, because our teacher, Leigh, told us to focus on the breath and be present.

Be present. Duh. It sounds embarrassingly simple, but I was struck by the reminder that no matter how many thoughts my brain can tick through in succession, I can be present in only one place at a time. So I have a new question to ask myself: *Where is your heart?* The only acceptable answer is *Right here.* If my heart is somewhere else, I'm going to go there and join it. So whether I'm pouring my love into a child, helping with homework, writing a column, combing out tangles, in Downward-Facing Dog, walking the dog, running up a hill, or being part of a conversation, the same answer applies.

The more I ask myself the question, the more present I become.

UNWRAPPED AGAIN

Spring break is just that—a break. A break from schedules, routines, to-dos, errands, and the general scurrying of life. I cannot tell you how much I am enjoying my children, not because they are any more enjoyable than they always are, but maybe because I am. Thank God my children can see me apart from running a household, meeting deadlines, supervising homework, driving the SUV, and all the hurrying. That's the main thing, the hurrying. We are taking a break from that.

I am letting my little people set the pace and letting my hair down, so to speak, carefree and windblown, cruising around in our old VW bug convertible. Aside from a couple of runs with my friends Jamie and Terra, and some sessions at my gym (with my trainer, Michael, whom I refer to as Sensei, because he benefits my head and heart as much as my body), my children have been my workout.

One day it was a run along the bike path, accompanied by children on scooters and roller skates. This might count as interval training, as I hurry up to catch up to one and slow down to wait for another. Another day it was a serious cycling workout in a rented double surrey. One afternoon Grace wanted to run to the courthouse and go to the lookout all the way at the top. Then Bella wanted to go for a run to the library, where we sat, sweaty and happy, reading books and coloring paper shamrocks. The run home, carrying our books, was pretty funny. One morning we held races on the sand, sprinting off our oatmeal and Mickey Mouse–shaped pancakes (speedwork, sort of?). Another morning was dog walking, tide pool searching, and shell and sea glass collecting with Nani and Papa (cross-training at its finest).

One of my favorite adventures so far was an afternoon hike we took with Terra and her children, Logan (5) and Lake (1). It was a 3-mile-loop hike, with the first half being a serious uphill (even harder for Terra, with Lake in the backpack). The kids were champs! They managed to avoid the poison oak, stay hydrated, and remain within shouting distance if we got separated, and they never once complained. It was pure delight. We reached the top and headed back down the shady side until we heard the sweet sound of a rushing stream. Some people and dogs were playing in the waterfalls below, and of course the kids wanted to join the fun. It was a steep grade down to the stream, and I held my breath as Terra worked her way down with ease, baby in tow. The kids scampered down like mountain goats and immediately stripped down to their underwear. Before my inner actuary could perform a risk analysis, they were in the ice-cold water, sliding down the mossy rock face, aiming for the little waterfall that made a water slide into a crystal-clear pool below. They paused when they saw how high it was, and Terra asked me if I was worried. I was, a bit, but more than that I was caught off guard, marveling at their lack of fear and inhibition. They were so beautiful; I wish you could have seen them. There are few things I dislike as much as freezing water, and Terra knows this. She, on the other hand, dislikes nothing about the outdoors. She strapped baby Lake onto me, peeled off her T-shirt, and asked me if her black Victoria's Secret bra would suffice as a bikini top. I concurred, and she hopped in, wedging herself into the cold crevice of rushing water at the top of the waterfall. She asked if she had any takers and my daughters hopped into her lap, and they disappeared over the side with a shriek and a splash.

I could not stop smiling, partly out of relief (when I saw their blonde heads and blue-lipped faces safely on the other side of the rock) and partly out of respect. I bounced Lake and watched Terra, in all her outdoor glory, doing something unforgettable for my kids. We need each other, you know, each of us sharing our gifts to forge experiences and make memories for our children and for each other's children. In this way, our gifts are unwrapped again, every single time.

30 STOLEN MINUTES

Frustrated in my love affair with running, I recently contemplated the idea of a breakup. As it turned out, we just needed some space to clear the air a little bit. Last week I did yoga, walked my dog, ran easy in the rain, and did 3 miles of speed work at the track. I had no method or motive; I just let my mood guide my effort and enjoyed every second of it.

I am busy with the momentum of the end of school as well as trying to edit my latest manuscript. When I get stuck in the middle of a chapter, it does me no good whatsoever to sit and brood over it. Rather than waiting for inspiration to strike, I opt for movement in hopes of clearing my head enough to make room for creativity. Creativity is a lot like love—if you try to force it, it eludes you. Better to busy yourself in other ways and let it tap you on the shoulder. So that's what I do. I go for a walk or a run and when the fog lifts in my head, I turn around and take my new idea back to my office.

I want to tell you about my most magical run last week. On Saturday my son Luke made his First Communion. We had family and godparents in town and everything was so exciting, which was probably why I was wide awake at 5 on Saturday morning, even though my alarm was set for 7. I stared into the dark and listened to the whir of my ceiling fan for about 5 minutes until I acknowledged that I was up for good and went to make a cup of coffee. I was hosting a brunch later that morning for my family, Lance's family, and the godparents, so I could have busied myself with hostess preparations. I didn't feel anxious at all, so the idea of busywork was unappealing. Mostly I was just excited. By the time I reached the bottom of my cup, I knew what I wanted to do.

My friend (and Luke's godmother) Peggy was asleep upstairs, and all the children were sound asleep, so I quietly slipped into my running clothes. I carried my shoes outside so I could depart in silence. The morning was balmy, almost tropical. I sat on the steps and pulled on my shoes. I set out in a random path that followed the streetlights, staying close to my neighborhood, where I feel safest in the dark. As I ran I could feel my body start to wake up, loosen up, and fumble for my stride. I rounded a corner and was greeted with a strong breeze. One of my neighbors has a gardenia tree in full bloom, and the gust of fragrance was intoxicating. Gardenia blossom is one of my all-time favorite smells; in fact, my wedding bouquet was made entirely of gardenias. I felt like God was smiling on me.

As I ran I thought of Luke. The combination of his First Communion and Mother's Day on Sunday made me reflect on moments of the prior 8 years of being a mother. It was like watching a montage of film clips in my mind, flashes of memory set to the soundtrack of life. It occurred to me that so many of the beloved aspects of my life, my writing and my running and my relationships, are all flavored by my love for my children. Where I had diluted areas in the past, I am now full concentration. Motherhood refines us. It forces us to refocus and reprioritize, leaving just enough room for what really counts.

I felt full, blessed to the point of overflowing. I checked my watch a couple of times, not because I wondered how much farther I had to go, but because I wanted to know how much more time I had to enjoy. The rest of the day was about celebrating Luke and honoring the special people who were invited to our home. But this time was mine; 30 stolen minutes in the dark, early morning.

I slipped back into my sleeping house in silence, my shoes in my hand. I padded in stocking feet to grab a glass of water and head to the shower. The day would soon be picking up speed. But my pace was already determined, my peace solid on the inside.

LITTLEST OF THE BIG GIRLS

This has been a momentous time at the Armstrong house.

This weekend Grace lost her first tooth. It was pretty loose, not as loose as they usually get with kids (i.e., hanging on by one persistent thread, moving freely with each breath), but she allowed her big brother, Luke, to yank the bugger out. After some bleeding, screaming, tears, and ice, she went to sleep proud and happy atop a lopsided pillow with the stuffed "tooth pillow" beneath it and a letter to the tooth fairy requesting the tooth be allowed to remain in her custody along with the little stipend.

Amazingly enough, the intuitive and kindhearted fairy also made a small donation to the underside of sister Bella's pillow, lest she feel forgotten in the frenzy of her twin sister with the gaping hole in her lower jaw.

All this—and today was the first day of kindergarten. We laid out clothes, trimmed nails, took showers, packed backpacks, remembered lunch money, and set long-forgotten alarm clocks last night before bed. I was up early, staring at my ceiling fan and praying that everyone (me included) would have a peaceful and wonderful first day. The kids came down already dressed (always a good sign) and ready to eat, brush teeth, and hit the road. The pink camo and polka-dot backpacks that the girls chose at Target seem to reach beneath their knees, so I sported both of them on my way in to school this morning. It was utter chaos inside—parents toting coffees and chatting, little kids crying, big kids roughhousing, and parents spying inside classrooms long after the morning bell. Luke gave a quick hug and raced down the hall to enter second grade with gusto. Grace and Bella had a little moment of uncertainty that hovered on the border of tears but never quite crossed over. I felt the tight squeeze of that "one last hug," hoping that their tiny little bodies were able to soak in whatever strength they needed to take from me, hoping it was enough to make for a great day.

I walked out of school and back to my car utterly drained.

I am not typically a public crier; I much prefer to save my outbursts for my car, my priest, my shower, or a darkened movie theater playing a chick flick. Yet my tears occasionally sneak up on me at the most bizarre and inopportune times and shout, "Boo! Gotcha!" Situations that normally send other mommies into sobs are usually okay with me, likely because I have had to practice the uncomfortable art of letting my children go (every other weekend) for the past 4 years. I am learning how to love with a looser grip than I would have otherwise, and this is probably not entirely a bad thing. Today, however, I was the littlest of the big girls. I really wanted to hold on.

I fled the parking lot and hit the streets running, me and my iPod making a little bubble to keep the world out. I ran hill repeats again and again up Scenic Drive until the tears finally came, and then I walked home. I flashed back on a mental photo montage of my kids since babyhood, set to the *Garden State* soundtrack playing in my ears. By the time I got home, I was refreshed and settled (and sweating profusely—I never run at 9 a.m.!).

I guess just like the hole where Grace's tooth used to be, sometimes it hurts a little to make room for something new.

AHEAD OF THE WAVE

I don't have my summer groove on yet . . . been fumbling to find the sweet spot between enjoying free, unstructured time with my little people and managing to tend to the basic tasks of home and work. So far it still feels like an extended Memorial Day weekend, and maybe it will stay this way through Labor Day.

When you have three kids in your house without the energy burner of school, you have to get creative. Mornings begin peacefully enough, jammies and breakfast and maybe some art . . . and then, out of nowhere, just as the people in *Jurassic Park* experienced with the approaching T. rex, the ground starts to rumble long before you see it coming. The peaceful breakfast eaters and Lego builders suddenly realize they have been caged inside too long, and *wham,* the crazies begin. The volume increases to jet-landing decibel level and chasing and fighting ensue, followed by inexplicable silliness that cannot be stilled or explained. Being a parent in this frenzy reminds me of surfing: You have to swim out ahead of that wave and ride it in or you will be crushed by it.

My best strategy so far is the same strategy that saves me from my own crazies—exercise.

This brings me to my relevant tale. Last week at my Wednesday running group, I brought Grace and Bella (5) with me in an attempt to burn off the crazies before they burned me. I told them to pack whatever they needed to be comfortable at the park where we were meeting and get their running shoes on. They packed a box of cereal, two wooden chairs from our outside table, a blanket to use as "carpet," and enough Capri Sun drinks to quench the thirst of a Third World nation. We were off.

It was hot and humid, the new status quo in Texas henceforth through November. And for whatever reason, I was dying more than I usually do at running group (this may have to do with my exhaustion from trying to swim out ahead of the waves?) as we did a series of 800-meter repeats followed by a crisscross drill through the grassy field that reminded me of some torture tactic by my high school soccer coach (run easy on the outside of the box and sprint the diagonals—something like that). On about the third repeat, I started to slide back behind the pack, much like the survival-of-the-fittest tales Luke watches on *Animal Planet,* in which the hurt, old, or sick animal loses ground and becomes lunch. I was quickly becoming lunch.

We had a minute and a half to recover, and I was tomato red and gasping for air, wanting to bend over with my hands on my knees, if Cassie would allow it (she doesn't). Bella and Grace came up and gave me water, and Bella wrinkled her nose at my sweaty, beet-red condition and sweetly asked why I was in last place. I found enough air to crack up laughing and tell her that

I'm not as much *last* as these other girls are *fast*. She said, "Why does Paige always beat you? I thought you ran with Paige." How do I explain that I do run with Paige, but just not so much at speed work on Wednesdays? I was formulating my answer when Paige came over, jovial and not splotchy red or wheezing, and she said, "Girls, your mommy does run with me, and don't you forget it. Now, c'mon, Mommy, let's go!"

We got back into a pack at the designated start line and began our final 800. I began to more closely resemble that injured antelope as we crested the final hill, my pack leaving me for dead once again. I was happy to be finished, proud to have stuck it out on a morning when every fiber of my being wanted to go out for pancakes instead.

Suddenly, there she was, snapping me out of my maple syrup reverie. Paige had pulled out of her usual lead and slid back to the bleeding antelope section. She smiled at me and said, "I told your girls you ran with me; now don't make me a liar. C'mon, let's end this thing." And we did, finishing together.

I am not sure if my girls noticed or cared that much as they joined in for the cooldown, but I know I did. It wasn't so much that I needed some redemption in my daughters' eyes—or even in my own—as it was a reminder of how lucky I am to have a first-place friend who loves me enough to happily finish last.

Later, we got our pancakes.

LIVING IN THE MOMENT

Like a great Italian meal that simmers all day on the stove and is gobbled in minutes, December flies by despite every morsel of resolve I have to slow it down.

My Christmas morning was spent with my parents and my brother, watching my children unwrap and promptly put together (I curse black plastic thingies with holes and the dreaded cuticle-thrashing plastic wires—can I hear an *amen*?) and play with some things off Santa's wish list. The best-loved gift was an air hockey table, which sent Luke and Bella into high-stakes competition. The one time Bella won, she did an end zone victory dance with one foot on top of each of the living room chairs. We lingered in pajamas as long as possible, dawdled over brunch and championship rounds of air hockey, and had some snuggle time by the fire. When afternoon comes, it's time to get dressed and take the kids over to Daddy's house.

I am getting smarter. This year I wore my running clothes.

When my kids leave my house, particularly on Christmas Day, it leaves a hole in my heart the size of, well, my heart. Lance and I get along well; the kids handle it fine; it's just me that aches on the inside. I drove home, parked my car in the driveway, and immediately hit the pavement running. I was glad for the cold air, because the tears on my face looked like winter splash instead of boo-hoo residue. About a mile into it, my breathing evened out and I noticed that it was sunny and pretty outside. About 3 miles in, I hit some hills and started talking to God, listing everything that hurt like an old person at a doctor's visit. I started to feel better, albeit hypoxic, so I turned back and did the hill again. And again. And once again.

And there it was. My switch finally flipped. I have to turn it over, flip the switch from Mommy to Kik. This is something that several years ago would take me a few days. I used to wander around my strangely quiet, clean house in search of something, as if I lost my purse or forgot something in the other room, feeling totally misplaced in my own home and skin. Now what took days is condensed to an hour or so, if I have my running shoes on. Isn't that awesome? My quickest route back to feeling like myself again is to run and keep running until finally I round one more corner or crest one more hill and suddenly there I am, waiting for myself.

We all have to get more adept at switch-flipping. Whether it's leaving the office and entering our homes, or leaving our homes to go on a date with our spouse, or leaving our comfort zones to try something new, we need to be able to purposely access the part of ourselves that is required in order for us to be present and authentic in the new moment.

You can't have a great date with your spouse if your head is still wondering if you turned off the oven after you took out the chicken nuggets and your heart is home tucking in the kids. No, you have to be with your spouse, living life where you are. You can't be a good friend to a friend in need if you are half listening to her and half wondering if you left the *Scooby-Doo* DVD in the player and returned an empty box. No, you need to focus on being a friend. And I can't enjoy my quiet time and be productive when I'm not with my children if I spend all my kid-free time pining for them. Running is such a catalyst for me, helping me learn how to flip the switch more quickly and expertly on my own. A friend of mine who owns a restaurant in France tried to explain this phenomenon to me one day over coffee about how the ideal husband/wife and father/mother is able to flip the switch, not in a matter of days or hours, but from moment to moment. If you could have heard Michel say it, in French, with his wise and compassionate eyes focused on you, it would mean as much to you as it does to me. In fact, it means more to me now than when he first explained it.

I want to be the kind of woman who can do that, *du moment au moment*.

I'm working on it.

CROSSING OVER

Last weekend we took a good old-fashioned family road trip. In classic Griswold style (*National Lampoon's Vacation*, circa

1983), so reminiscent of my childhood years that it was almost eerie, we (my parents, me, three kids) piled into the family truckster and headed north on Highway 101 to San Francisco. The main difference between my childhood road trips and those of the present day is in the more relaxed nature of my father. When we were kids, he would let us stop to pee only if the car needed gas or we had a doctor's note confirming imminent bladder infection (kidding, but it seemed like it). With my kids, however, we can stop as needed. So we paused at interesting places along the way, including a place called the Madonna Inn, where they apparently specialize in cakes covered in bright pink curls of shaved chocolate instead of frosting. The men's bathroom there has a fountain for a urinal, so naturally the kids spent more time in the restroom than at our table.

We did all the classic San Francisco fun. We rode cable cars (yes, I let them dangle off the sides; yes, I had numerous heart attacks); Luke tried crab; we toured Alcatraz, watched crazy street performers, visited the wharf, the aquarium, Lombard street, Union Square, Chinatown. We ate our weight in sourdough bread. I woke up early to run, wandered the hilly streets with my people all day, and usually collapsed midmovie at night. So many memories were made; it was a perfect trip. The grand finale was a detour through 17-mile drive on our way home, stopping in Pebble Beach and Carmel.

Out of all the memories (and my kids each made a list— Grace had 86 things), one thing stands out for this mom.

One day we decided to have lunch on the water in Sausalito, so we had to cross the Golden Gate Bridge. It was a cold, gray morning, and the way the red of the bridge was cutting through the fog was spectacular. My parents pulled over before the start of the bridge, and the kids and I hopped out. I took a couple of photos, like the dorky tourist and devoted mother I am. And then we started running.

I have to preface this memory with the background information that a couple of years ago, maybe Isabelle would have happily run with me, but there would definitely have been
complaints ("I have a cramp," "My leg itches," "My shoe is
untied," "My lung collapsed," "I'm gonna barf," etc.) from the
peanut gallery and numerous stops. This phase was totally normal and had a vague charm all its own. But I noticed this year
as we were crossing over the bridge that we've crossed over an
even bigger bridge. *My kids and I ran across the Golden Gate
Bridge together.*

From my mother's pretrip lessons for the kids, I know that the
Golden Gate Bridge is 8,981 feet, or 1.7 miles. (My mother is a
teacher; every experience has a preparatory lesson behind it and
a report or journal entry after it—we are so lucky!) We relished
the entire distance, pointing out the city, the sailboats, and the
suicide warning signs. We talked and trucked along in our
going-out-to-lunch-in-Sausalito clothes paired with running
shoes. We looked ridiculous. I was wearing skinny jeans and an
unzipped thick fleece jacket, and I forgot a hair tie, so my hair
was whipping in all directions. To all the runners out for their
Saturday morning long runs with Garmins, hydration packs,
and Gu belts, I looked like a crazy lady out for my first (and
last) run. Don't worry, Rodale, I did not wear my "I work for
RUNNER'S WORLD" T-shirt—okay, it was dirty.

I know I grinned for 8,981 feet. I ran ahead and turned
around, snapping a picture of my people. I snapped one for the
eternal roll inside my head as well. Although I can't possibly
know at this point what their relationship will be with running,
I can tell you now that they each have one. We were out of
breath and talking over each other when we reunited with my
parents, cheering for us on the other side.

I have a lump in my throat just sharing this with you. I almost
didn't want to write about it, because I thought that somehow

putting it out there might diminish the intimacy of the experience. Or that it might lose some sparkle if I tried to translate it. Some personally significant things are best kept personal.

But in the end I decided that just like crossing over the bridge together, the best memories of all are the ones you can share.

7 KIDS

Nothing in my life has ever motivated me more than my children.

Never have I wanted to be stronger, healthier, more present, or more intentional with my heart. When I come up against a challenge or tough spot on a run or in life, I consider the implications of how my decision will translate to my children. Simply put, when I want to give up or give in, I think of them and I dig deeper. Because of them I am aware that there is more to me, more within me, than I ever imagined possible. I never thought I could love this big, be this fierce, this devoted, this real. Raising children is raw. It's the most vulnerable, humbling thing I have ever done. As they grow older and I have had a few experiences of watching them race or even running beside them, I realize that we are constantly training, constantly building endurance, for this, for them. What I mean is legacy. When we run we are showing our children, teaching without words, that we value ourselves, our hearts, our fitness, our health, our friendships, our clarity, and our balance. They see us push, and with every stride, they learn a measure of what it is to prepare for their own races. We are passing the torch.

BEING HERE

Last week my kids had Friday and Monday off for Presidents' weekend. Since it's not my year to have them for spring break, I decided to make an exodus. The stars were aligned, because I found a great airfare and my brother was in town and could house-sit the Ark (lots of animals; it rained the entire week we left). The fact that I had been saying "Hurry up" more often than "How are you?" was the truest indicator that I needed some time away with my little people.

When I get alone time with my kids, away from the have-tos and hurry-ups, I feel like we all get a much-needed break from the side of Mom that gets things done. Part of it is my personality and part of it is necessity, but I can literally pack more in and get more done than a person and a half. I say this not to boast but to lament and repent. Who cares if we get it all done if the people I love most aren't all that thrilled about getting it all done with me?

I promised my people that we would be taking our time. I turned my cell phone to silent and left it on silent. I turned the bedroom clock to face the wall. I left my watch in my carry-on bag. We never asked "What time would it be in Texas?" We were in Santa Barbara, on California time. We ate when we were hungry and slept when we were tired. I ran every morning in a pack of scooters, a bag of fresh croissants from our favorite bakery attached to Luke's handlebars. We stopped and ate on the grass when we felt like breakfast. We hiked through a eucalyptus grove, through a field of wildflowers and butterflies, along the bluffs above the beach. We wrote messages in the sand with a stick. We found sea glass and strung broken shells from a piece of driftwood. I got breakfast in bed delivered on a teetering cookie tray. We invited friends to dinner and walked to a pizza parlor instead of cooking. We fell asleep in a tangled pile of family and books. We walked to the movies and ate popcorn for dinner. The kids found a cool way to sneak up onto the roof, and instead of busting their chops, I made them a picnic and passed it up in a basket. We sang loudly into the wind, top down on the 101. I let the kids go to the little store across the street alone. (Okay, so I spied on them.) I didn't complain (too much) that they bought Dibs and Ring Pops for a snack. My fingernails, toenails, and their surrounding flesh received a valentine-red mani-pedi. We wandered the farmers' market and sampled berries. We couldn't get reservations at our favorite Italian restaurant on Valentine's Day, so we crammed four people into two seats at the bar at our favorite seafood joint on the pier and had root beer, sourdough, chowder, and fish and chips instead.

Something happened while we were away. I noticed that I wasn't the full-time referee of sibling WWF. I stopped shrieking "Put your shoes on!" as the precursor to every departure. My vocabulary blossomed beyond *no* and *stop*. I stopped responding to every beep of my phone like a mindless, drooling participant in a Pavlovian conditioning experiment and started responding to my children. For real.

I felt decidedly, delectably, profoundly present.

After I got home I realized I don't have to go away to be present; after all, being present is about being "here," not "there." I carried a small, round rock home, one we picked up on a beach run one morning. It fits in my closed fist and has just enough weight to feel substantial.

It is my souvenir, which in French means *remember.*

ROOM 304

This week Paige's daughter Layne had surgery to cut her heel cord. She has mild cerebral palsy and her left side is affected, particularly her hand and her leg. Without her brace, she walks on tippy-toe on her left foot. This surgery is a periodic one in Layne's life (once several years ago, this time, and likely once more when she stops growing), and the intent is to lengthen the tendons by cutting them and then casting her leg into more of a 90-degree position while it heals. My description is highly unscientific, but you get the idea.

My Tuesday schedule was clear, and I was able to go up and wait with her family while the surgery was underway, then return again in the evening to spend some time with Layne and Paige. I was expecting her to be groggy, in bed, in pain. When I arrived, she was hopping along in a child-size walker, talking animatedly to her friend Ella, who was visiting her, and wanting to go play Wii in the kids' lounge. Paige, on the other hand, was exhausted, the weeks of worry, anticipation, and preparation finally catching up with her. Other friends were visiting, so we pulled up chairs and sat on Layne's bed and talked in the quiet of the hospital room, with dim lights and the hum of the nurse's station as our backdrop. I love the way close friends convene when the situation warrants solidarity. The atmosphere and love in room 304 felt more like a slumber party than a hospital stay.

Paige borrowed my jacket (having been inside since 6 a.m., she had no idea how freezing it was outside) and went to her car to grab a movie for bedtime entertainment. Meanwhile, I got to help Layne brush her teeth and ease her little body from the walker into the bed, propping her wrapped leg up on a pillow. I love that girl like a daughter, and she let me brush her hair and apply balm to her postsurgery dry lips. She looked like a little angel tucked into that bed. I wondered if she was in pain, and she wondered if her IV bag had a goldfish in it. She never talks about her pain.

We have a friend in our running group who ruptured her

Achilles tendon, and based on her description, it was horribly painful. Her recovery has been long and slow. And here was Layne, whose Achilles had been severed in multiple places, and she was smiling at me and wearing my lip gloss.

At running group the next day, we did 3 miles' worth of hard interval training at the park. I was out of breath and out of steam with another 800 meters to go. We were close to where we parked; it was tempting to say uncle and call it a day. But there she was: Layne popped into my mind in classic Layne montage fashion, the way she does anytime I feel close to wimping out. I see a series of images: Layne as a preemie newborn gripping my finger in neonatal ICU; Layne trying to learn to walk and falling every other step—scraped and smiling as she chased Luke around in France; Layne racing a kids' K, still casted after her first surgery, beaming in last place, crowds roaring, her cast unraveling in the puddles on the course; Layne in her brace toting an oversize backpack heading off to kindergarten; Layne turning 10; Layne completing the 5-K for her Girls on the Run program 2 days before her surgery; Layne hopping around in her walker hours after a surgery that would render me hopeless and hopless and desperate for a morphine drip.

Maybe Layne doesn't feel pain, frustration, or limitations the way the rest of us do. Or maybe she does, but she just gives them less of her attention. However she does it, whatever the spark is that makes her utterly unique, I crave her company and I conjure her image anytime I start to think that I can't do something. Because that statement is not a part of her being; the only thing bigger than that girl's will is her heart.

I refocused and finished that last 800 meters. And another 200-meter sprint after that. And a cool-down lap after that.

After all, Layne was getting out of the hospital that

afternoon. I wasn't about to call it quits knowing the long road of recovery ahead.

I have to stay fit if I plan to keep up with her.

WORTH FIGHTING FOR

We went to a family friend's 7th birthday one evening this week, and when we arrived, their house was full of food, friends, and festivities. The mass of children started playing a game—some version of war, boys against girls. They ran in a pack from the backyard through the house, while the adults somehow managed to visit over the din of the wild rumpus. It wasn't long before Paige's daughter Riley came in crying; a boy had hit her on the forehead. We hugged her and got her some ice, assuming (correctly) that it was accidental, a normal play-time casualty. Well, Grace didn't see it that way. She came storming in, screaming all kinds of unflattering words at the boy who harmed her precious friend Riley. Her words were mean, though luckily nothing stronger than PG, and I should probably add that Grace is extremely loud. It was like the old E. F. Hutton ad in which silence falls over the crowd. (Remember the tagline? "When E. F. Hutton talks, people listen." Whatever happened to good old E. F. anyway?) It was a classic record-scratch moment. *Oh my.*

After her outburst, Grace made a dramatic heel turn, fled into their office, and crumpled into a chair, sobbing. I managed to collect her, locate Bella and Luke, mumble something to the parents of the little boy who was the recipient of Grace's wrath, hug the birthday boy, and make a hasty exit. Grace sniffled most of the way home, and I could see her splotchy, stern face reflected in the car window as she stared into the night. At home we made the frantic effort to recoup from a school evening out of the nest, cramming for spelling tests, filling out reading logs, showering, and tucking in. I saved Grace for last. She was already in bed curled into a ball with her stuffed animal and her blanket.

"Hey, girl, how you doing?" I asked when I walked into her night light–lit room.

"Okay," she said quietly, not turning toward me.

"You know, I know you had a rough night. I want you to know that I am not too happy about the mean words you used tonight, but I am proud of you for the way you love your friends."

"Mom, Riley is not just a friend, she's like family."

"I know, honey. I just think that you could have come and found me instead of yelling—"

She cut me off. "Mom, when someone hurts someone I love, I don't care about nice words. I don't care what anyone thinks of me. At. All."

She couldn't see me very well in the dark, but I was smiling. She waited quietly for a reprimand or consequence, but I had made my required parental remark (check in box) and had nothing more to say. Just a kiss, a tight hug, a blessing, and a good night.

"I love you, Grace. I really do. Everything about you."

"I know, Mom. I love you, too."

I walked out of her room and down the hallway, still shaking my head and smiling. *Grace.* She may be just shy of 8 years old, but she is already a full inhabitant of herself. I am not quite sure how that much person can fit in the confines of a child-size body. I totally get her. I can't punish her for being just like everyone else in my family, nor do I want to. I am aware that the mama bear that lives in me is fierce and unstoppable—I have seen her only on a handful of occasions, and she scares me, too. We tell our children to play nice, to be sweet, to share, to say thank you, to let others go first, to eat things they don't like without complaining, to say I'm sorry (whether they mean it or

not). And while these can be good things, they are not everything. There is a time to fight for what you believe and on behalf
of the people you love. Although this night and this particular
situation perhaps didn't warrant her full-armored verbal war-
fare, there is a part of me that is proud to know that she isn't
afraid to step forward, raise her voice, and lift her sword. She is
exactly the kind of person I would want for a friend, and I hope
to eventually earn that grown-up friendship.

I have thought of Grace on every subsequent run this week,
thinking about the things that matter to me, the things I will
fight for, the things I will lay it all down for. The things that rise
to the top of my heart and overflow. The moments when I don't
care what anyone thinks. At. All.

BELLISSIMA!

Last week as I was getting dressed to run a local 5-K race, my
daughter Bella appeared in my room wearing a running skirt,
running shoes, and a shirt. She asked me to put her hair in one
ponytail in the back, like mine.

I said, "Honey, you look cute. Are you going to come cheer
for me tonight?"

"No, Mama, I'm running with you tonight!" she replied with
a big, toothless smile.

I had big ideas about attempting to beat my previous time, and
those thoughts went immediately and happily out the window.
I made the ponytail and we headed to the beach. We were a bit
late, parking was nuts, and she wanted to fill out the registration
form herself in her very best handwriting and sign her name in
cursive. Then there was much debate about whether she liked
her number (545) on the front or the back of her shirt, or maybe
on her skirt in case she wanted to take off her long-sleeved shirt
if she got hot. She thought it would be best on the back of her

shirt, because most people might be trying to catch up with her. We carefully pinned the number on the shirt, twice. (The first time, it was crooked.)

Then we started walking to the start line at the top of a big hill. We passed a couple of people who said, "You two better hurry; they already started the race!" Oh dear. Bella took off at a full sprint up the hill to try to chase down the pack. This was before I had a chance to tell her about the importance of pacing herself because the first half of the race is uphill—a steep uphill. Even steeper if you are 6. I caught up with her and breathlessly (no warmup for me) told her about the importance of pacing, even though I already conceded the fact that at this rate we would likely be walking most of the hill. We passed the usual starting point, and there were no runners to be seen.

"Where is everyone, Mommy?"

"Honey, I think we missed the start. Let's not worry about that and run our own race. This is something very important to learn how to do if you really think you might like to be a runner."

So we slowed down a bit and ran side by side, at Bella pace. Which, I might add, is not slow. We talked about breathing in through our noses and out through our mouths. We talked about how pretty the sunset was and how it looked exactly like a red playground ball. We talked about how nice and clean the air is when you are by the sea. I asked her how she was doing and told her she got to choose if we ran fast or slow or if we walked or stopped and stretched. She said she was just fine, so we continued as we were.

Finally we came across the race leaders, who had already made the turn at the crest of the hill. They looked even faster on the downhill. We cheered for them, and Bella had concerns about being in last place, so she picked up the pace. I followed suit. When we could see the cones indicating the turnaround, I told her we were almost there. She was smiling so big that her air intake was coming entirely through the window created by her missing top and bottom front teeth. By this time we were back in the pack, and people started to cheer for cute little number 545 with the blond ponytail. Every time she heard her number, her smile got impossibly bigger.

We turned the corner and she let out a huge "WAHOOO!" as we started going downhill. I was incredulous that we had climbed that entire hill without stopping once.

"This is much better," she said. I had to agree.

But better than better, undeniably best of all, was the sudden awareness I had that I was running next to my daughter. I was sharing one of my most treasured passions with another of my most treasured passions, and my eyes filled up with tears at the glory of it all. The red sinking sun cast the entire hillside and coastline in a warm glow that matched my heart. My sweet reverie was broken by number 545 making a hard right and rolling very dramatically (classic Bella) onto the grass. I plopped down next to her, breathing hard.

"Mommy, I am *so* tired! It hurts right here." And she pointed to a spot under the left side of her rib cage. I explained that she had a cramp and that we could stretch for a bit and walk it off. I taught her how to poke at it and take deep breaths. She thought this was funny, and a tickle war ensued. We got rid of the cramp and kept walking down the hill together, holding hands and talking. Anytime anyone cheered, "Go 545! You can do it! Looking good!" she would pick up the pace long enough to sustain the compliment and then go back to walking. We did this for the rest of the race—until the finish line was in plain view. There she saw her cute little friends Kate and Sammi cheering from the sidelines.

"Bella," I asked her, "do you want to know the most important thing about crossing the finish line?"

"What is it?"

"You have to smile."

And so my sweet little speedster got her second wind and went full throttle for the finish line, smiling the whole way. From there it was full-body hugs, high fives, a million kisses, and ice cream to celebrate.

I am quite sure she slept well that night, with echoes of "Go 545!" in her mind. The next day I saw her number stabbed into the bulletin board in her room with one of the safety pins from her shirt.

I have a feeling that number won't be her last.

AMAZING GRACE

Our entire Bible study group, plus kids and spouses, went camping last weekend at Camp Deer Creek in Medina, Texas. I never went to an organized camp as a kid, so the whole experience of cabins, canoes, archery, fishing, and campfire s'mores with my children was especially delectable. (I did go camping with my dad and his friends with backpacks and tents, so I wasn't deprived of the great outdoors.) It was the perfect way to enjoy time with family and friends before we head to Boston at the end of the week.

To illustrate the notion that you have to earn your fun, there is a tower to climb in order to enjoy riding the longest zip line in central Texas. The tower is made of wood and is about 50 feet high. One side is a climbing wall and the other side is an obstacle course of sorts, beginning with a rope ladder, then a tire, then a log, then a trapeze, then a telephone pole with metal pegs. Climbers wear helmets and have a safety rope attached to a harness.

It's one thing to do these team-building activities as part of some annoying HR ploy to foster camaraderie and trust in the office (been there, done that). It's quite another to experience something like this with your children and friends you already love and trust. To understand the underlying dynamics of the story, you need to know something about the dynamics of my family. Luke is the oldest, the big brother; he (in typical first-born fashion) gets to do things first, and he usually does them well. He was recently voted best running back of his flag football team. Bella is adept and agile, a natural athlete who excels at every sport she tries. She tossed her own training wheels in the trash at age 4, or was it 3? Grace has more charm, humor, and insight than most adults I know, but when it comes to physical things, these days she has to work harder than her sister. She reminds me so much of myself that I bite my own lip when I watch her concentrate.

Luke was quick to suit up in his harness and helmet, excited about riding the zip line. He made it as far as the top of the rope, which swayed under weight and with the pull of the wind. He wanted nothing more to do with it and was lowered back down. Bella made it to the trapeze bar before she adamantly decided she was afraid of heights. Grace was the little child that could not stand to go upside down in toddler gymnastics, so I was surprised when she suited up to climb the ropes. I stood on the ground nearby and watched her (pitting out, lump in my throat) as she began her ascent. If any of my children needed a win, it was this one. When the rope swayed under her, she steadied herself and moved when she was ready. She found firm footing above the net and pulled herself up onto the tire. From there she had to balance on a thin rod that tilts and spins unless your weight is equally distributed between your feet. She struggled there for a while before she got brave enough to throw her arms over the log above her and slowly pull one leg over at a time. I could see her shaking with effort and determination. From there, she reached for the trapeze bar, one hand at a time, then pulled herself onto the telephone pole. She climbed the rest of the way up and hoisted her body onto the platform at the top. I saw this whole last part through blurry vision, because I was sobbing and screaming her name loud enough to make sure she could hear her mom above the din of all her other fans. She peeked over the edge, her toothless grin and cavernous dimple appearing under the thick, white helmet, and I was utterly undone.

Next up was Paige's daughter Layne, who has weakness in her left hand and leg from cerebral palsy. It took 30 minutes for her to reach the top, and it was humbling to watch, thinking about how easily most of us give up when our only obstacle is frustration. I was already an emotional wreck at this point, so Paige and I were good company for each other.

When I watched our brave little girls fly together across the field on that zip line, screaming and laughing into the afternoon sun, a piece of my heart flew with them.

In classic Paige fashion, she readily accepted the challenge to climb the rock wall. In classic Kristin fashion, I dreaded climbing the ropes so much that I figured I had to do it. I can't remember much about my climb except that I did it as fast as I could because I was shaking so hard.

Flying on the zip line ranks pretty high on my list of fun. Not as fun, of course, as watching Grace.

Isn't it cool how people can surprise us? Even people we know as well as our own children. Even as well as we know ourselves . . . there is always plenty of room for surprise. When it comes down to it, determination has a greater impact than giftedness. This is the thought that I will carry with me to Boston this weekend, as I watch Cassie and the other women run the Olympic trials. This is the spirit I will carry with me when we run our race on Monday. I am actually starting to get excited.

FRESH EYES

Every once in a while I have to change it up—so my kids don't think they have a dull mommy, and so Mommy can shake off her dust. This was one of those weekends.

After a beautiful run with Paige on Saturday morning, the kids and I got cleaned up and packed the car. I had a small overnight bag for myself, and the rest of the Volvo was packed to the hilt by the kids: all the pillows from my bed, more movies than would fit in the hours we would be away, a "picnic" that would feed three families, three Razor scooters, one DVD player, three puffy down jackets (it was 75 degrees when we left, wearing shorts), and a stack of books.

First stop was Enchanted Rock, just outside Fredericksburg, Texas, about an hour and a half away. This is about the perfect road-trip distance with my kids, long enough for one movie and the early whining of bathroom break insurrection. The entire picnic was consumed during the drive, so with that out of the way, we made straight for the Summit Trail. I was chosen to wear the backpack stuffed with snacks, water bottles, and sunscreen. It was so hot out that it wasn't long before I was drenched with sweat beneath the backpack. People up on the top looked like scurrying ants from our puny vantage point at the bottom. We started hiking up. The terrain is mostly sheer rock face, very little trail, which makes Enchanted Rock look like an outcropping on a barren planet. The kids started panting and complaining about the heat and their aching legs about halfway up, but this was cured by a water break and by seeing a smaller child scamper by, totally unaffected. I told them we could stop and turn around, but they insisted that they were Armstrongs and would not stop until they reached the top! Unless we saw a rattlesnake, was Luke's caveat, and the girls agreed. So did Mommy.

We finally reached the summit and enjoyed the view and another water break before heading back down. It was a steep and gravelly descent, and I admit I was a little worried about someone losing their footing and taking a tumble. They walked slowly and stuck together, and as I lagged behind watching them I was quietly stirred by their teamwork and camaraderie. These are the same kids who slugged each other over a Webkinz toy on the drive over, so it was very encouraging.

There is something about a little adventure that brings out the best in all of us. The kids need to see me in a new light, to remember that the lady who packs their lunches, flosses their teeth, and folds their laundry is also a rock climber ("Mom, this is like Mt. Everest, only in Texas!") and expert navigator. (Ha. Luke sat up front and recited my MapQuest printout to me.) And the lunch packer/teeth flosser in me needs to remember that I am parenting their spirits just as much as their tummies and teeth. An adventure sets us all free.

After we chugged our remaining water supply and set the car's AC on high, we set out for downtown Fredericksburg, where I had reservations at a little stone cabin. This overnight was originally a gift certificate for a romantic getaway, but since it had twice nearly expired and been renewed (yes, I got it in December '05—now hush), I decided it was time to quit waiting on romance and enjoy the darn thing with the people who love me the most.

We cruised the town, ate a casual dinner at the local brewery, and rode our Razor scooters under the lights of the covered picnic area in the park until past bedtime. I am not bad at scooter tag, if you want to know. Back at the little stone house, we made use of the big, romantic bathtub in our bathing suits and goggles with plenty of bubbles. We all passed out before the end of the movie, three in one bed and one on the couch. It was heavenly, an early Valentine celebration with my sweethearts.

Sometimes a little escape offers the perspective we need to see that the love we love most is right in front of us. And a little adventure ensures that we keep seeing each other with fresh eyes.

8 ENDURANCE

If I had to pick between speed and endurance as a training (or life) goal, it would be endurance. Maybe it's because I'm heading into my forties and have a richer perspective about time. Or maybe it's because the longer I'm a runner, the stronger my desire becomes to remain a runner—for as long as possible. It is not lost on me at long-distance trail races that many of the people passing me at the end are women who are older than me, going longer than me. It's a window of possibility opening, like arriving on a beach vacation at night and opening curtains to the sea in the morning. The view makes you want to get outside. I want to go longer as I get older. I want to learn to tame the beasts of doubt and discouragement. I want to figure out how to push myself through the thin membrane of *I can't do this* and pop into the wide, open space of *maybe so*.

I think there are few more potent metaphors between running and life than those derived from the subject of endurance. When we consider what we are really training for, why we care so much, why we are willing at all, it becomes as obvious as a

black bra under a white T-shirt. *We want to be able to endure.*
When life throws us some difficult miles, we want to know that
we can suck it up and prevail.

I don't know about you, but I get chills just thinking about it.

GLORY

Last night was my first Nite Moves of the summer season with
my kids! Nite Moves is the ocean swim and 5-K held every
Wednesday evening. This year the organizers added a special
kids' mile, so there is a distance in between the full 5-K and the
little-kid run on the beach. It's a perfect distance for my kids,
and we were so excited to get out there. We packed our usual
pile of things: a big blanket to spread on the grass, some warm
hoodies and jackets, sweatpants to pull on over our shorts when
the ocean breeze turned cold, a football for Luke, and some red
wine for the adults. (They have dark beer for the postrace
concert, but sometimes we are in a wine mood.)

I debated about whether to run the 5-K myself, but after an
early morning bluff run with Terra and some PT work on my
psoas and hamstrings in the afternoon, I decided to take it easy.
Speaking of psoas, I was not aware that (a) I had one or (b) it
needed work. Apparently the psoas is the key link between the
trunk and the legs; it is imperative for endurance, and core stability
resides there. Why I am just learning about this after 37 years is
beyond me. My initial report on psoas work is *Ouch*. Emily
is a wise and delightful PT from Britain, and I think I am able to
endure this kind of suffering only by focusing on her accent. She
says step one is for me to become aware of my psoas (this will
take a while), and then eventually the goal is to learn to engage it.
Oh my, something else to add to my work-in-progress list.

It ended up being a blessing that I didn't run the 5-K, because
I felt compelled to trail behind my sweethearts running in the

kids' mile. Two of my kids raged at the head of the pack and one lagged behind, having a rough race. I saw my beloved athlete slow to a walk and take on the dejected shoulder slump signifying defeat. I came up from behind and said, "Hi, honey. Want a friend to run with?"

I was met with tears, heavy breathing, and a sniffled response. "I am not a good runner. This is terrible. Everyone else is better than me."

Oh dear. Not this.

Mommy: You are too a good runner. There is a big difference between being a good runner and having a good or bad race. Rough races happen to everyone. A good runner is anyone who has fun and tries her best.

Bummed-Out Athlete: I *stink*. [*sniff*]

M: It's okay. We can walk for a while.

BOA: Do you think everyone else is finished by now?

M: No, there are still kids behind us.

BOA: [*more tears*] I bet you never cried in a race before.

M: You want to make a bet? Come check me out at mile 23 of any marathon if you want to see some tears.

BOA: [*small smile*] Really?

M: Really. You can ask my friends.

BOA: Were you embarrassed?

M: No way. I was just focused on trying to finish, not really caring so much what I looked like at that point or even what my time was. I just wanted to do my best all the way to the end, and it wasn't easy for me. It's usually not easy for me; I guess that's why I like it so much.

BOA: We can run some more. My cramp feels better now.

M: Okay. You stay ahead of me so that way you set the pace, and I'll just be here.

BOA: Mom?

M: Yeah?

BOA: Thanks.

M: Anytime. You know you can't be a good runner without handling some bad races. I'm really proud of you.

We were close enough to see the finish line at this point, so I veered off the course and watched my runner take it on home. It isn't easy to be present for three people, cheering for some without going overboard and bolstering others without making them feel coddled. We walk a fine line as we shepherd these precious people into becoming. But anytime they cross a finish line, a piece of my heart crosses over, too.

It made me think later, when the moment had passed. It is impossible to be a good runner without bad races. Just like it's impossible to be a good artist without messy creations, or a good parent without fumbling, or a good friend without failing, or a good spouse without missing the mark. We can't do anything well, not one single remarkable thing, without reaching far enough beyond ourselves that we are bound to fail from time to time.

The glory is always somewhere in there.

SACRIFICE

Yesterday was Ash Wednesday, which marks the start of Lent, the 40 days before Easter. I got in late on Tuesday night after a trip to Dallas to tape a television program, and I was tired but happy to wake up in my own bed, with my dogs snoring on the floor, instead of in a hotel room. To me it's always worth it to make it back to the nest whenever possible after a business trip. So I woke up sleepy and a bit drained on Wednesday morning.

I met Paige at her church for the early morning Ash Wednesday service and sat with her and her kids (mine were with Dad) for the brief service followed by the dispensation of ashes, marking a small, gray cross on our foreheads. Soon after, we reconvened at Cassie's running group, which her e-mail described blithely as "something fun in nature." Frankly, I was hoping for a trail run. Nope, her idea of something fun in nature was a brutal hill workout. We did three small loops that included one whopper hill that left us all breathless and vaguely nauseated. This was followed by two longer loops, each about twice the distance of the smaller circuit. This longer loop included two hills, one medium and one that felt like scaling a stadium wall, at least to me. It's interesting when you have already expended yourself in other ways—things like work, parenting, taking care of life's business—and then you have to find something in reserve within yourself to complete a workout that is truly beyond your capability in that moment.

About halfway through the first long loop, I began to think I really should have stayed home and respected the fact that I was already worn out before the day began. On the second half of the eternal climb (which was really two hills separated by a small lull, a false sense of breathing respite and quad relief), I honestly felt like crying. It has been a long time since I felt close to tears from running; occasionally, running might release some tears stuck in an emotional holding tank, but rarely do I feel so pathetic during a workout that I want to cry or give up. I mean really give up—not just placate myself with the *option* of giving up. But I didn't give up. A quiet and tenacious voice spoke to me and told me to take my time, go whatever pace I needed to go, but under no circumstance was I permitted to quit. At first I thought it was Cassie running beside me, but I could see her at the top of the hill. No, it was me talking to me.

I got close to the top, finally, and heard the familiar and supportive voices of my friends yelling for me. I ran through the stop sign at the top of the hill and sucked in great, gasping breaths like I had been held underwater for almost too long. I wiped my dripping face on my shirt and saw the smear of gray ash. I looked at Paige's face and saw her forehead in a gray wash, and I had to smile. *Of course*. Of course today of all days would not be a relaxing trail run, of course today of all days I would not have the rest or the energy to excel at this workout. Normally I love hills, with a weird, reverent sort of love. But today I would nearly be brought to tears by them. Of course.

After all, Lent is a season of sacrifice. Even those people who have no observance of or interest in Lent can appreciate the timeless, noble act of sacrifice. Maybe it means sucking it up when things hurt and you can't breathe and completing the effort on a day when you don't have what it takes. Maybe it means going to work and supporting your family when your career is in an unfulfilling rut. Maybe it means honoring your marriage even when it doesn't feed your soul the way it used to, right now. Maybe it means taking the time to visit or call your parents or grandparents because it's the right thing to do and it makes them happy. Maybe it means biting your tongue when you feel like lashing out. Maybe it means boldly speaking up when you feel like shutting down. Maybe it means being generous when you feel like hoarding. Maybe it means taking a deep breath during the inevitable periods of frustration and chaos in raising children, and taking the time to figure out what's really going on or to figure out how a moment can become teachable instead of punitive. Anytime we can acknowledge our selfish desires or feelings of inadequacy with a nod and move beyond them, that is sacrifice. And the season is upon us.

SUBSTANTIAL ALVEOLI

I have a race on my calendar this weekend: the 3M Half Marathon in Austin. This race is special to me because it holds my half marathon PR (1:36:26) from 2006. For that race I had a specific training program that Cassie designed for me, a full calendar combining longer distances, hill work, and speed work. I didn't drink red wine for a week before the race. I carb-depleted-then-loaded. I remember being very nervous. I also remember being mystified and elated when I crossed the finish line.

That pace is about the same pace I have run almost every 5-K since then, which makes me laugh.

Prior to my 50-K in December, all my training was lo-o-ong and slow, with my attention focused on nutrition and not wiping out on the terrain. I still attended my Wednesday running group because I love those girls and because I didn't want my body to forget true suffering in the face of all my off-road glee. I have still kept up my base with longer weekend runs. And I still nurture my friendship with the trails; just last Sunday I logged more than 2 hours on the greenbelt trails, not realizing when I set out that the cedar count was astronomical that day.

I felt fine (great, actually) while running and was planning a picnic outing in my head on the final climb back to the car. I was filled with the happiness and peace of time spent in nature and was high-fiving myself on the inside for not tripping, getting lost, or turned around even once. But as soon as I got in the car I was hit by the 18-wheeler known to Austinites as cedar fever. It sneaks up and smashes into you without warning. Before I could get my car back on the freeway, I was sneezing in machine-gun succession, my nose was running like a Texas creek after a storm, and my eyes swelled shut, one with a welt in the corner that looked like a mosquito bite. It's a wonder I got home without an accident. I showered, did a sinus rinse, took a Benadryl, abandoned all picnic plans, and returned to bed for an afternoon alternating between napping, nose blowing, and bad TV.

I really want to run well this weekend. I don't know that I am where I was with my specific training back in '06, but I have

3 more years of miles and life in my tank since then. We'll see. I went to my Wednesday speed work at the track this week and still had a handful of Kleenex at my disposal.

Cassie had us do three sets of 4 × 400 (those not running 3M did five 400s per set; if I were them, I would've signed up for the race on my BlackBerry after drills once I heard that), and our first lap set the scene for the rest of the workout. Every lap in each set had to be the same or faster than the one prior, and (drum roll) every set had to be faster than the fastest time of the previous set. Um. Okay.

I was bordering on panic when Cassie told me to go out at a 1:36 lap pace. I have a memory of my 400 typically being a 1:42. I raised an eyebrow at her, but that was as far as I dared go. If you complain to Cassie, she doesn't react, she just makes it harder. I could imagine her not even making eye contact, saying, "Okay, 1:34, TFB." (TFB is her customary sweet and sensitive abbreviation for "too *flipping* bad.") I have trained with Cassie since 2003, so I have learned to keep my complaints to myself. She and I are on a last-name basis when it comes to the track.

We set our watches. I could feel my heart in my throat, already overexerting, and we hadn't even moved yet. Speed work, like giving speeches, makes me have to pee. If I had been wearing a heart rate monitor, it would have melted and fused to the skin around my rib cage. Cassie could likely smell my fear from where she stood with her clipboard, so she reminded us that each lap stands alone and not to think about the next.

The first lap was good—whoops, too fast, panic pace. Cassie was not pleased. "You made your bed, now tuck in." Oh my. I tried to keep Ellen in my sights a few seconds ahead of me. We had a brief respite (45 seconds) between laps. I walked off into the grass, trying to keep my gasping and wheezing from frightening the other runners into calling EMS. The third lap of every set was a total mind game—my body made painted signs with ugly slogans and was rioting and picketing on the steps of my inner capitol. I had to shift into dictator mode. It wasn't pretty.

By the third lap of the third set I was certain I would barf up a lung, or at least substantial alveoli. (I love that word, *alveoli,* and, sadly, I rarely get a chance to use it.) By the last lap, the angry mob within had grown. I could hear shouting: "Why are you doing this? Who are you kidding? You are not getting paid for this, missy! Stop the madness! We're going on strike! That's it; you're on your own." Then silence. All I could hear was the pounding pulse in my ear, my breath choking in heaving sputters like an old car, the *slap slap slap* of my feet. I survived the second curve, then the final approach on the runway to my destination: Cassie, her serious expression, and her waiting watch. *Let's land this sucker.* I gave what I had left and flung myself across the line. This time I'm not kidding about the alveoli.

I cooled down for a couple laps, slammed some water, tried to clear the stars from my peripheral vision. I grabbed the soggy layers of clothing I stripped from where I'd tossed them on the bench, and my car keys. Cassie stopped me.

"Nice work today. You are looking strong."

A compliment from Cassie is the equivalent of a prom date, a fresh haircut, a real letter in the mailbox, an anonymous flower left on the windshield wiper of your car, and breakfast in bed, all lumped together. I melted.

In that moment, the mob inside turned friendly, cheering, hugging, and slapping hands.

They put their signs away . . . at least until Sunday.

A DAY'S WORK

Last Friday I became Forrest Gump. In his running phase, I should clarify (as opposed to the infantry, shrimping industry, or Woodstock phase).

I dropped my kids off at school—hugs, kisses, buh-byes, extendo waves as they traversed the crosswalk, air kisses from the bottom of the stairs, the tap of the horn. My gear was in the backseat. I met my friends Jon and Nancy Hill at the trail head by 8. Bodyglide, sunscreen, hydration backpack stuffed with snacks and filled up with H_2O—and we were ready to roll. We started slowly, picking our way carefully over the rocks, knowing that we were not yet warm or agile and that we had a long day was ahead of us. Nancy was also nursing a sore ankle—an unfortunate mommy-injury, an ankle-rolling wipeout over a tricycle. I hadn't run with these two since we trained for the New York City Marathon together back in 2004. Running is the best way to catch up with old friends. (Or to get business done, for that matter; I met with my publisher last week in Austin over a 7-mile run! That's the kind of meeting I like.) Our conversation, like our route, was meandering and comfortable. Old friends have ways of easily settling back into a groove.

Jon led the charge, knowing the trails better than we do. He took us out and back covering 19 miles, stopping a few times to refuel and replenish our backpack stash. We shared food, anecdotes, and wisdom. I picked Jon's brain often, since he is no stranger to endurance training and racing. Neither is Nancy—she has run Sunmart and other trail races before and loves it. They have the kind of marriage I imagine I would like to be part of one day. They have a respect and ease between them that is at once inclusive but also clearly their own. They go on *adventures* together—alone and with their two children. They have camped in the Grand Canyon, done altitude training camps in Leadville, taken their RV all over creation and explored. We talked about these adventures over the miles, and I felt happiness for them and also a vague wistfulness, thinking of how incredible it must be to share the experiences that build you as a person and as a couple. A few miles later and gratitude had settled into my empty places, and I was thankful for my children, family, and friends. It isn't the same as being part of a couple, but it is way more than enough to slosh over any cracks and wear them smooth.

We returned to our car, quickly shared some peanut butter sandwiches and Gatorade, and ventured on. It was hard to leave the car, knowing we still had 7 miles to go to complete our total of 26. And it was hard to transition from the varying terrain of the trail to the continuous slap against the asphalt. Some of these miles were quieter, each of us in our own heads, working it out. We got to our turnaround point and stretched briefly. I tried to stretch my quad by picking up my foot and pulling it behind my knee, first the right, then the left. The left side was like an ornery horse getting its hooves picked. I instructed it to lift and got no response. It was like a synapse was clogged and the message wasn't getting through. I shrugged it off and we shuffled on. We imagined how we must look to normal people running the 4-mile loop—slogging along, backpacks, water bottles, salt-encrusted faces, and chapped lips, weary warriors returning home from battle. We had to laugh at our own brand of weirdness. This is where the Forrest Gump image came to my mind, when he had long hair and a scraggly beard after endless weeks of running. And then the energy mysteriously returned, our banter picked back up, and we made it to our cars at the trailhead.

It was 2:10 p.m. I had an extra 10 minutes before I had to go back to school and pick up my children. We took the time to soak in Barton Springs pool, peeling off our dirty socks and shoes (never would I have imagined that this girly-girl would tolerate having her perfectly good pedicure outlined in brown dust) and walking carefully over the mossy rocks to find a seat. We eased into the cold water, letting the current rush over our feet, legs, and hips, tilting our faces back to the sun, breathing deeply. We did it. The realization that we had just run a marathon while my children went to school ran over me like another current, this one on the inside.

I wrapped my soggy, salty, mossy self in a towel and drove shoeless to the pick-up line. I opened the windows and sunroof and read my latest installment in the *Twilight* series (my Stephenie Meyer addiction; yes, I know it's meant for teenagers, but I don't care) until I heard the familiar stampede of backpacked children rushing for home base. Luke found me first, slung his backpack in the back hatch, and hopped in the front seat beside me, taking a big slurp from the hydration pack nozzle. "How was your race, Mom? You do okay?"

"Better than okay. And it wasn't a race, just a run."

"Same thing." He smiled. Maybe he's right. It's all part of the journey.

I took the girls to gymnastics like any other mom, smiling softly on the inside, still shoeless and soggy on the outside. *All in a day's work.*

STEADILY MAINTAINED

Our Saturday morning long run was the 2-hour variety that felt like 20 minutes. It's funny how time expands or contracts in relation to our enjoyment, to our presence in the moment. It felt more like a moving conversation than a workout. We are training for a series of half marathons, which could be my favorite distance. I am hoping to have one race that beats my best time of last year. I ran the 3M Half Marathon at a 7:23 pace. That is pretty zippy as far as this body is concerned, so we shall see. I intend to enjoy every second out there.

Later that morning, Lance and I were talking about running as we watched Luke's flag football game (the way parents sit, side by side, talking but looking at the field). He is running the New York City Marathon in a few weeks. We were talking about the perfect running weather, and I mentioned that my friends and I ran 2 hours. He responded, "Why? Do you have a marathon coming up?" No, I said, we just ran.

We just ran. It got me thinking. I want to be fit and ready for whatever seems fun or challenging. Oswald Chambers has the *best* quotation for us: "Preparation is not suddenly accomplished, it is a process steadily maintained."

Isn't that just perfect? Was Oswald a runner?! Like anything in life you love enough that you want to honor it by being your best, you can't just wing it. Things of passion are not to be checked off a list. You aren't "done." Health, fitness, balance, faith, the building and nurturing of relationships, parenting . . . these things do not end. There is no star for completion. Even a task well done or a milestone met is not a conclusion; it is simply a transition to a new beginning.

When we embrace this mind-set and accept the mobility of the unset finish line, we can begin to grow into people who are *manifested in the moment*—people who relish equally the process and the punctuation!!

9 BODY

O h, girls. This subject, specifically as it relates to body image, is one of those doozies that can make even this shy girl shake it off and step boldly up onto the soapbox. I do it for myself and the long, roundabout journey I have made to finally feel delicious in my own skin. I do it for my daughters, because I would pick up a giant sword and stagger beneath it if I could slay the dragons of self-criticism, mean girls, and food weirdness on their behalf. And I do it for you, because I feel that our sweat sisterhood is sacred, and victories in this area are harder to come by on our own.

I have a dear runner friend whose thinness these days makes me ache and worry. Her formerly glorious body has been reduced, withered, as if she has been held hostage and starved or ravaged by illness. Only she is held captive within herself, and her illness is rooted somewhere between her eyes and her mind, when she sees her reflection. I miss her strength. I miss her springy stride beside me. I miss her steadiness. She has no idea how much I miss her, even though I try to tell her. I want my friend back, dammit.

I used to complain, in a semijoking kind of way, that my thighs and my calves were practically the same size. This haunted me when I lived in Europe, because all skinny-leg jeans and supercool boots were for people with slender calves. Mine are not slender. Mine are strong and curvy. The last time I saw my friend, with her cablelike veins and muscles that looked like Ace bandages stretched across protruding bones, I made a promise to myself: I will never say one more thing that is ungrateful or uncomplimentary about my body. And I mean it. Even if I'm joking. It isn't funny to me anymore.

Did you know that studies have shown that the best way to foster positive body image in girls is for their mothers to speak kindly and positively about their own bodies in their company? When I pull on a swimsuit or check out my rearview in a pair of jeans in earshot of my daughters, I make a point to say, "Right on, girl," and wink at myself in the mirror. After all, if I don't think my own aging booty is cute, how on earth will my girls ever appreciate their own?

OUTLINES

My speech this past Thursday evening to my daughters' running group, Kids in Motion, went well. I asked the Coach, Melody, beforehand if any of the speakers had talked with the girls (ages 7 to 11) about the subject of body image. Not so far. I decided it was going to be me.

Body image is a daunting subject, riddled with nuances and fraught with meaning. I was equally intimidated and honored to talk to such young women about something with lifetime impli-cations. I did what I usually do when the stakes are high: I asked an expert. I e-mailed Molly Barker, the founder of Girls on the Run International, and I asked her how her groups handle such a delicate and colossal subject. She offered amazing insight.

I began to feel equipped as I drove around town, filling the back of my VW with a roll of butcher paper, markers, tagboard, glue, stickers, and granola bars.

We arrived at the park, and Coach Melody led the girls in a series of warmups and exercises. Then it was my turn. I gathered up my supplies, took a deep breath, and settled in, sitting cross-legged in their circle on the grass. I started, in an attempt to foster some connection, by telling them a tale about when I was their age and living in the Bay Area. Because I was the new kid, a pretty good student, and relatively uncoordinated, I was picked at the end of the pack when we chose teams in PE. One athletic kid, Chris, used to pick on me, saying, "Aw, man, I don't want her! She stinks in sports!" I am still not sure why our PE teacher never intervened. Anyway, I told them how bad that felt to me and how the idea that I stunk in sports stuck with me for a very long time.

Then I showed them an exuberant photo, taken moments after I crossed the line of my 50-K trail race last December. I explained how the woman in that photo (*moi*) just finished running 31 miles off road. I posed the question "So, tell me, do you think this woman 'stinks' at sports?"

"NO WAY!" they answered. Yep. My point exactly. I used that example to illustrate the power of words and how other people cannot use their words to define us. We hold that power for ourselves alone. It's crucial to understand that power so that we use positive words when we speak to others, or perhaps even more importantly, when we talk to ourselves. I showed them a collage of some images depicting good friends, playfulness, fitness, nutrition, family time, sports, balance, etc., and we talked about these words. Then we moved onto the activity that Molly suggested I try.

I asked the girls to pair up, and I handed each girl a piece of butcher paper and some markers. They traced the outlines of each other's bodies, and we held them up for review. We talked about how this was our "outline," our "shape," our "container." And how this shape basically was the one God gave us, having a lot to do with heredity (we defined this) and history and a bit to do with our healthy choices—we eat healthy food so we can grow, we exercise so our muscles are strong, etc. Then I had them take their outlines, find a private spot in the park with some markers, and write all the things that were special and unique that they liked about themselves—on the inside of their outlines.

I wasn't sure how this would go—if they would be shy or at a loss for words or have short attention spans. I was, frankly, blown away. I don't know if I have many adult friends who could come up with words about themselves that were so gracious, thoughtful, interesting, insightful, introspective, and honest. I saw words like *good friend, honest, responsible, loving, good sense of humor, disciplined, good student, smart, athletic, strong, loyal, good reader, adventurous, brave, silly, good daughter, good sister, thoughtful, kind, helpful, generous, fast, good runner, focused, dramatic.*

We gathered back in our circle and shared some of our words. This conversation started more shyly, but after a few girls shared, almost everyone wanted in on the action. We revisited the idea of the power of words, how the words we choose for ourselves have the power to define us, protect us, and keep us strong. I handed out stickers and treats, and our time was up.

I walked slowly back to my car, carrying my roll of paper, markers, and the rolled-up outlines of my daughters, holding the words that mark who they think they are, right now at age 7. The words they chose were so bold, so true, and so pure—no hiding, no deprecation, no games, not diluted or distorted by anyone else's careless words. I want to roll them carefully, tie them with ribbon, and guard them on their behalf. But I know I can't; I know the glare of the world will somehow get in. I guess I can only hope that each lesson, taught by me and many wiser than me, will take root and grow into something that offers some shade.

And I had to wonder about my own outline—if I could lie still enough, without wiggling self-consciously or making remarks while being traced. I wondered if I would be completely at ease with my image on the paper and what words I would choose today to fill in the description of the woman inside.

THE CRUST ZONE

I always floss my teeth, even when I've had a glass of wine too many and sleep in my mascara.

I would rather overprepare, underestimate (myself, not the task), and overdeliver.

So considering these things about me—my inherent nature to prevent rather than fix—my nutritional patterns are a mystery to me.

I can go for weeks, months even, making wise choices about food, and then it's like I hit a slump or a rut. It happens so innocuously that I don't notice it, like subtly drifting on a boat or raft only to lift your head and find the shore seemingly miles away. Next thing I know, I start to graze instead of preparing meals for myself. It goes like this: For breakfast (after coffee, of course), I might eat a couple bites of Eggo waffle in syrup off Grace's plate or a Ritz cracker with peanut butter while packing lunchboxes, or maybe I'll steal a bite or two of soggy Rice Krispies as I'm doing the rapid kitchen one-two into the dishwasher on the way out the door. Then I drop the kids off, go to speed workout, or run 7 miles or try some hill repeats, and I just bonk.

I finish my workout poorly, slam some water, run some kid-unfriendly errands, or shackle myself to my computer to meet my deadlines. I look up, see lunch has passed, and hurry to get the girls from school. Bella, my 5-year-old budding fashionista, berates me for still being in my running clothes. (She has actually said, "Mommy, no one will marry you if you wear those clothes. Running clothes are for running and pretty clothes are for walking on the town." I nearly died laughing, then duly noted the small possibility that she has a point. Clean hair and a baseball-cap-free head might yield a more fruitful dating life.)

By now the girls want a snack, so maybe I'll eat the crust that has been cut off a peanut butter and honey sandwich or eat a spoon of cookie dough if we are in a baking mood (read: Mommy has PMS). Later, Luke comes home and wants a snack, so I'll grab a handful of his popcorn or some of his "nachos" (these are Tostitos with ripped-up American cheese, melted in the microwave—*very* lame by Tex-Mex standards). Then I cook dinner, snacking continuously on random ingredients, and by the time it is on the table, I am sick of the meal before I sit down. I wonder why I am exhausted and starving at 10:30 p.m. when I finish working in my office.

Does this sound familiar? Or are you far more deliberate and disciplined than I?

It startles me to find myself back in this place again, the Crust Zone, as I call it. I am tired and cranky and have no snap at my workouts. Then it hits me: *Duh, you're doing it again, eating like crap.* Then I go to Whole Foods, restock, reset, and start over. A few days later I start to feel better again.

The Crust Zone is about more than laziness, I think. It is a way of disrespecting and undermining our bodies. How can I expect to go run 15 miles effortlessly when the previous day I ate the crusts of peanut butter and honey sandwiches as a meal? Cassie, my coach, summed it up the best way. When I explained my backsliding to her, she said to think of food the way we are instructed to use oxygen masks on an airplane: adults put the oxygen masks on first, then on their children. Why? Because if you are suffocating, you can't very well help your little people, now, can you?

Well, ditto for energy slumps and exhaustion. How can we take care of the business of life if we haven't fueled ourselves? We simply cannot provide for others when we are shortchanged.

So I'm trying to get out (and stay out) of the Crust Zone. I am trying to plan ahead and prepare when I know I'll be pressed for time, on an airplane, or on the run. I'm keeping healthy snacks in my car and making dinner earlier, before we all start raiding the pantry. More than merely avoiding the rut, I'm trying to figure out why I end up here. Perhaps I have a distorted view that generosity means putting everyone ahead of self, when true generosity and thoughtful caretaking require an even application across the board—meaning it has to include me, too. Love, like sunscreen, if not evenly applied, can burn in weird patterns.

As I type, I'm snagging bites of my lunch. It's a spinach salad with grape tomatoes, pine nuts, cottage cheese, and a chopped-up veggie chicken patty. I ran almost 2 hours with Paige and Katie this morning . . . and you know what? I feel great.

DETOX

Last night was Cassie's birthday.

We had a small dinner party at my house before going out on the town. We made homemade pizzas, rolled our own dough (thanks to Chef Nancy), and had all kinds of fun toppings to go with plenty of birthday bubbly and some nice wine. It was all so much fun.

Until this morning.

I woke up and my head felt like I needed to remove my brain, put it very gingerly into a deep bowl of ice water, and let it soak. Why do I think I can still drink champagne and feel normal the next day? It must have some type of amnesia-inducing quality that inhibits memory of my advanced age and my last experience with the bubbles. I woke up and shuffled to the kitchen in search of Motrin and some ice-cold water. (If I could not literally soak my brain, I wanted to at least try to drown it.) My house smelled vaguely of smoke, and my bare feet stuck to the dusting of cornmeal that covered my kitchen floor. (It was initially sprinkled on the counter to prevent sticking while we worked our dough.) I thought of the pizza toppings from the wayward sliding pizza that had an unfortunate transfer from the wooden cutting board to the pizza stone, frying on the bottom of the oven instead. Luckily, I got ahold of my security company in time for them to turn the fire trucks around. It's never good when your neighbors know you are having a dinner party and then emergency vehicles block your street. (Especially since I actually *can* cook.)

I stood in my messy, wine-glass-littered, cornmeal-covered kitchen and looked at the clock: 5:50 a.m. I thought I might dust off my feet, jump back into bed, pray for deliverance via Motrin, and hope to wake up later and start over. 5:55 a.m.: Thought maybe I needed just a little more water first. Made futile attempt to wipe off feet with wet paper towel. 5:59 a.m.: Remembered that Melissa was going to run at 6:30 down at the lake. 6:05 a.m.: Slammed half a cup of coffee and scarfed one toaster waffle with divots filled with maple syrup, dripping, while standing over the dirty dishes in the sink. 6:06 a.m.: Caught a view of myself reflected in the kitchen window over the sink and diverted my glance immediately. 6:10 a.m.: Threw on clothes and searched for my other shoe. Grabbed another water for the road. 6:15 a.m.: Exited driveway.

I secretly hoped maybe Melissa would be a no-show. But *Melissa* and *no-show* are incongruent. She arrived at 6:30 on the dot and said, "Looks like it's just us." I inwardly groaned, because while I love the wisdom and humor of conversations with Melissa, I was feeling more like hiding in the middle of a pack and hanging on by a thread, sans conversation. She asked how I was, and I told her I had a few glasses of bubbly the night before and needed to repent. She said, "Well, a detox will do you good. Let's get on with it." *Groan.* I think I was so dehydrated it took 5 miles to work up a sweat; either that or the bubbles themselves were trying to escape through my pores. Melissa is very fast, very funny, and very smart. I don't know if it's harder to keep up with her mentally or physically; it's usually both. Today I was feeling sluggish in every capacity.

When I finally broke a sweat, I was like Albert Brooks in *Broadcast News.* The sweat came like a torrent, and my shirt was drenched in places that formerly, to my knowledge, did not have sweat glands. Like a little kid whose fever breaks, I finally started to perk up and I wanted a Popsicle. We rounded the final bend in the trail just as I was starting to get my groove back. I thanked Melissa for her patience, gave her a hug (I think she winced, due to my amphibian slippery-slimy condition), and dripped all over my car on the way home. I was purged, vindicated, still tired, but blessedly clear.

Thank God for running. It is the ultimate detox for me, whether my poison is champagne bubbles, a foul mood, or a bad attitude. If I overcome inertia, get out, and get moving, eventually every kind of toxin works its way out.

MIRROR, MIRROR, ON THE WALL

One of my close friends is walking precariously close to the edge, and I am afraid that any warning I shout or any abrupt move I make to reach out to her will startle her and cause her to tumble.

My friend is one of those girls. By this, I mean she is so startlingly beautiful that people do a double take just to make sure they don't know her from some magazine. She is fit (a great runner) and sexy and fresh and stunning. She stands out in a crowd. Usually women like this are off-putting to other women, that old jealousy thing, but something about my friend makes her beauty magnetic instead of repellent. Initially it might be a bizarre form of curiosity, like: Is this woman really equally pretty on the inside? Once you realize that her beauty goes all the way through, curiosity turns into comfort, and there you are—lucky to be in her good company.

Except for one, hopefully short-lived, problem.

She doesn't see herself this way. Someone said something negative to her (an inane comment: "Really? You don't look like a runner") that should have come off in the wash, but it stuck. It somehow set off a chain reaction of other long-buried mines of doubt and delusion. And now it's like someone has replaced her mirror with a circus funhouse mirror and she can't see anything clearly anymore.

Everyone can relate. It's like the sad hostility, the PMS feeling of trying on 10 different things, all of them insufficient and stifling, while trying to get ready to go somewhere. Everything feels unflattering, but the only useful thing to change is our perspective, not our outfit. But no one can hear that when she is in her closet with her clothes in a heap, clock ticking, time to go or else be late.

I run with my friend, listen to her, pray with her, pray for her. But I can't make her see herself the way everyone else sees her, especially God. Why do we do this with our beauty? We stuff it, warp it, minimize it, starve it, berate it, and then wonder where it goes. I know that one day when she's a 70-year-old woman, she will come across a photograph of herself from this era, and she will weep as though seeing this woman for the very first time. She will weep for time lost, for days spent worrying about nothing and chasing something that she possessed all along.

And so here I stand, on the periphery of my friend's sadness.

I wish I could use my creativity for her healing . . . paint her, sketch her, describe her with words, illuminate her from the inside out, so that she could finally see. Or run with her, so far and so fast that everything false would be burned as fuel.

Our culture breeds such insecurity; it runs rampant across our femininity, taking hostages in its wake. Let's run counter to it, circle round the other way, surprise it—take our people back.

10 FREEDOM

There are many words in my repertoire to describe a good run; it's a cleanse, a respite, a reset, a connection, a prayer, a challenge, a passion, a pleasure. But if I were forced at starting-gun-point to choose one thing, just one thing, that sums up my affinity for running, it would have to be *freedom*. Freedom is the thing I'm after when I pull on my shorts and lace up my shoes. And even though I wear a watch, it is more about reclaiming time than measuring it. Regardless of the weight of my responsibilities, no matter how sluggish or choppy my stride feels at the outset, I eventually even out and lighten up. Just like the stray layers of my hair work their way out of any ponytail, the inner parts of me that are pulled too tightly somehow manage to escape their confines as well. I love the wind in my face, the burn in my legs and lungs, the smell of sweat mixed with sunscreen. I love the knowledge that I would rather brave the elements—rain, heat, cold—than stay home and miss my liberty.

There is a restless place inside me, and if I don't intentionally access and relieve it, it groans at me, distracting me. There are too many thoughts in my head, too many feelings in my heart, too many things I want to do and say—and if I'm not careful, I can get overwhelmed with myself. Running restores my equilibrium, quiets the noise within, reprioritizes my list, repairs my state of gratitude, and returns me to myself, but a better version, nice and roomy in my own skin.

Taking off on a run isn't about leaving the rest of my life behind. It's about departing just long enough to fuel the desire to pick up the pace when I head for home. Like a freshly swept porch with a swing, a hanging fern, and a glass of sweet iced tea, my life welcomes me back and invites me to rest a spell.

SHAKE IT OFF

On the topic of why I run, a major reason is to "shake it off." I bet you are doing it too.

Here is what I shake off:

My foul mood

A lousy night's sleep

Indecision

An unsettling phone call

A hangover

Tight legs from the gym

Feelings of inadequacy

PMS (*see also:* My foul mood)

Travel funk, including jetlag or just general airplane odor

A cold (I mean, I could feel lousy enough to debate getting out of bed, yet somehow after a run I can breathe and find a reason to go on)

Spiritual malaise

Parenting pressure

A day of decadent eating

Relationship quandary

Routine

Allergies

An argument

Doubt

A mistake

Germy children

Limitations, self-imposed or otherwise

Lack of gratitude

Constraints

Excuses

Fog

Sound familiar?

When I think I have no time to get out there or that taking time to run could be the most selfish thing to do in that moment, my feet start slapping the pavement and my lungs fill with air and I remember once again, just like always, that there is nothing selfish about being clean. Running is one thing that allows me to be everything I need to be for everyone else and not resent it. With so many time constraints and limits and rules and routines in the hectic pace of daily life, we need another place where we set our own pace, even if it's just for 5 miles. We need a simple and acceptable route to freedom. We need to shake it off.

JUST GIRLS

One of the best things about running is that it cuts across the crap that litters life and relationships in other areas.

I mean, tomorrow morning, after I take the kids to school, I'll head to the track for my weekly speed work. It's not like I'm training for the Olympics or to win a race or even to win my age-group—none of those things motivate me. I just want to improve, period, in every area of my life, in equal measure, and running happens to be important to me. It is a catalyst for many other things. And my week would not be the same if I didn't get some quality time with some like-minded, ball-capped, ponytailed, strong-spirited, quick-steppin' ladies. Half the time I am too winded to talk and only see the back of their Nike shorts, or they see the back of mine, but it doesn't matter.

I just want to be in their good company.

Which brings me to my point, which came up in discussion on a run. The point is that to me, running offers a respite, a zone free from the conflicting, competitive, disheartening, punitive, and sabotaging behavior that brings us all down.

I am not sure where or when it begins, though I see it already in the relationships at my daughters' preschool. And I can only speak of it from a female perspective, because this is all I know intimately enough to dare comment on it (though I am quite certain that men deal with it in different ways). There is something about women that permits us to vie for a better impression of and for ourselves by belittling someone else. It rages through the gossip and social strata of adolescence and should by all means end when we "grow up," but somehow it does not end, it only mutates.

Think about it.

Some woman might excel in the workplace and someone else is quick to call her a witch or worse. Someone is pretty and someone is not; they are both equally cursed. Someone who's skinny is obsessive; someone who's curvy has let herself go. Someone has a baby and we make judgments about her choice between natural childbirth and using an epidural. Someone breastfeeds and someone gives formula, and somehow it is everybody's place to comment. Someone stays at home to take care of her kids and she is second-rate intellectually, or she gets the "it must be nice" routine. Someone else works outside the home and she is second-rate maternally or a slave to materialism. Even if we have no idea what motivates either choice or what makes it possible.

We judge if someone has a nanny. We judge the poor person who never gets out much. We judge other people's relationships, even if our own are crumbling. We judge other people's parenting, even when we are all hanging on by a thread and we are all far from expert. Someone who speaks her mind is grating; someone who doesn't is a wimp. Someone with a successful husband is a kept woman; someone who struggles is a poor thing. Someone who never exercises is lazy; someone who does take time for herself is decadent. Someone who hides her feelings is cold; someone who is authentic gets picked apart. We judge who has what job, who is busier, who has more stress, who has it "rougher." Like what—she who complains loudest is the best martyr? Or she who enjoys and is grateful is a simpleton who has no idea of the "real world"? Someone tells us bad news and we secretly rejoice that it's not us. Someone shares good news and we call her arrogant.

The funny thing is, no one ever wins—because, ladies, *we are all on the same team.*

Can you imagine if we acted like it? If we treated each other like it? This is why we love to run together! Just for a glimpse of it! For the blessed 30 minutes, 1 hour, 2 hours, however long we run, it's our modern-day red tent. Because regardless of who we are, what our bank account has in it or doesn't, what we do for a living or don't, if we are married or not, if we are emotionally broken or healed, if we breastfeed or not, if we eat meat or not, if our hair color is real or not, if we believe in God or not, if we are sullen and introspective or freewheeling and hilarious . . .

there has to be a place to just *be*. And in a sport that requires only shorts, a jog bra, a shirt, socks, shoes, and some heart, we are probably about as equal as we are going to be. Why not enjoy and appreciate each other for once, plainly?

After all, we were all just girls, and we are all getting old.

FIREFLIES

An interesting thought occurred to me about photographs.

Have you ever noticed the way people, particularly women, look back at old photographs of themselves and are wistful? "Oh, I looked so *young* then!" "Look at my *skin!*" (*Sigh.*) "Good grief, I was so *skinny*! And here I thought I was heavy at the time!" "Awww, look at us—just gorgeous. *We had no clue.*"

No one ever really mentions that just as we had no clue at the time, there might exist the possibility that we have no clue right now. Captured moments of today are the wistful memories of tomorrow. I guarantee that just as we can look back at a photo from 10 years ago and appreciate ourselves, 10 years from now we will look at a photo from today and think the same damn thing. How come nobody brings this up? Wouldn't this awareness bring us a certain measure of peace?

Can you imagine the liberation if we could just appreciate ourselves right now? Who we are, where we are, what we look like? If we could just look in the mirror long enough for a basic once-over and a smile-wink and be done with it? If we were too content and confident to critique?

I saw my daughters growing up before my eyes this weekend. Isabelle sang in a kid rock band on Friday night, with a music school that teaches music by ear. She played keyboard and drums and had lead vocals on two songs. I watched her up there, mic in hand, smile on her face, totally at ease, and I wanted to scrape some of the confidence oozing from her pores and bottle it up, save it to dab on myself sometimes or anoint her later, if she forgets what she's made of. This was followed by my girls' First Communion on Saturday morning. Watching them, poised, pensive, and peaceful, walking down the aisle at church—my breath caught in my chest. *Are these really my girls? When did they get so tall and beautiful?* The contours of their faces are losing the roundness of youth. Their features are distinct. No longer kid paws, their hands have assumed the unique shape that I will recognize for the rest of my life. I know the next time I see them walking the aisle dressed in a white gown and veil I will say to myself, *Her First Communion seems like yesterday . . .* Where does the time go?

At running group this week, Amy and I were following the pack. I asked her if she noticed how unbelievable the legs were loping in front of us. Really, these women looked more like a college soccer team than a group of 40-year-olds. "Do you think they have any idea how lovely they are?" I asked her. "They have no clue," she laughed. I wanted to tell them, but I couldn't catch up without popping a lung, so I'm saying it now.

Savor yourself. Cut yourself some slack. Appreciate your beauty. Wink at yourself in the mirror. Tell your husband he has nice buns. Tell your wife she's hotter than she was yesterday. Tell your children how you see them. Tell your parents thank you. Remind your friends who they are.

After all, 10 years from now, right now will be 10 years ago. Moments are like fireflies. You are a runner, so go chase them. Cup them carefully in your hands and watch the glow seep through your fingers. Don't miss it.

2 YEARS TO PREPARE

Sometimes the best kind of party is the kind that moves. And this was exactly how we celebrated our friend KT's 40th birthday this weekend—wearing leis and stopping for doughnuts, racing the hills of Austin in the Run for the Water 10-Miler.

My favorite part was a thread of conversation that wove its way through our group during the race: "What is the best part about being 40?" Being 38 with 2 years left to train, I was highly intrigued. Here is the wisdom I have to look forward to at 40.

You get to say the things you used to think about but would never say. Other times you choose to keep your mouth shut, because it just doesn't bother you anymore. You aren't afraid of having a preference or an opinion, no matter if anyone else agrees with you or not. You do the things you used to talk about doing but never did. You quit playing small. You learn to forgive. You learn the difference between when to let go and when to hold on tight. You stop rushing. You aren't intimidated to say it like it is. You eat what you want; screw it. You aren't as worried about getting hurt because you know you can bounce back. You rarely feel like a fraud in your own skin. You have earned the right to be an expert in something. You stop apologizing all the time. You see the humor in things, especially yourself. You finally wake up and realize you are as hot as you're going to get in this lifetime, so you might as well enjoy it. You stop blaming people and get to work. You learn to say no, so your yes has some oomph. You stick up for people who are too young or feeble to do it right. You buy clothes that fit you today and get rid of the old ones in your closet that taunt you. If your marriage has made it this far, you really love it and take better care of it. If you're single, you don't settle. You spend time with the friends who lift you up and cut loose the ones who bring you down. You stop giving your power away. You are more concerned with being interested than interesting. You see the value of being on time. You get to be in a new age-group at races. You are old enough to appreciate your freedom and young enough to enjoy it.

You finally know who you are.

11 IDENTITY

I am a runner.

How many times have we said that? To a new acquaintance at a business function or cocktail party, on a first date, to a fellow mom in one of our kids' classes, to a new friend . . . We say it by way of introduction, explanation, as a means of finding connection. We say it because every time we do, it reminds us of who we are.

No matter how mired or muddled our identity can become through the transitions of womanhood—becoming a wife, mother, stepmother, or grandmother, juggling work and home, blah, blah, blah—we always have running as a touchstone. It brings us a sense of clarity, peace, purpose, accomplishment. It gives us a blessed window of time-for-self that somehow makes the rest of the day easier to carry. But it is even more than that.

I contend that when we breathe deeply into one passion, we provide oxygen for others. When we remember who we are and what we love to do and take steps in that direction, we move into a realm of hopefulness and possibility. We have momentum.

We are inspired. We harness energy. We remember how to aim. We shake off fear. We are so sexy.

Reconnecting with our passions, the things we have loved since we were little girls, is more than remembering who we were. It is the culmination of who we were, who we are, and who we are becoming. It is the evolution of a life. It's your *I am* statement. Chase it down.

THE ATTIC

I spent the morning following my friend Katie in her first triathlon. Watching her dripping wet and running by us with a smile and a wave, transitioning onto her bike, making loops around downtown, figuring out how to fix her chain, running a 10-K in the brutal midday heat and humidity, and heading home to nurse her baby . . . It was humbling to me. I am so proud of her I can barely stand it.

Lately my friends have done some pretty impressive things. One recent Saturday morning we ran with our friend KT, who was competing (after several years on hiatus) in a local 1-mile swim. Our run was her warmup. She just turned 40—she won her age-group. For Paige's 43rd birthday last week, she competed in a local horse show. She borrowed a horse and a trailer from a friend and spent her birthday in a hot, dusty riding ring, the stands filled with friends and children cheering her on. Her smile lingered for 2 days afterward. My friends Amy and Stacey got accepted into a prestigious writers' conference at Columbia University in New York; they went several weeks ago. My friend Leticia is taking a leap of faith and starting a new business with her husband. My animal-loving friend Christi is releasing her first book, benefiting the Peninsula Humane Society. My friend Saskia just fulfilled her dream of having a home birth—and, ahem, her daughter weighed more than 9 pounds. My daughter

Grace hiked to the top of Ajax Mountain with her dad this weekend—amazing.

Just to think about these women and tell you about them fills me with awe and wonder. These aren't indulgent women who have nothing else to do—these are women like all of us, who are juggling family life, career, finances, relationships, homework, challenges, and changes, and yet, still they are finding ways to bring life to their passions. It's so easy to come up with excuses: I'm too busy right now, it's not my season, things are complicated enough, it's too much trouble, the kids, my job, my travel schedule, my this, my that. If we aren't careful, we come up with all sorts of ways to creatively dilute our passions, shift our uniqueness to simmer on the back burner, stave off our desire by placating it with counterfeits, starving our talents until they are withered and weak, and ignoring our restlessness in hopes that it will take a hint and go away.

Remember what you love to do. Don't put it in a chest in the attic of your being and leave it for your kids to find long after you are gone. *Mom liked to write? Mom was a runner? Mom could swim? Mom did ballet? Mom had a beautiful voice? Mom painted? Mom could act? Mom climbed mountains? Mom liked camping? Mom played guitar? Mom was a good photographer? Mom spoke French? Mom rode horses?*

Let your children see you do your thing. Let your friends come watch you. Let your husband fall in love again with that cool, interesting chick he married. Let yourself be you.

I AM

Since I was a young girl I have always wanted to be something preceded by the words *I am.* I tried on many ideas in my mind before finding my Cinderella slipper: *I am a teacher. I am a ballerina. I am a veterinarian. I am a doctor. I am an artist. I am an oceanographer.* I like the way the words *I am* are simple, bold, and clear and roll easily off the tongue. In 36 years I have been most content when my life was an *I am* statement rather than "I manage . . ." or "I sell software that . . ." or "I work for a company that . . ." Perhaps it has always seemed beautifully noble to me to cultivate a craft or pursue a title that signifies identity rather than occupation.

Today I live peacefully (and gratefully) as an *I am*. I am a mother. I am a writer. I am a runner. It has taken me a while, but at last (thank you, God) my identity ties directly into who I am rather than an action I perform. Even though I mother, I write and I run; these verbs are less important to me than what the nouns signify.

I say all this because this topic has weighed heavily on my mind this week. Katie has been having some stomach issues lately, and after our half marathon, she didn't feel well. Katie is so tough that where she would say "Um, I don't feel so good," I would be screaming for morphine, an acupuncturist, an epidural, and my priest and mumbling incoherently about sciatica, gout, asthma, Ebola, rickets, and scurvy. (This flair for drama usually occurs at about mile 17 of any marathon.)

Our darling "I don't feel so hot" Katie ended up in the ER the morning after the 3M Half. She was too sick to keep down any food or hydration and too weak to care for herself. She spent 2 days and 1 night in the hospital getting IV fluids and being tested for everything under the sun. We still don't know the final results, but it looks like colitis is part of the diagnosis. We think this means an overhaul of habits—food, drink . . . and running. My beloved friend who exactly a week ago was blowing past me in the half marathon now tires after a walk around her block.

Katie can do whatever she puts her mind to, so an alcohol-free macrobiotic diet is just something new to learn and grow accustomed to. Her sadness this week was not about eating brown rice; we all like brown rice. Nor was it about not drinking red wine or coffee; well, okay, maybe a little.

Her sadness was part of her perceived identity adjustment.

This brings us back to the idea that every single one of us connected here today understands the implication of the *I am* statement below.

I am a runner.

This has nothing whatsoever to do with race results, placings, PRs, split times, training programs, gender, age, racing schedule, weekly mileage, or pace bands. This has to do with something deep, something tender, something profound, something powerful, and something untouchable about who we are in our hearts. This is why we recognize each other, on the road or in coffee shops, and we nod and smile. This is why we are never alone, even if we are training far from our hometowns or way outside our comfort zones. Even if no other *I am* statement about our life feels good at the moment, we always have that one.

I have no doubt that Katie will regain her health and her strength. Likely she will be able to eat something besides brown rice and to run around her block rather than walk—hopefully, with Paige and me by her side. Sweetheart, in the meantime, you are not left out or left behind. You are simply pacing yourself. What I want to tell Katie and anyone else out there struggling with injury, illness, delay, or disappointment of any kind, is that even if you are healing or taking time off, you are still, and always, a runner.

GIDDYUP

This morning Katie and I ran for 2 hours in humidity so deep and drenching, we felt like we were cutting through the underbrush of the Amazon. We were a little concerned about running without Paige, because Paige is the one who always keeps track of minutes and miles. Not to mention that Paige's nickname is Rand McNally, because she has an unfair and uncanny sense of direction. I, however, was unfortunately born without the GPS upgrade package. Somehow Katie and I managed to suffer through the swamp and find our way back home after a decent run. The reason Paige wasn't running with us today was that she had to tend to her other passion, one that has been dormant for 25 years.

Paige entered a horse show today.

I found my way (with explicit directions from Rand McNally) to the Travis County Expo Center and wandered around the stalls and trailers until I found my friend and her posse. I learned that flip-flops are not the footwear of choice for a horse arena. I hung out there most of the day, watching the kids, admiring the fancy horses, and observing my friend in her element. It was like watching a wild animal being released into its natural habitat on a TV nature program: riveting and sweet. I see Paige in one light, the way I know her—as a mother, a wife, a daughter, a friend, a runner. She is one of those lovingly annoying people who are pretty much good at whatever they attempt, so I'm used to that. But to see her on the back of a horse is like finding the missing piece of a puzzle you have worked on for a long time. I have been friends with her for 10 years, but I missed three-quarters of her life. Today she seemed like a teenager, utterly immersed in her world with her horse. (And her three prize ribbons! Yee-haw!)

She showed me a journal she kept as a young girl, which cataloged all her horse events, written in multicolored markers, with bubbly letters that have dots on the stems. Because she and I have so many clash-worthy differences, I sometimes wonder how we connect as easily as we do. But when I saw this journal, I caught a glimpse of precisely why I would have loved her way back then exactly as much as I do now. Despite the fact that she is as freewheeling as I am measured and studious, we are both equally focused and equally devoted when it comes to the things we love.

She entered almost every event today (clearly she's a jump-in kind of girl, while I prefer the steps), in categories that are too numerous and too unfamiliar for me to properly recount to you. But I can recount that she was beautiful out there! She wore a bright blue shimmery top, black pants, chaps (which fit her when she was 16—excuse me?!), a belt buckle the size of a Big Mac, a black Stetson hat worthy of a country music video, red lipstick, boots, spurs, and a smile bigger than Travis County. She looked so young and free and happy that another friend and I decided that the world would not need Botox if people simply did what they love.

We all need to find the thing we love to do as much as Paige loves to ride her horse. And we need to know the passions of the people we love. Because if we can't articulate and activate our heart's desires, what exactly are we doing anyway, marking time?

Sometimes running is that thing for me, unleashing me from my yard and allowing my body to chase down my thoughts. Sometimes running is the vehicle for my passion—when it plugs me back into my spirituality, or when it frees my mind of entanglements and provides the perfect insight or angle for my next writing assignment. Paige is carried away by her love of horses, and I am carried away by my love of words.

We have to know what carries us away.

12 CONFIDENCE

My mother always told me the most beautiful woman in the room wasn't the prettiest one, the skinniest one, the best-dressed one, the most talented one, or the most popular one. Without age and without fail, the most beautiful women of all time are the ones who radiate confidence. These are the women who are so magnetic that people of both sexes are inexplicably drawn in. These are the women who are so comfortable in their own skin that the rest of us immediately relax in ours. These are the women who are so free with the best they have to offer that they call others to bring forth the best in themselves. They do not puff themselves up, nor do they play small. They laugh, often, and often at themselves. Confident women are captivating women.

How do we become more confident women? How do we help our sisters and friends grow in confidence? How do we raise confident daughters?

Like every other worthwhile pursuit, we begin by putting one foot in front of the other—and move in the right direction. And if we're really lucky, we do it together.

WILLING TO BE SEEN

I did my normal Wednesday running group workout on Tuesday this week—solo—because I was giving a speech on Wednesday morning. I ran in the misty morning after school drop-off.

Normally I account for my pace and my effort by my slot in the pack. It's very primal, really; we have an alpha dog, or two, in the pack. I am somewhere like an epsilon dog, if I can remember my Greek alphabet correctly (likely drowned out by bad keg beer back in the early nineties in Ohio). Anyway, since I'm not alpha and I had no pack, I felt a bit like a lost dog. I couldn't remember how bad this particular workout was supposed to hurt, so I pushed until I was empty when I got to the stop sign at the top of the hill, gasping like I had been punched in the stomach. (Cassie later said that was probably about right.) On my cool-down jog back to my car, I thought about the topic for my speech the following day: Confident on the Inside.

It occurred to me that it's important to separate from the pack sometimes and reacquaint ourselves with how it feels to push it all alone. It's good in general to know what you are willing to give when no one is watching.

Because it's who you are when no one is watching that builds the confidence and the comfort to give your best in the moments when it's time to be seen. And the fraud-o-meter could definitely go off during my talk about confidence if I weren't trying my best to walk the walk in my ordinary days. My audience, in addition to the amazing coaches and volunteers at the National Summit for Girls on the Run, included Paige, two of her daughters, and my girls, Grace and Isabelle (who prefers this to Bella now, as it is more formal, more serious, not some nickname).

To the best of my knowledge, the picture my girls have of Mom at work is a pajama-clad woman huddled over her computer screen. Seeing Mom take the microphone is a view of a part of my world that's usually relegated to the days when they are at school or with their dad, or occasionally with my parents if I absolutely, positively have to travel on my mommy time. It was such a sweet gesture on Paige's part to wrangle four girls from school and bring them to see me speak. This is a gift we give each other, making sure all the facets of Mom are seen and intimately known by our children.

With my own daughters as well as Paige's girls, who are practically daughters, in the audience, I really, really wanted my message to be "ageless." If we can't speak words of confidence to our girls, who will?

Here is how I defined Confident on the Inside.

Confident on the Inside means: You are wise enough to accept God's definition of who you are, and you are strong enough not to accept counterfeit messages. You know your own beauty and are grateful for it, never needing to promote or pollute it. You possess awareness of your talents, as well as the humility and generosity to share them. You can say yes and no with equal certainty. You live and love big—never needing to play small or belittle others. You can say "Thank you" to a compliment as easily as you can say "Forgive me" or "I forgive you" to a mistake. Confident on the Inside means that you feel so comfortable in your own skin that your very presence is an invitation to freedom for others. Confident on the Inside knows no age.

And here's part of how I think it has to be developed.

I want my girls to see me out on a race course, both sucking wind and struggling as well as flying across the finish line. I want them to see me shake off my shyness and get up in front of a room full of people and talk about the things that matter so much to me that I am willing to offer a piece of myself in the hope that they might matter to someone else. I want them to see me eat and enjoy food—with the appetite of a woman who prefers to push rather than deprive. I want them to see me try new things—fail at some and fall in love with others. I want them to go on adventures with me. I want to be a team. I want them to know what it means to put your heart out there, all of it, and be happy with that, regardless of how it is received.

We have to live it out, ladies. *We have to be willing to be seen if we want to earn the relationship to be understood.* If our lips are moving but our actions don't match, we become a badly dubbed foreign film, without the benefit of subtitles.

We show young women how to be confident on the inside by first being confident on the inside ourselves.

BLIND SPOTS

I missed my yoga fix last week and my body was creaky and grumpy about it, so I went to a class on Monday taught by a new friend named Kelly. I have been to her class before, and I love the way she speaks, love how the workout is for my core in a physical sense as well as a spiritual/mental/emotional sense. Kelly emphasizes total presence, which is nearly impossible for a woman with thoughts that ping and crackle in my head like Jiffy Pop on a campfire.

This class started out normal but quickly took a turn for the unexpected. After a brief meditation, she handed out scarves to each student and announced that the class would be conducted with blindfolds on, and we were to tie our scarves on tightly.

Gulp. The thoughts started popping: *I can barely do yoga when I can see! I can't balance when I don't pick a spot on the wall to stare at! I don't know the names of many of the poses, so I can't do them without cheating by looking at other people!*

I can't do it right if I can't compare myself to someone else!

She entered the hallway of my mind and said on the loud-speaker, "You are probably thinking that you can't do yoga without your eyes, but you can. It might not be perfect, but it's not about that. Whatever you are doing is going to be just right. We waste so much time comparing ourselves to everyone else, and today is going to be a departure. Relax and breathe." It took me a moment to realize she said that out loud, to all of us.

At first my breath eluded me, and I could feel the sweat pooling around my blindfold. I tried to cheat and look beneath it, but sweat dumped in my eyes when I opened them, which I took as a sign to stop doing that. I felt awkward and wondered if I was doing something completely different from the rest of the class, if they had moved on without me, or if I was the only one facing the wrong way. My knees wobbled and slipped off my triceps in a feeble attempt at Crow Pose, and I knew that I had to stop thinking and start being present or I was going to fall on my face for real. I started breathing, this time with intention.

I had a brief flashback to my children as babies, to the inno-cent way they thought they were hiding when they covered their own eyes. *Inhale. Exhale.* The room fell away. Kelly's voice was nearby, and I could hear the regulated breathing of the students around me. Sometimes I could feel her hands on me, steadying me or repositioning me—but oddly not *correcting* me. Next thing I knew, our time was up and I was sweaty and content in a shut-eyed savasana, aka Corpse Pose (no teacher really calls it that, thank God). After bidding namaste, I handed in my soggy blindfold, retrieved my flip-flops, and walked out of the studio into the glare of the afternoon sun. Everything looked too bright.

I drove home slowly, thinking about how smart and creative it was to make us do that, how totally, uncomfortably important that was for me. In yoga and out, I spend too much time and energy trying to do things right, working to figure things out, trying not to look like an idiot, judging my efforts and my results, and comparing myself to other people, usually unfairly. What if I really could surrender and trust? What if I could accept that whatever I'm doing and however I'm doing it is just right for now?

Maybe once in a while we need to close our eyes in order to see.

DOG BONE

Ever notice how easy it is to find fault in others? There are plenty of timeless metaphors for this very human phenomenon—from the pot calling the kettle black, to the Bible verse about the hypocrite who can't see the speck in his brother's eye because of the log in his own, to how those in glass houses should not throw stones.

I hear the playground war stories from my children—who was mean to whom, who called so-and-so a name, who wouldn't share, who wouldn't let them play, etc. And I know it in my own life, in my own so-called grown-up heart, when I feel attacked or slighted or ignored. Sometimes criticism can be an invitation to growth, especially when the critic speaks truth with deep knowledge and love. Other times, particularly when it's just a matter of mean-spirited people getting their kicks or nursing their own insecurities, it serves no good purpose at all. I console myself the same way I comfort and bolster my children. I remind them that the best way to not get picked on is to do nothing. Be nothing, learn nothing, do nothing, stand for nothing, and talk to no one. I say this with a smile.

"But Mom," they say, "that's really boring."

"Exactly."

A surefire way to get picked on is to speak up, act out, try new things, make mistakes, say what you feel, risk, reach out, put it out there, have opinions, ask questions, be deliberate, be hasty, be vulnerable, be real. An image comes to mind of an overweight person running: red-faced, perspiring, angled shorts surely chafing, slowly working her way around the track. Would any runner worth the salt on her sweaty face scoff? Are you kidding me? No way. When I see someone like this, I smile and nod as I do anytime a runner passes by, except that on the inside I am cheering. Every runner knows how hard it is to begin, to motivate, and to fight inertia. Our instinct as runners is to encourage.

And most runners carry this same sentiment even out of the shower and into normal clothes. And that is the gift we share, our offering to the world, especially to those who cannot run a mile (or 3, 6, 13, 26.2) in our shoes, so to speak.

I keep a quotation from writer-comedian Katie Goodman, ripped out of a magazine and framed in a dog-bone-shaped frame on my desk in my office. I read it any time I need to "throw myself a bone." It says: *There will invariably be people who do not accept you. And in that case you must be your own badass self, without apology.*

Wink.

DRESSING ROOM GLASS

My mother hates to sweat.

For all the ways we are alike, this is one major deviation in our personalities. I should clarify, she definitely prefers to be hot than to be cold—after a childhood spent in northern Minnesota, she took her college degree and fled to sunny California. But she does not like the kind of sweat caused by exertion, which is of course my favorite kind. I almost feel that a shower is wasted if I don't stink first. She totally supports my running passion (with affirmation, sideline cheering sections, and baby-sitting) even if she doesn't always understand it.

My mother has always had a beautiful figure without trying. She is tall and thin but not too thin, with curves in the right places and the kind of olive complexion that pisses off her yellow-toned, easily sunburned, freckle-spattered daughter. She always told me her weight management included a balanced life-style during the week and free-for-all fun on the weekends. She watched how her jeans fit and adjusted accordingly. This worked fine until the year she both stopped smoking and hit menopause. Then she welcomed some unfamiliar pounds. She never made a big deal about it—she isn't an obsessive person by any stretch—but I know it bugged her.

Recently she has reclaimed her figure—with careful nutrition and discipline, if not with sweat. She is 66 years old (and couldn't care less if you know that) and absolutely lovely. She is at a college reunion right now. Before her trip, we had a mother-daughter date; I brought her with me to a speaking engagement, and we went shopping afterward. Shopping with Mom is not about shopping, not about buying things at all. It's about wandering around a store in a time warp where I forget how old I am and so does she. I could be 8, I could be 13 and eye rolling, I could be hunting for a prom dress, I could be home from college, I could be taking a break from my first job, I could be in a postpartum haze . . . With her I am all these ages at once, and in each case she is simply 28 years older.

Because of her svelte new bod, all her clothes are too big. I can't remember the last time, if anytime, we spent more time searching the racks for her than for me. I loved it. I directed her to the rack with expensive jeans, some of the brands I like for when I feel cute or want to treat myself. Not my regular Old Navy collection but the going-out kind. I pulled out a pair and handed it to her.

"I don't know about this," she said. "Skinny jeans? I am not wearing low-rider jeans that slide down the back. Please."

"Just try them," I said. I know full well she would not tolerate crack-exposing jeans or even the threat of exposure. She is a refined woman with tailored style who wears her thick, dark hair in a classic 2-inch low ponytail at all times. We headed to the dressing room.

It's what happened next that lingers in my memory, days later.

I tapped on the door, wanting to check her out. She stood in front of the mirror in perfectly fitting, expensive skinny jeans, with heels on. At first I said nothing. I just looked at her. And then I asked her to spin around. And then I told her she looked gorgeous. And then it hit me.

For my entire life my mother has stood in the dressing room with me, usually with a heap of clothes on her lap that I toss on her and make her hang back up. (What a pain I am.) And she has told me for going on 39 years that I am beautiful. And because she has always thought that, even at times when I have hated myself, a part of me has given myself the benefit of a doubt. To stand in the doorway of her dressing room and tell her how I see her, tell her how lovely she is, was one of those moments when every nice thing I could ever have uttered collected in a lump in my throat. To be 66 years old and be elegant, sexy, and comfortable all at once, in a kick-ass pair of jeans—*are you kidding me?*

As women, we mark the passage for those who come after us. My daughters are watching how I define and respect my beauty as I navigate from young mother to middle-aged mother, and what they see and hear will affect how they evolve from children to adolescents to young women. In the same way, I am watching my mother as she makes transitions through her seasons, and she is affecting me.

I saw her, really saw her, reflected in dressing room glass, and just as I often marvel that these beautiful girls are actually my daughters, I marveled that this beautiful woman is actually my mom.

13 FEAR

Trying to understand your personal relationship with fear is like unpacking a suitcase after a long trip. There are things in there you don't remember packing. There are dirty clothes mixed in with clean clothes that are so funky you may as well wash everything. There are things you packed but never wore. You mutter under your breath as you start the laundry and swear to travel lighter next time.

Fear can constrain us and compel us, sometimes in equal measure. It can tether us to our past or catapult us into our future. It can force us outside our comfort zones, or it can tuck us in to our comfort zones and pull the covers up over our heads. It can hurt us. It can heal us. It can warn us. It can wean us. It can propel us. It can stop us dead in our tracks and render us useless.

One thing is certain about fear: We cannot ignore it. The braver we are about examining and identifying it, the more victorious we will become.

THE ROCKING CHAIR TEST

My new friend and mountain guide, Terra, has been showing me the ropes with my new addiction: trail running. Terra is fit, wise, interesting, passionate, funny, strong-minded, strong-willed, and up for anything. She has two children, including a 7-month-old baby girl, yet she scrambles up these mountains billy-goat-style, while I (who can no longer claim postpartum fitness levels when my girls are 6) huff and puff like the Big Bad Wolf. She also manages a serious case of diabetes, running with a monitor and pump to control her own insulin levels. This means I cannot comfortably complain about my own erratic blood sugar and mood swings. One day we did a long run up Romero Canyon Trail, and when we headed back along the single track, she pointed out the route we had just ascended from across the canyon. When I saw the winding path we had traversed, I got chills. *I ran up that thing? Who, me?* I had to stop and admire the accomplishment, squeal, and hug her, totally erasing any semblance of cool. At least that was out of the way.

Another day Terra asked me to consider running a local race called 9 Trails in late November. It is 35 miles long, on trails, some of which I have seen and attempted, and I cannot even imagine stringing them together and running an ultra. She did not settle for my usual attempt to use humor as my way out of answering difficult questions. She wanted to know what I was afraid of. *How did she know I was afraid? Did my chattering teeth, goose bumps, and lack of eye contact give me away so easily?*

I have avoided answering this question for at least 2 weeks. It has made headlines in my journal, though, and I'm still working through the answers. Like anything of magnitude (and 35 miles certainly qualifies), the answers have implications beyond surface level.

I started to respond to her via e-mail, then figured I may as well share it with you.

TOP 10 REASONS WHY I FEAR 9 TRAILS
(OR ANY OTHER ULTRA)

1. I am a newbie. I need time to progress before making an utterly enormous and seemingly unfeasible commitment.

2. Ultras are for ultra people. I am regular. Happily so.

3. It's 35 miles. 'Nuff said.

4. I can barely survive 26.2 flat. My calves cramp up. I have cried before—total chick whiny-baby. Not sure how or where this fits in with tough, outdoorsy culture.

5. I am a homework girl. Need more reconnaissance. At least a year. And would have to make headway with trails in Austin to show my devotion.

6. I thought I did not like dirt or flies or sweat mixed with dirt becoming paste. But I think I actually like it. But not the flies.

7. My sense of direction (or lack thereof). I could get utterly dropped and become a pilot for a whole new *Lost* series. Or an episode of *Without a Trace*. Or, gulp, *CSI*.

8. I don't live here. I would need to run these trails over and over and over and over until familiarity trumped fear.

9. What if I liked it? Or was good at it? Then I couldn't hide behind my veneer of wimpiness—what then?

10. What if I can't finish what I start? The old adage of biting off more than I can chew really matters. The older I get, the more this means to me.

Terra said something intriguing to me about making decisions.

She applies the rocking chair test to life's more compelling questions. She explains: "When you are old and sitting in a rocking chair talking to your grandchildren, how would you want to tell the story?"

I am not sure how this story will be told or when this particular chapter will be written; it might be a couple of years from now. But I do know that trying new things and meeting new friends is one of the best adventures of all. And I plan to tell my grandchildren all about that.

ORANGE SHORTS

This week I went on one of those whirlwind overnight business trips that go by so quickly that you wonder if they really happened. I flew to New York on Wednesday for a dinner with the great folks at my publishing company, and then I was part of a magazine editors' luncheon where three other authors and I had a chance to generate some advance interest or possible publicity for our upcoming book projects.

I got up Thursday morning, and like anytime I have to get up and talk, I wondered what the heck I was going to say. Being a nerd at heart, I crafted some notes on a sheet of the hotel notepad. My notes were so outlined, dry, and boring that I almost fell back asleep. ("The evolution of the project came about . . ." Blah, blah, blah. It was awful.) I had to escape my hotel room and my head, so I went to the gym. Ideally, I would have gone running in Central Park (the weather was gorgeous!), but with my sense of direction, I figured I would likely end up getting lost or getting mugged (and missing my luncheon entirely), so I hit the treadmill. Once I started moving, my brain fog began to lift. It's amazing how a run can do that. As I stared out the window and watched the fast-paced New Yorkers hoofing it up Seventh Avenue, my thoughts started to move as well. I got enough clarity to remind myself that the only time anyone ever cares what I have to say is when I speak from my heart. If I couldn't share why this manuscript was special and important enough to me to devote a year of my life to it, why on earth would an editor care to read it, publicize it, or print an excerpt from it?

After 5 miles, I went back upstairs, showered, dressed, and threw my notes in the trash. When it was my turn to talk, I am not sure exactly what I said, but I do know that I was myself.

I guess the thing that keeps me from doing this sort of thing more often (like scrapping my notes or losing my shyness and being myself) is fear. I have another recent example, this one of a personal nature. My kids "took me" to the Hyatt Regency Lost Pines for an overnight on Mother's Day weekend. It's a great getaway, not far from home, with a waterslide and a "lazy river," which is a manmade river surrounding the pool. People float around it in inner tubes all day long—it's kid, and mommy, heaven.

I have to say that I rarely, if ever, see anyone of the opposite sex that stops me in my tracks, but I did about 5 minutes after we got to the pool. Usually, I am the person at the pool who is so preoccupied with slathering sunscreen on my kids or on me, ordering Sprites and chicken fingers, locating errant flip-flops, and keeping track of small people as they bob around the lazy river that I don't see anything or anyone. But this guy, well, he was so beautiful and so my type that God might as well have put a bow on him with a tag that said "For Kristin. Love, God."

We stood on the steps watching for available inner tubes, because the lazy river was packed. I saw him and I froze—the odd sensation of recognizing someone you have never seen before. He floated by and said to me, "If you want a tube, you kinda have to hijack one." I thought to myself, *I'd rather hijack you.* Only the problem was, I didn't just think it, I accidentally said it out loud (apparently I left my filter in my beach bag?) and felt my face turn as red as a sunburn. He laughed, luckily. I saw him throughout the day, floating nearby or playing basketball or goofing off with his friends. I think he was there with a wedding party, but I couldn't tell for sure. I didn't see any wife or any children. At one point he said something funny to me, and I had the courage to say, "So, are you enjoying a nice weekend with your wife and children?" And he smiled and said, "No wife." At least that much was clear.

But here's the thing. I never really talked to him. I was brave enough to throw out a (questionably) witty remark, but I never had the courage to be real—to say hello, introduce myself, find out his name, and actually get to know him. On one hand I am a mother of three awesome kids, a writer, a marathon runner; I have sat and dished on Oprah's famous white couch, for goodness' sake. But yet when it comes to a cute guy, I revert to eighth grade—I suddenly have braces, my arms are crossed over my chest, and I can't make eye contact. What is my deal?

I think we all have something (for me it's the phenomenon of the guy in the orange shorts) that snags us, a fear that comes back from childhood to haunt us and keep us from stepping outside our comfort zone. I could rationalize and say that maybe he never wanted to talk to me because I was surrounded by family, being motored through the lazy river by three small sets of kicking feet. Or maybe he loves children and I will never know because I was too shy, too afraid to find out.

It's the catch-22 of being a grown-up, simultaneously wanting certain things but being scared to death of them at the same time. We have to own whatever is our equivalent of the guy in orange shorts and realize that until we are brave enough to acknowledge the desire (for love, for friendship, for a promotion, for a chance at adventure, for a shot at pursuing a dream), we will never, ever have the opportunity to see it blossom in our life.

My brother, while laughing at me in classic sibling tradition, tried to comfort me over the "loss" of my unknown sweetheart by quoting a song lyric from the Robert Plant–Alison Krauss album: "Let your loss be your lesson." It bugs me when he goes Yoda on me, but he does have a really good point.

Let's not let life float by.

P.S. If you happen to know the handsome, dark-haired man with the great smile in the orange shorts and aviator sunglasses who was last seen on May 10 at the Hyatt Lost Pines in Bastrop, Texas, please tell him I want to start over and say hello. My name is Kristin.

YOUR ANTARCTICA

I love to read as much as I like to write, which is why I recently joined a book club that meets monthly here in Austin. This past month was our fourth meeting. We read a book called *Swimming to Antarctica: Tales of a Long-Distance Swimmer* by Lynne Cox.

If you are sportier than I am, perhaps you know that Lynne Cox is an anomaly of an athlete. She specializes in long-distance swimming, particularly in waters that have never been braved before. She swam in places like the English Channel (where she set the world record at age 16), the Bering Sea, the Strait of Magellan, Cook Strait of New Zealand, the Cape of Good Hope, the Nile River, and eventually Antarctica. She wears only a swimsuit and goggles, no wet suit. Her body fat is uniquely and uniformly distributed so that she can sustain temperatures that would kill other people in a matter of minutes. Many of the studies done on hypothermia today have been tied to research done on Lynne Cox. She is truly an amazing woman and athlete.

I was looking forward to the meeting and the discussion, particularly because Lynne Smith, an Austin distance swimmer and triathlete, was planning to attend. Smith completed the English Channel swim just last August. She added her personal perspective and anecdotes to what was to us an unfathomable feat. To prepare for weather and water that cold, both Lynnes had to gain weight, sleep with windows open and no covers (or crank the AC to frigid, here in Texas!), and wear impossibly minimal clothing on cold-weather days. The intent was to prepare the body for a colder core temperature and prepare the mind to deal with being uncomfortable for long periods of time.

We asked Lynne about how she dealt with the cold water. She said simply, "It's pain. You just have to get used to it and eventually stop fighting it."

Not everyone can relate to a cold-weather, long-distance, open-water swim—true. But everyone can relate to the handling of pain, physical or otherwise. Whether we are training, racing, or living through a difficult season, the idea of not fighting pain as a legitimate method of coping with it is very interesting to me.

Then came the question of the evening, posed to the group: "Okay, so what is *your* Antarctica?"

Silence fell across the table. Slowly, in lieu of hastily revealing any answers, we discussed the question. Did it mean "What is the physical challenge that has me intrigued and ready to push my parameters?" Did it mean "What am I truly afraid of?" Did it mean "What am I being called to prepare for?" Did it mean "Where is my courage manifested in my life today?"

Did it refer to the physical, the relational, the intellectual, the emotional, or the spiritual depths?

I am still mulling over my answer. Perhaps it's not something that can be given an immediate response. Perhaps it can't be verbalized at all, only revealed. Or maybe the answer is there, but I'm not ready to acknowledge it yet. I am not sure.

ONE THING

Recently my friend Dawn gave me a quotable card that says

Do one thing every day that scares you.

—ELEANOR ROOSEVELT

I got the card and set it on the windowsill above my kitchen sink. I stare at it every time I wash my hands, scrub dishes, drain pasta, or peel apples in one long, twisty strip. I tried to throw it away but couldn't, then decided that maybe if I tried putting it into practice, it would stop haunting me. And so for the past 2 weeks I have done something every day—in varying degrees, of course—that is scary.

One day I had a conversation that was so difficult that it left me breathless, puffy-eyed, and congested for the rest of the day.

One day I apologized to my children for not keeping a promise.

One day I did interval work at running group. (I start dreading Wednesday speed work on Monday.)

One day I spoke to a class of senior high school AP English students. (That scared me more than doing the *Today* show, by the way.)

One day I made a cold call about publishing some of my work.

One day I went to a different kind of church.

One day I held my ground in a fee negotiation.

One day I helped someone who is homeless.

One day I stood up for someone in a conversation, and everyone got silent.

One day I said "No, thank you" when I normally might have said yes and resented it.

One day I entered a hilly 5-K (and nearly died, FYI).

One day I kept a boundary in a relationship that has the potential to usurp me.

One day I was completely honest about my intention in a situation and did not apologize.

One day I let silence be an answer and let it go.

Being really honest, trying something new, or doing something old in a new and improved way—all these things, in one way or another, scare the crap out of me. When I was sitting in front of that classroom and trying to translate my passion for writing into something meaningful to a group of 18-year-olds when so much of my journey with words has been forged in adult-size fires, I felt utterly exposed, totally vulnerable, sweaty, and tongue-tied. When I finally realized that I did indeed belong there and I relaxed into the moment, I actually enjoyed myself. I tried to explain to them that I could no more separate myself from running, writing, mothering, and praying than you can separate a single ingredient from a loaf of baked bread. Sooner or later, we just have to own and enjoy who we are, the whole crazy concoction.

And this weekend, when I left my post at the registration table for the 5-K at my church, ran past my car to ditch my heavy cotton shirt, and pinned my bangs back with a barrette as I raced through the start line, I realized how much I love training and hate racing. Why? Because I'm afraid of hurting, burning, bonking, and running out of air. Yet I have, to date, survived every single race, so why the fear? Start-line fear makes my heart race faster than the effort of racing itself.

It has been a worthwhile experiment, doing my One Thing. *Facing fear is ultimately easier than constantly navigating around situations that provoke it.* I'm thinking that if I can train myself in this way, expand my comfort zone and my threshold in the presence of fear, my new reaction to it might become second nature, the way an athlete practices a certain play or sequence of motion over and over again until her body knows it by heart. I want my default set to honesty and courage and openness.

It starts with One Thing. Try it for yourself and see what happens.

T MINUS 1 WEEK

There is something about the tail end of a taper (the decline in training intensity and mileage prior to race day) that can make you feel edgy. Perhaps it's the excess energy, usually expended in miles, now turned into vague restlessness. This, combined with a heavy dose of doubt, new and unidentified outcroppings of aches and pains, kids with ominous runny noses, and the pace of life traveling at a velocity inversely proportional to the desired rate of rest, makes for an interesting final week before race day.

Rest is like a cold pool or a hot bath; you gotta ease into it so you don't shock the system.

Meanwhile, I try to wind the kids down early for bed so I can unwind myself. I try to eat well, though the only thing that really sounds good is peanut butter on Ritz crackers—what's up with that? I try to drink more water, keeping tally by tossing empty plastic bottles on the floor by the passenger seat of my car. They rattle around these days, both the bottles and the thoughts in my head.

I worry about race-day jitters, race-day pace, race-day food, race-day hydration, night-before sleep, night-before-the-night-before sleep. I worry about calf cramps and side stitches, bonking, and crashing headfirst into the wall. I worry about letting my friends down. I worry about my friends having a good day. I worry about a speech I'm giving in Minneapolis and the possibility of freezing to death on my trip, if I don't freeze to death when I'm handed the microphone. I worry the way I did when I had these little worry dolls as a child. They were little primitive dolls, made of brightly colored wound string, kept in a tiny balsa wood box, the idea being that you should tell each doll a worry before bed, and they would stay up all night with it so you didn't have to.

The idea of worry dolls is childlike and sweet. Yet my need for relief is as real now as when I was a little girl. The days of dolls have been replaced by a more reliable and true source of anxiety alleviation: faith. My taper includes a great deal of prayer. Any approaching marathon (this is my fifth) feels like final exam week—like a countdown until I have a serious evaluation of my understanding of the lessons taught in recent months. A marathon is one of God's prime workshops for me. I have always been one who learns by the book but must practice in order to become. For me it's not just about muscle strength, lung capacity, and the trained experience of facing fear. These things are daunting enough, of course, but the true lessons for me are always the soulful lessons of the heart. I don't know the Professor well enough to know what questions will be asked of me, or if they will be multiple choice or open-book essay.

Multiple choice might look like this:

Kristin, it's mile 18 and you are losing your edge, feeling the rumblings of the body's hostile takeover of spirit. Which of the following do you do?

(a) Have a full-blown panic attack before the next aid station.

(b) Breathe in and out and frantically try to find the Ziploc with your salt pills and Motrin.

(c) Let your friends know you are fading by making sounds like a gorilla in the mist.

(d) Crank up your iPod and start praying.

(e) All of the above.

Open book might be this:

Kristin, describe how running has changed you. Has it made you a better woman, and if so, how? Describe in specific terms how the humility of your impending breakdown at mile 20 will affect your daily life going forward in terms of your compassion, your relationships, your insight into self and others, and your view of the world. How will the acute awareness of your own weakness affect your reverence and your ability to submit; that is, to turn over the challenges that prove to be greater than you?

The old test anxieties never really go away, even if you think you are a more grown-up student or have better study habits. Even if you have done all your "homework" and "attended class" without fail, you still don't know for sure how you will do on marathon day.

It's just like big tests in life: We read and study and try to live out our learning, but when trials come, they come in fast and hard and unexpected. (At least with a marathon, we know the date when we sign up.) We want to be living true and living well, doing the best we can with what we have before us, and we want to be aware that at any time we could be tested (a trial separation, a fight with a close friend, the loss of a job, the death of a parent, a lump in your breast, an accident, a sick child, anything). When the test comes, like Oswald Chambers says, we want to have done our work in the workroom so we will be ready and will not be a hindrance to others.

That's really what I want to be, to the best of my ability: ready and not a hindrance to others.

T minus 1 week and counting.

14 BURDENS

Burdens are the things in life that weigh us down—things like complicated circumstances, struggling relationships, career and parenting challenges, illnesses, disappointments, grief, or the discomfort of change. They are the proverbial rock in our shoe, thorn in our side, chip on our shoulder, speck in our eye, or load on our back. In any relationship worth its salt, burdens are divided and joys are multiplied. This applies to good marriages, strong families, loyal friendships, and devoted running groups. As runners we have vast educational opportunities on the subject of burdens. We hear about them and speak about them as we log miles together. And we train ourselves to carry them, as we bear up under the weight of our own burdens as well as the pieces we carry for one another. We carry pieces for people who can no longer run but wish they could. We carry pieces for our beloved comrades struggling beside us. We carry pieces for people we love and for the people loved by the people we love. This is why we train. This is why it all makes sense—all the time and energy expended, all the aches, and all the weariness.

Because it really matters that we can go on, we can endure, when the load is heavy and the conditions are not optimal.

As runners know intimately, you cannot rely on endurance that has not been built over time. You cannot rely on either fitness or relationships when you have not already invested. The time to build is now, today.

SPRING CLEANING

I was invited to give a speech this week, and the theme was spring cleaning. I was hoping no one was going to ask me about helpful solutions for organization or stain removal, because my house often does not reflect that state of order that is my heart's deep (unmet) desire. I might have things somewhat clean if I have been home during the day and not holed up writing in my office. This is always short-lived, lasting until approximately 3 p.m., when the kids burst through the back door and the formerly orderly surroundings become a sea of backpacks, old papers, new homework, lunch boxes, water bottles, shoes, and balled-up stinky socks. Soon the entire inventory of the pantry is expelled, evaporating into a trail of wrappers and crumbs, the dogs following close behind. When someone can't find her jersey for practice, the neatly folded contents of full laundry baskets are unfurled onto the laundry room floor in a mosaic of color. Before bedtime, the bathing process yields heaps of discarded dirty clothes, soggy towels, dog hair, and a waterlogged bathroom floor. Typically, at least one of the dogs finds his way (unconfirmed whether this is forced or voluntary) into the bath or shower and needs at least two towels to get "dry," or at least it takes that many towels to wipe the walls down after he has a good shake. (Is anyone else aware that a wet dog and scrambled eggs smell exactly the same?) Real life is messy, people.

So for my speech, I neatly avoided the subject of household

cleaning and focused instead on spring cleaning in terms of an inside job—mainly, letting go of some unnecessary things we hold on to and getting a better grip on the things we really need. To provide some visual aids for the beginning of my talk, I did an archaeological dig in my closets. I was able to showcase the following items:

1. An Ann Taylor blazer from the early nineties. This is proof that I am unable to fully let go of my former corporate identity. If my writing gig flops, I will at least have this blazer for the interviewing process, and this offers some measure of comfort. If it still fits.

2. Maternity jeans. Yes, the kind with the belly pouch. I have not been pregnant in 9 years; yet if I manage to meet a great guy before my biological clock runs out, date him repeatedly, fall in love, somehow merge our lives and schedules, fortify my courage and sense of optimism enough to say yes to a proposal if he makes one, then follow through on the wedding and marriage part, then have unprotected sex at exactly the right moment to conceive, I will have jeans with a belly pouch. This is proof that I am unable to fully let go of my young mother identity despite the fact that I am no longer a young mother.

3. Nursing top. Gross, I know—the kind with discreet (ha) slits in it. Guys, move to number 4. I keep this hideous shirt for unknown reasons, likely tied to the fact that I am still in shock that I ever nursed twins. Or that I ever nursed them in public without landing myself smack on the pages of *National Geographic* magazine. No matter what happens, I will never again wear a white turtleneck the size of a barn with boob slits big enough to do a puppet show through them.

4. Skinny jeans. Small enough that my daughter Grace could probably wear them today, and she's 8. This is proof that I am unable to let go of my skinny-as-a-rail era. I keep the jeans around in case I ever get that skinny again, which hasn't yet happened. I have to be truly miserable to stop eating, and I haven't been that miserable since, well, back when I wore those jeans. Meanwhile, whenever I feel fit and fabulous, I try them on just in case, and all this does is to limit the amount of time I feel fit and fabulous. They need to go, but I keep them. This is proof that no matter how much I think I have evolved and made peace with my body, I can still manage to torment myself.

5. Superhigh-heeled rhinestoned gala shoes. I vowed to avoid galas, in deference to my allergy to inane small talk and silent auctions. Yet I keep the shoes just in case, in a warped Cinderella affliction—as if Cinderella had size 9 feet with calluses from running, which I am certain she did not, or the handsome prince would not have held her foot in his hand and fallen immediately in love.

I did move beyond these superficial items in my introduction, and I talked about deeper things than shoes and jeans. But the symbolism of the silly things we hold on to was not lost on me. They may seem shallow, but they tie into something much more profound.

If you take a look in your closet, your attic, your storage space, or your garage, what do you find? What does it say about you that you still have certain things? Is the thing a sentimental piece of personal history that you hold on to for nostalgic purposes—or is it something that has a hold on you? Do you need to let it go or, finally, after all these years, dust it off and put it to good use in your life today?

Either way, this is some food for thought for your next long run, whether you are logging some solo miles or meeting up with your friends.

FLORIDA SNOWMAN

I am not sure it bodes well when you begin a 20-miler with a small Ziploc bag containing ibuprofen, toilet paper, and cab fare.

This was my sad state at the start of my long run last Saturday morning. I had just flown in from New York the night before and had a margarita to reclaim my Tex-Mex heritage and set my nerves to neutral after two concurrent flights in less than 48 hours with enough turbulence to create keg-beer-quality fizz in my bloodstream.

I woke up with my stomach churning and a bad case of what we affectionately call liquibutt (I never claimed to be pleasant or mature) from 4:30 a.m. until I grumbled and muttered my way to meet up with my cronies at 6 a.m. With my Ziploc bag.

With my oddly clenched gait, general fatigue, and foul mood, I was not anywhere near the front of the pack. (Maybe people were picking up the pace so they wouldn't run behind me.) I silently trudged along for most of the miles, trying to hang on to the last shreds of my resolve and keep a bead on the familiar shorts in front of me. (Uh, I think they turned right up there . . .?) Finally, when my last calorie was burned and the last person (think straw/camel) asked me an honest question about how I was doing, I lost it. I don't think I'm a pretty crier. You know how some girls well up with tears that somehow illuminate the brilliant color of their eyes but glisten just short of any possibility that they will come into contact with mascara? The overall effect is stunning: They seem vulnerable yet strong enough to hold it together. Add to that a couple of delicate, well-timed, feminine

155

sniffles and you are on your zippy way without a speeding ticket, or your unsuspecting significant other is on his way to buy you ice cream, diamonds, or a ticket to Paris. Well, this is not me.

My sobs catch me by surprise, like grabbing a hot door handle on the back draft of my emotion. I suck air in manic gulps, wheezing in a drowning attempt to stave off panic. This always causes a telltale gap in conversation, at which point innocent bystanders politely try to avoid eye contact and wait patiently for the remainder of my response, or at least the mandatory exhale. This comes out more like high-pitched wail, like something I once heard on a Discovery Channel program about migrating whales. Then come the tears and runny nose, mixed with more choppy verbal attempts to explain myself or cover my tracks. Forget the ticket to Paris; I'm lucky to get a Kleenex. Saturday I used my sleeve. It was a make-do kind of day.

By the grace of God, and Paige and Katie's Navy Seal–level of loyalty to a fallen comrade (*At least we can bring the body back to her family, SIR!*), I finished the run and made it back to my car. I wanted to kiss the bumper of my dirty Volvo. After we guzzled Gatorade and did the mandatory (albeit insufficient) calf stretchy-stretch, another friend, Melissa, asked me if I was okay, if there was anything she could do. I smiled and told her she already had by getting me through those long miles. I made it, humor and humility intact.

Paige, Katie, Courtney, and I went and stuck our gimpy legs in my freezing, leaf-covered swimming pool. It was so cold we screamed upon entry, on step one. After about 5 minutes, unable to feel our lower extremities or stop laughing, we decided that there are times when the only way to get through it is to do it.

Provided you are in good company, of course.

MT. BURDEN

If I had a Doppler Emotional Weather Radar Man, he would have predicted cloud coverage of unworthiness, with continued chance of doubt and fear for the next 48 hours.

On the morning of day 2 of mood fog, Paige sent a text that a group was meeting the next day at Courtney's house for a run at 5:30. I woke up sans alarm at 5:20, and Courtney lives around the corner from me . . . so there was no plausible excuse not to go except that there was no time for coffee. I sucked it up, threw on my clothes, and jogged around the corner in a disheveled daze, wishing I had brushed my teeth and hoping I wouldn't have to go to the bathroom before I got home.

Little did I know what I was in for, because if I had, I would have stayed home in the biscuit, nice and warm and cozy. Apparently, these tough chicks do this run every Monday morning, as a way to usher in the week ahead (and from my perspective, they show the week who's boss). It involves running *both* Balcones Drive and Mt. Bonnell and navigating lots of other beastly hills between them. For those of you who do not live in Austin, think of me as the Rice-A-Roni cable car, hanging on for dear life to some unfathomable incline, half asleep.

One of the hills dead-ends, and I wondered why we were running all the way to the end. I was too out of breath to question them or complain, so I followed along. When they got to the end, they declared it was time to pay homage to Mt. Burden, and each woman picked up a rock and set it on the ledge at the end of the street. My morning head cleared enough for me to realize the magnitude of the opportunity at hand; naming and unloading my current burden was particularly wonderful news. I picked up a rock and hoisted it up, depositing my "boulder of unworthiness" and leaving it there.

It might have been a placebo effect, it might have been that we were headed in direction *casa* and my morning coffee was calling my name, or it might have been that there is something to this Mt. Burden idea. Maybe the experience of literally naming the fear, doubt, or problem and leaving it at the end of a difficult, sweaty climb is effective therapy. I don't doubt the efficacy or care if it is a placebo, because I ran home a lighter woman. As far as I know, my unworthiness is still sitting on the ledge, and I hope it stays right there where I put it.

Ditch your burden and start fresh.

Doppler Man predicts sunshine.

BONDED BY BURDEN

Paige's father is sick, really sick. Cancer. She went to see him yesterday.

I could tell she was struggling by the way I was struggling—to keep up with her—on our run this morning. If you have ever run beside a beloved sweat sister (or brother) who is working through something big, you know what I'm talking about: The way they attack every hill as if it personifies the thing they're up against. The way they pump their arms in warning, churning their legs against the terrain. The way they want their legs and lungs to burn, because any self-inflicted pain is like an acupuncture needle, releasing the torment of deeper, unreachable areas. The way they steel their faces and set their jaws and position themselves against every mile, honing their skills, making themselves ready. I don't know that runners attempt to outrun or run from a challenge as much as we try to generate momentum to sustain the pace required to match it. It can't roll over us and carry us away if we can keep up with it, stride for stride. We don't know how to face anything other than to fuel for it, strengthen ourselves for it, and add the mileage necessary to endure it.

If you run next to someone in that place, there isn't much to say—mostly because you can't breathe. So you listen. And for as much as you want to prevent pain or alleviate circumstances when you love someone that much, you can't. And in fact, to do so would eliminate the specific growth divinely appointed by the challenge. Just like you can never really help someone run (in the literal sense—it has to come from her own body, her own strength), you can't really help someone endure in any sense of the word. *But you* can *run beside someone.* Sometimes your words can offer insight, levity, or community. But most of the time the solidarity of your silence, the sound of the footfalls and the breathing, is the greatest comfort in the world—knowing that there are people alongside you in your journey.

If your running group has not yet been bonded by a burden, keep training, because it's unavoidable. And although heartache is never fun, experiencing it together is at the core of sweat sisterhood and brotherhood. Once you have run those hard miles together, you are permanently altered—the group becomes a team.

And over time, the team becomes a family.

15 PEACE

Peace can be as elusive as love when we pursue it with ravenous need. We need to ease into it, recognize it, cajole it, make space for it, and welcome it. Most of us, most of the time, go through life with a vague restlessness, a lack of peace that goes unnamed and unresolved. We try to make do. We distract ourselves and busy ourselves; we buy things and do things in an attempt to make that lack seem less nagging, less obvious, but of course this is about as subtle and helpful as applying concealer under sleepless eyes or spraying flowery spray in a stinky bathroom. We get tired and we go broke, all in the name of resolving something—except that we aren't seeking resolution with the thing we need most of all—peace.

Some of us find peace through cultivating stillness. Others have to work our way there through movement. Some need silence. Others need the right kind of noise. Some need to be alone. Others need to be with specific people. Some need to cloister themselves inside. Others will never find it unless they are out in nature. What you need isn't nearly as important as *knowing* what you need.

And that is the first step in the direction of peace.

GIVING IT UP

Several weeks ago, in anticipation of Lent, I pondered the theme of sacrifice. Raised as a Catholic, I grew up thinking that Lent meant giving up something you like for 40 days—things like chocolate, teasing my brother, watching too much TV, etc. I have had variations on this theme over my "grown-up" years, giving up much more profoundly dear items like caffeine or wine. It wasn't easy, but it seemed much more like fodder for humorous complaining than a spiritual exercise of self-denial.

This year I wanted something different, something more.

My answer came to me, as it usually does, on a run. Sacrifice for me this year has something to do with fasting—not so much a fasting from food but a fasting from things that break my spiritual connectedness. Every day looks a little different. My morning run reveals the item for the day; there is something about these clear spring mornings that inspires me to clear my head. It has been quite an awakening, like a spring cleaning for the soul.

One day I fasted from busyness and I stayed home—all day. The initial feelings of stir-craziness or the compulsion to tend to my list evaporated by 4 p.m., and I finally got comfortable with my pace at a screeching halt. Another day I fasted from my cell phone. This was harder than I expected. At first I felt an odd disconnectedness as I drove quietly in my car, battling the notion that I need to be multitasking at all times. This disconnectedness evolved into a giddy sense of freedom as I remembered what it was like before I could be reached by anyone at any moment. Another day I fasted from judgment and practiced giving anyone and everyone the benefit of the doubt. I have fasted from my need to have a program and have run easy miles in solitude just because I can. I have fasted from my obsession with my own plan to tend to the needs of a friend. Another day I fasted from stress and took a break from hurrying my children and being a slave to the clock. We were oddly on time anyway, but it was remarkably more pleasant getting there.

Each day has held something revealing about me and my life. I don't know why I have never thought about doing this before. It seems to me that runners know a lot about sacrifice. We sacrifice time to fit our running in around work and family life. We sacrifice comfort for the pain required to improve. We sacrifice indulgence for the happiness of being light on our feet. Usually we sacrifice these things easily and willingly, knowing that our passion to hit the ground running is the very thing that keeps us grounded.

WORKING IT OUT

I am going to let you in on a secret fetish of mine. It's not something I like to tout around town or talk much about at cocktail parties, lest people think that this single mother of three, age 35 (that's halfway to 70), is going to end up a total spinster with a houseful of cats (yes, I do have a cat).

I like to knit.

Okay, there. Now you know. It's not like I am embarrassed to like knitting; it is actually very cool. But it is embarrassing how much I like it despite the fact that I am highly untalented. I have no pretty sweaters to wear or cutesy hats to show off. I have no patterns or variations in types of stitches; I just sit and knit . . . miles of "scarves." A couple of family members will be receiving these snuggly wonders for Christmas presents, and I apologize in advance. I couldn't resist. Plus, the wintry weave made for good packing material around the framed school pictures of the kids.

Besides, how many of these do I really need, in Texas weather?

What does this have to do with running? Well, everything, of course, because everything relates back to running when you are a runner. Lately I have realized that they are quite similar pursuits. They are both means of resolution and relaxation. They are both monotonous repetitions of activity that loosen the knots of mind and spirit, resulting in a clear channel of consciousness. When I am tense, I can feel the hot, bundled mass of confusion or angst rumbling around in the pit of me. I can't just sit like that, even when there is no clear solution in the immediate future. I have to move. I have to work it out; whether it's through sweat and the metronome of shoes on pavement or the comforting, rhythmic clack of knitting needles, I need release. When my body is engaged, my mind is liberated. The inner tangles can jostle free when I quit struggling against them.

One night I was particularly uptight and found myself with a mangled knot of yarn that looked frighteningly similar to my ponytail after a humid run. Frustrated, I was tugging at it from every thread, looking for the path to its undoing, and having no luck. I stood up and dropped the balls on the floor (my childish response to my own impatience and inability; this needs to be addressed at some point—when I'm more mature, perhaps?), and they miraculously untwisted. My act of letting go, literally dropping the ball, created order.

(Attention, fellow lovers of order and control freaks: *epiphany.*)

The same applies to my running. The mere act of taking my mess to the road, pounding my problems, moving into my questions, and changing my momentum in the face of fear shakes the knots out and generates purpose, perspective, and peace.

I wish you and I could have a cup of coffee so I could ask you about your "other thing"—the thing you do besides running that untangles you. I bet you have one.

I have a couple more: baking (maybe it's a good thing I run!), painting (oil on canvas), reading, walking on sand, vacuuming (the noise drowns out fighting children and the action offers a sense of order in a chaotic, uncertain world), driving with windows open *avec* music and *sans* destination, grocery shopping (with no list, rush, or children, at Whole Foods), swaying in a hammock or rocking in the rocking chair on my screened-in back porch, and, of course, my favorite—writing.

PEGGY ANN McKAY

I was out until 11 last night at a good-bye party for my dear friend KT, who is moving. I was asleep by 11:20 and don't think I even took off my mascara. The alarm clock rudely assaulted me at 5:20, and I showed up at 6 to meet my usual posse.

It was cold at 30 degrees but clear, with a full, shining moon above Town Lake as we ran a flat and easy 12 miles. When I got home, I lay down on the floor by Mercy's dog bed to love on her for a little bit before I took a shower. I woke up an hour and 15 minutes later, spooning Mercy on the dog bed, in cold, sweat-soaked clothes. I stayed in the shower for a very long time, trying to defrost and wake up. The kids are with Daddy this weekend, so I could allow myself the luxury (?) of sleeping on the dog bed and lingering in the shower as long as I wanted, without children's faces pressed against the steamy glass door demanding cinnamon rolls and for me to push "play" on the DVD player.

Y'all, I am tired.

It hit me after my dog bed siesta that I really need to rest. I am not the resting type. I am more like a multitasking, efficient, anal-retentive, neat-freakish, task-oriented, list-making, checkmarking, time-managing (annoying?) (never mind—don't answer that) person. I am the kind of woman who folds clothes during *Animal Planet,* makes phone calls while driving instead of at home, flosses her teeth while the kids are bathing, packs lunches before the kids wake up, writes thank-you notes immediately, works while the kids are in school and after they go to bed, travels for work (or occasionally for fun) on Daddy days, and shops for Christmas in October and November. Once in a blue moon, when I sit down (usually to read or do homework with Luke), I can't recall whether I have sat down once all day aside from driving. This includes meals (except dinner), which I eat standing up at the kitchen counter, usually while reading something or writing notes in my journal or calendar.

I worry that I, we, are forgetting how to relax.

As I toweled off after my shower, I decided that I needed a pajama day. I put my PJs back on, with my robe and fuzzy slippers for good measure. I closed the drapes on the front door to dissuade visitors or neighborhood kids in search of my kids for Nerf dart war. It occurred to me that there is a part of me that enjoys when my children are sick (with the exception of stomach flu) because we all take a day off. No school for them, no appointments or obligations for me, just a total cancellation, a complete departure from our schedule, a hiatus from daily life. We hunker down in pajamas and read. (Our favorite is *Where the Sidewalk Ends*—particularly a poem titled "Sick," which begins, "'I cannot go to school today,' said little Peggy Ann McKay, 'I have the measles and the mumps, a gash, a rash, and purple bumps . . .'") Or we snuggle and stare at the TV. I don't feel compelled to do any chores, and I spend my day happily giving back tickles and making grilled cheese sandwiches.

So I am sitting here, talking (typing) to you with greasy, grilled cheese fingers, wrapped in my favorite robe, my slippered feet resting on Mercy's snoring torso under my desk.

For the record, it is 3:18 p.m.

16 PURPOSE

As women we can get so caught up in defining ourselves by our relationships (we're moms, wives, grandmothers, daughters, sisters, friends) that we push our purpose to the back burner of life and leave it to simmer. Sometimes my purpose is left to simmer for so long that by the time I remember to stir it, it has burned to a blackened crisp on the bottom of a scalded pan. I soothe myself (and rationalize my neglect) by reminding myself how essential my relationships are, and I feel better for how I've spent my time. This lasts until the nagging feeling returns—the desire for something deeper, something more, some kind of relief. I cannot ignore it. It's like an itch between your shoulder blades that you cannot scratch, regardless of what crazy angle you bend your arm into. It's a sore throat that you want to ignore because you have no time to go to the doctor, but it makes itself ruthlessly apparent every time you swallow your spit.

It's a cop-out to say "I'm too busy right now." Or "I don't have the luxury to pursue that right now; maybe later." When, exactly, is later? Later, when the kids are in school? Later, when you are working fewer hours at the office? Later, when the kids go to college? Later, when the nest is empty? Later, when you aren't busy babysitting your grandchildren? Later, when you're dead?

Just like an interrupting child, your purpose will poke at you relentlessly until you turn and give it some attention. I've written before on this subject, about women who say they were "born to be a mother" or "meant to be a wife." To that I reply, "Of course you were; you have a uterus and a ring finger. But those are your *roles,* not your *purpose.*" And that distinction is important, because a purpose is a higher, broader calling than a role. But together, the culmination of our roles and our purpose becomes our life and, eventually, our legacy.

And that, my darlings, is something worth passing down.

CALLING

On the day that I got a shipment of boxes from my publisher, some advance copies of *Heart of My Heart*, about motherhood, I was terrified to open the boxes. I carried them in from my car and set them on the counter. Then I unpacked my groceries and put them away, taking time to clean out the refrigerator just to stall. Then I unloaded the dishwasher. Then I put breakfast dishes in the empty dishwasher. (Yeah, it was after 2 p.m.; so what?) Then I responded to a couple of text messages. Then I made half a turkey sandwich since I forgot about lunch. I looked at the morning paper while I ate, standing up.

I took a deep breath and got a knife to open the packing tape. For all my stalling, I love a box of crisp new books. I slid one copy out and took it over to the sofa and plopped down. I shut my eyes for a second and said a prayer. And then I looked down.

A writer holding her book in her hands is like a mother holding a baby, a dog breeder holding a leash, a carpenter fitting a cabinet, a chef carrying a platter, an architect unrolling plans, an artist hanging a canvas. It's the culmination of every year of your life up until that point, the amassed personal experience and the effort and courage required to bring it to fruition. It's empowering and humbling in equal measure. It's a revelation of self, full of hope and full of holes. My brother always reminds me that holes are how the light gets in. I'm pretty sure that comes from a Leonard Cohen or Tom Waits song, like lots of Jonisms. (He also regularly draws upon the movie *The Big Lebowski*.)

I spent the next couple of hours reading my book, pretending someone else wrote it, seeing if I might like it. I couldn't get out of my head enough to successfully pretend it came from someone else, likely because I was searching for errors and typos like a stern teacher with reading glasses on her nose and a red pen. I can't help it. But I liked it; I liked my book. Relief settled over me like a worn blanket knitted by my grandmother. I closed the book and sat a while longer. The wind pushed the leaves outside the family room window, making patches of light play across the carpet. I sat a little longer, thinking.

I would never have been brave enough to write anything besides my personal journals if my friends (Paige and KT) had not told me that my words were good—and that day I held my fifth book in my hand. If you have a friend who has a gift, tell them, quickly. It really matters.

If you have a gift you have been stuffing or hiding away, waiting for a more "feasible" time, stop stalling. Dust off that dream; reclaim that passion; pull it out of the attic trunk, shake it out, try it on like a musty old garment, and see if it still fits. Because it probably does. It's probably the most natural-feeling thing you have ever worn.

I don't know what I would be doing if I weren't a writer—probably logging hours in a company someplace, unsatisfied but good at what I do, bringing home a paycheck (probably much bigger than the one I bring home now). But there would be a part of me, restless and itchy and relentless, calling.

GOOD INTENTIONS

I ran early with Paige in the dark, damp mist that marked this Thursday morning in Austin. We decided that it was part run, part facial, and we were sure we would look 20 again by hour's end. We felt younger, anyway.

After drop-off this morning, I went to my weekly yoga class at 8 a.m. I still cannot get my heels anywhere near the mat in Down Dog, but I actually attempted a handstand (still terrifying, albeit wall assisted) today. In the middle of my lopsided handstand, I had a Tourette's-like outburst, shouting, "I am FREAKING OUT over here!" I'm sure the class was impressed with both my lack of coordination and my lack of filter. I don't like being upside down, off balance, and bordering on out of control. That's exactly why I made myself try it. But I might wait a while before I do it again.

Other than the word *namaste,* my favorite part of yoga is when Leigh asks us to "set an intention" at the beginning of class. She explains that it can be anything we want as long as it's something worthwhile and positive. I have had all kinds of intentions: peace, openness of heart, patience with myself and others, surrender, creativity, lightness, freedom, authenticity, forgiveness, etc. We go through all of our moves, and then 10 minutes before class ends, she dims the lights and we get to utterly chill in savasana. We can sprawl out whatever way feels comfortable on our mat, using a bolster, sliding our feet up the wall, or just lying full splat, which is what I do, with a heavy Mexican blanket draped over me. I melt into nothingness on the floor like a chalk drawing at a crime scene. Leigh has a playlist that I covet, and as I lie there luxuriously, decadently resting, I think about . . . *absolutely nothing.*

It may be the only time on record that I ever think about nothing. I am usually thinking about my kids; my list; a conversation that I had, will have, or don't want to have; work; plans; my family and friends; my life; or I'm thinking about thinking about something—but my mind is rarely idle. I sometimes do so much during the night in my dreams that I wake up in the morning vaguely tired.

But for those 10 minutes my mind goes on hiatus and I transcend myself. When Leigh's voice beckons me back to consciousness by asking me to slowly wiggle my fingers and toes, I resent the disturbance but I comply. I curl up on my side and stay there too long before I slowly join the rest of class in a cross-legged, hands-pressed-together namaste position. I breathe and try to save the pocket of Zen in my mind for later.

Leigh often asks us to check back in with the intention that we set at the beginning of class. I like that part; it means something to me. I have begun to incorporate this idea into other areas of my life. I try to set an intention before I run, work out, write, meet up with a friend, make a speech, eat a meal, discipline my children, state my opinion, or say yes or no to a request. The more I set intentions, the more I realize how many opportunities I have to do so in the span of a week, a day, or even an hour. I realize how often in the past I have not checked in with my intention or even made one to begin with. How easy is it to waste time, get off track, or miss the moment when I forget where my heart is?

I can use my intention if I have to regroup or reassess: "What I meant to say was . . ." or "My intention before I arrived was . . ." to connect, apologize, inquire, support. When I clarify things out loud, it helps other people understand where my heart is, even if I have totally botched my delivery. It also helps me clarify my goal in any given situation. For example, I had to remind myself of my intention (which was *completion*) halfway through running group yesterday when I wanted to quit and go eat pancakes. Syrup tastes much sweeter on top of victory.

Try setting intentions today with your work, your relationships, your running. Perhaps the truth behind the acknowledgment has the power to affect results.

Namaste.

DICTATORSHIP BY DEFAULT

I love the start of school. If I could be accused of trying to live vicariously through my children in any aspect of their lives, it would be at the start of the school year. I love the crisp, new backpacks and lunch boxes; the sharpened pencils and stiff boxes of brand-new, unbroken crayons; the new notebooks with empty lines waiting to be filled; the class lists, cafeteria menu, and schedules and assignments. It feels like anything is possible when school starts, like a slate wiped clean.

My birthday has always fallen either just before or at the beginning of school. For some this might be a tainted childhood memory: the cupcakes that couldn't be delivered to the classroom or the birthday excitement lost or diminished in the hype of returning to school. Like a Christmastime baby, I have grown up knowing something bigger than me is going on. Rather than grieve any perceived slight or injustice, I have always considered the start of school to be perfectly timed to celebrate two simultaneous new years—for academia and for me.

To alleviate any school-supply envy, I purchased some nerdy treats for myself. I went to Office Depot and bought a few new file folders, a new highlighter, new decks of sticky notes and list pads, and two new notebooks, and I shamelessly indulged my penchant for trying out new pens for as long as it took to find just the right one—then bought a handful of them. The kids are off to school and I am newly 38. I have a brand-new year, and with it, the potential to reprioritize and recalibrate my use of time. This is savory to me. Summer Mommy gets her groove back.

After drop-off in the morning, my day sits before me in a chunk—an expanse of free time that looks as vast and unencumbered as a Texas sky. If I am not purposeful about filling it wisely, my time will become nothing more than a blip between drop-off and pickup, disappearing in a wash of errands, e-mail, and wasted time. And so I am reminded of Hugh Grant's character in the movie *About a Boy* (if you haven't seen it, it's adorable and funny) when he talks about time in units, saying things like "Make breakfast, one unit. Watch TV, three units." It's humorous and vaguely pathetic in the movie because his character is rather depressed and lacks motivation, but it makes me smile to think of units when I'm planning my day in my head or making my list in one of my spanking-new notebooks.

My biggest desire as far as my time goes is to choose how to spend it purposefully rather than have it chosen for me by the dictator known as Default. If I don't choose to plan my running and my exercise, thinking, *I'll get to it later,* then Default will decide that it's too hot, I'm tired, and there's not enough time before I have to pick up the kids. It won't happen. Since I am a writer and work for myself (meaning I do not get paid unless I produce words, and not just any words but words someone actually wants to read), if I don't allocate specific office hours when I am unavailable to the outside world and the plethora of distractions it provides, then Default will decide that my deadline can wait until I have more time or feel more creative. In other words, the page will remain blank.

If I don't allocate a specific time frame to respond to voice mail, e-mail, and text messages, then Default will decide that I should look and listen to them all day, responding at whim, constantly distracted, not truly present for anyone, anywhere, ever. If I don't think ahead and make a plan of what's for dinner, Default will decide that we don't really need to sit down at the table as a family, that it's perfectly acceptable to eat at the kitchen counter at separate times, between activities and homework, whenever we're hungry, eating whatever we're hungry for, exchanging snippets of conversation and calling that connection.

I refuse to be dictated by Default. So I have been running early this week—thanks to my brother, Jon, who comes over at 5 a.m. I have set my office hours. I have a summer notebook full of notes for my first novel. I am remembering to turn my phone to silent mode. I signed up for a long-talked-about-but-never-followed-through-on French conversation group that meets for lunch on Mondays. I blocked off an hour on Tuesday mornings for yoga. I blocked off running group and Bible study on Wednesdays. I picked up old magazines for the girls' science collages, due on Friday. I know I am grilling salmon and corn on the cob for dinner tonight, and we're going to sit down together at the table and talk about all things pertaining to second and fourth grades.

I've wiped the slate clean and boldly wrenched my life back from Default.

17 PASSION

These two mile markers—purpose and passion—have to be sequential, because you can't realize your purpose without passion. They go together. Purpose without passion falls flat and yields nothing. Passion without purpose is at best a floundering, directionless expenditure of energy, and at worst just plain dangerous.

Passion comprises a few key ingredients: the ability to recognize the things that really stir you, the courage to go after them, and the steady internal fire to press on even when the dream has phases of drudgery. The manifestation of a passion involves something all runners know and love well: work.

My father sent me this quotation from Logan Pearsall Smith: "The test of a vocation is the love of the drudgery it involves." If Mr. Smith would allow me, I would like to replace the word *vocation* with *passion* here. "The test of a passion is the love of the drudgery it involves." Every single one of my passions involves a measure of drudgery: mothering (Packing lunches!

Laundry!), writing (The blank page! The looming deadline! The elusive perfect word!), running (Low morale! Bad weather! Fitness plateaus! Hills!). If I didn't deeply love these things, I would be discouraged and deterred by the drudgery. But because these are my passions, I love even the most menial and mundane work required to bring them forth. Because these are my passions, I am willing to take a risk. Because these are my passions, I am willing to chase after them and not let them get beyond my sight.

It is impossible to really live your life or embrace your truest destiny without passion.

GETTING A GRIP

Today at running group I decided the end of the school year is just like running strides. You start out steady and quickly pick up speed until you are hauling at full throttle, arms pumping, legs flying, chest heaving, then you thunder across the finish line and want to collapse. If I am this tired, the teachers must be zombies, God bless them.

The workout at running group today was the pupu platter fitness assortment: a long warmup in the park, followed by multiple hill repeats up a steep grassy hill (forward and backward, ouch), two long tempo laps, four strides, and the same cooldown as the warmup but in reverse direction. On Monday Cassie killed me with a weight workout in the gym, and I have been taking Advil ever since and gimping like I just finished a marathon. I have no idea what she did to me, but my quads and glutes ache pitifully and my abs hurt when I sneeze. For me it's usually a good idea to move when I least feel like it and try to get a little blood flowing through. Today I still was so sore that I could feel the impact of each footfall rattling muscles that groaned back at me, clearly wishing to be left undisturbed. Even though I love seeing my friends, I was glad when it was over.

It's Track and Field Days up at my kids' school this week, so the whole campus is on excitement overload. Today grades K through two convened in the afternoon for the ultimate challenge: Tug for Fun.

I can't tell you how much I love watching Tug for Fun. It really is more like Tug of War, but they try to make it sound sweeter. I will probably be the total dork who still comes up to watch it even after my kids have long departed for middle school and high school. You would have to see it to understand. Each class is divided into two groups, and they challenge other classes in their grade. Excitement and emotions are running high as the sweaty kids walk out in line formation to assume their spots on the rope. The crowd has to stay quiet until the PE teacher shouts "PULL!"—at which point the cheering section explodes from the sidelines. The kids' faces are what gets me, their serious expressions set in firm concentration, brows furrowed and their mouths etched in a grim "don't mess with me" line. They dig in their heels, straining fiercely against the rope, often leaning back so far that they are pulled across the dirt on their bottoms. Some even turn around and attempt to run in the opposite direction. I tried to worm my way as close to my daughters as possible when they were on the rope so they could hear me screaming for them. I am such a sap; whenever they are trying hard at anything, I am on the verge of tears, blurry-eyed behind my sunglasses and growing hoarse and lightheaded from my sideline antics.

We can learn a lot from watching children play and compete. They have no inhibitions about what they look like when they try hard; they lay it all on the line without fear. They don't really know their limits, so they have no awareness or anxiety about approaching them. If they know someone believes they can do it, they are certain they can. Watching them work together toward a common goal reminds me of everything that is pure and good and redemptive about humankind.

Some food for thought for your next solo run, or your next conversation with a moving gaggle of girlfriends . . .

When was the last time you gave something your all? When did you pull so hard for a dream that you got red-faced and your hands hurt from your simple and adamant refusal to let go? When did your effort simultaneously exhaust and invigorate you? For what (or whom) are you willing to dig in your heels, get rope burns on your palms, and slide across the dirt on your behind?

When did you last pursue something with the abandon of a child?

ADVENTURE

Paige and I have been talking a lot about the fact that we have no real fitness plans set for the immediate or midrange future. Usually we have a marathon on the calendar, even if it's many months away, to consider. Or we plan some trip for a destination race, usually a half marathon. After our recent local half marathon, we realized that we had no set plan.

We dished on the subject over some miles, comparing ideas, goals, options, and dreams. She is even floating a vague desire to run the Austin Marathon next weekend, even though we haven't consciously prepared for it at all. I do not harbor this same desire, vague or otherwise. In fact, nothing specific jumps out at me and says "Pick me! Go here!" She and I agree on one very important fact, and that is that we both want to keep our health and fitness at a sufficient level to be able to make quick decisions if something does suddenly sound appealing or feasible. If our training is strong, we can decide to do a spontaneous half marathon, or even ramp things up quickly for a marathon or trail adventure.

Adventure. Now that's the word that starts to get to the heart of things.

"Adventure" describes more accurately what I need to put on my calendar. I need to know that at some point in the future, I have booked an appointment outside my normal routine, maybe even outside my comfort zone—an appointment defined not so much as a race but as an experience ahead that reminds me that *I have it in me.* It could be trying something new, something old in a new setting, something playful, or something challenging. I can flip to that date on my calendar and dream about it, plan for it, and prepare for it.

My friend Misty's father-in-law passed away last week. I read his eulogy in the paper yesterday, and something jumped off the page about this man's life. His philosophy about living well was that you "have to have someone to love, something to do, and something to look forward to." Yes, that sounds amazingly simple. However, if you can reflect back on any time in your life when you didn't feel like you were living well, it's pretty easy to see a gaping hole in one of those three areas.

We live our lives, love our people, and do our work. We can get into a fairly absolute pattern with these items, forgetting that we were designed to need adventure, too. We need the new experiences that stretch us and call us higher. When we ignore this need, it's easy for our passions to get clogged and then erupt or morph in other ways that are harmful. We were not designed to thrive under restlessness or complacency.

Some friends and I are thinking about getting a guide and making the rim-to-rim trek across the Grand Canyon. I have considered going to a high-altitude training camp in Leadville. I have never been to Big Sur. I want to take my children camping. I surf Web sites for RVs when my writing feels blocked.

It's in me, just like it's in you—the hopeful flame of possibility that keeps our mind-set warm and our view long.

OUT OF THE RUT

If you have ever gotten your car stuck in mud or snow, you know what it's like to try to get out. You alternate between forward and reverse, trying to accelerate the proper amount at the proper time to get enough momentum and traction to get out of the rut. Too much or too little and you just dig a deeper groove into the earth, going nowhere.

The same applies to fitness. We have all said or heard the expression "I'm in a rut right now," meaning "I'm doing the same old thing, and I can't see how to change or find the motivation to make it happen." It's like writer's block for the body. There is nothing more intimidating than a blank page, a blank mind, and a deadline. But pressure yields no fruit. Pressure doesn't seem to help a physical rut, either—"Ugh! I have a race coming up and I am out of shape" or "Oh great, my jeans are tight" or "I have to drop this baby weight, fast!"—at least not for me.

I have been discovering a way out of my rut this summer, and the funny thing is that I wasn't acutely aware that I was in a rut to begin with. It was a combination of routine, habit, the Texas heat, and the unspoken, unrecognized agreements made with limitations. I do these things this way because that is what I always do—so there. I started off my summer finding new ways to enjoy fitness with my kids. It got me thinking outside the box and subsequently escaping routine, lifting pressure, and having fun. When my kids had a few days with Daddy, I felt energized, healthy, and happy. I was ready to get out there.

I started going to a new gym twice a week, and I'm working on core strength. One day I train with Michael and one day I go to a family workout, which means daddies supervise a kid boot camp downstairs while mommies get a workout upstairs. I feel so lucky to be included. Last weekend Luke did the elliptical trainer, ran an obstacle course, and hit a punching bag. He loves it! Afterward we go for smoothies.

One night last week I raced a 5-K; I felt motivated to try without my usual start-line anxiety. Afterward I saw a table advertising a trail run on Saturday morning led by a local trail runner and trainer for my favorite group, Moms in Motion. (It's nationwide! Find a group near you; it's awesome.) In my post-race elation, I signed up. Then I changed out of my sweaty race clothes and into jeans and a sweater, teetering on a pair of wedge sandals in a sandy beachside public restroom stall. I pulled the ponytail out of my sweaty hair, shook it out, splashed water on my tomato-red face, slapped on some deodorant (not like it helps without a shower; the masking effect is the equivalent of chewing gum instead of brushing your teeth) and some lip gloss and called it good enough. Then I went out for wine and chowder.

Friday night I started having second thoughts about my trail run bravado. It had been a long time since I ran trails and then there I was, committed to meeting up with very fit strangers and already worried that I would get dropped on a long climb and then (with my amazing sense of direction) get utterly lost. I e-mailed Lance that if I was late to get the kids, he would need to send out a search party. But I was curious, and I had already signed up, and the girl in charge called me to follow up, so, okay. I went.

I loved it! You know the way we are apt to forget the things we love? Silly us. Trail running is amazing. It's like regular running, but more playful and with better views. I sounded asthmatic on the climb and had to stop twice to walk a bit, but Terra assured me that I wasn't awful and that it was okay for me to hope that by the end of summer, I could make the climb without stopping or constant wheezing. I am going to go for it. My rut is officially over.

Game on.

GREAT BALL OF FIRE

We celebrated Paige's birthday on Friday night at my house. The party ended with a Texas-size rainstorm, so we moved outside to the screened in porch, where I lit some candles, and we finished our wine and lingered in conversation into the night. It was ideal.

It was not ideal, however, when my alarm rang at 5:30 a.m. for our usual Saturday morning run. I was like the Peanuts character Pig Pen, traveling around in a cloud, mine caused by wine fog. When Paige came out of her silent house, she was carrying a bouquet of flowers. Saturday was the anniversary of the death of Katie's grandmother, so we concocted a great plan to hide a bouquet of flowers and some Gatorade somewhere near the cemetery so we could run there with Katie in the morning to honor the day and her grandmother.

But we never quite got that organized, and Katie had no early morning childcare, so it was just Paige and me and a fistful of lilies. The Texas State Cemetery is on the east side of town, across I-35. We had to weave around downtown a bit first until it got light enough to feel safe running with just the two of us.

The gates were locked; apparently no one normal visits the dead at the first light of dawn.

I was certain I was going to be creeped out, but instead I was awestruck. The cemetery is absolutely beautiful—a wide expanse of lush green lawn, a path lined with Texas flags blowing idly in the morning breeze, and the comfort of the orderly rows of small white markers.

I could tell that Paige planned to enter, valid visiting hours or not. She and I always find ourselves in these moments—the clash between our personalities made evident when she wants to break the rules and I want to cling to them. I was thinking about the horror of getting arrested for trespassing on state property. She was likely thinking about the pointlessness of running for over an hour while carrying a sweaty flower bouquet and not getting to place it in the intended spot. Her logic (or her personality?) prevailed, and we hopped the fence like a couple of naughty high school girls.

It was so worth it. The section where Katie's grandparents are buried is full of huge headstones and monuments, all of them so incredibly crafted and thoughtfully placed that you fall into a hushed admiration for the sanctuary of these important souls. The Texas State Cemetery is not an ordinary cemetery; it is reserved for those who have significant roles in Texas history. Katie's grandfather was John Connally, the former governor of Texas, and his wife, Nellie, is buried beside him. Paige placed the flowers on the headstone, and we sat down on a nearby bench and prayed.

It was inspiring to be surrounded by the reminders of so many great and powerful lives. It made me wonder about what it is that makes the difference between the ordinary and the extraordinary, when we are crafted essentially the same. The answer came to me in a quotation on the back of Katie's grandparents' headstone, from Theodore Roosevelt's "Citizenship in a Republic" speech, given in 1910 when he addressed the Sorbonne in Paris.

It is not the critic who counts; not the man who points out how the strong man stumbles, or where the doer of deeds could have done them better. The credit belongs to the man who is actually in the arena, whose face is marred by dust and sweat and blood; who strives valiantly; who errs, who comes short again and again, because there is no effort without error and shortcoming; but who does actually strive to do the deeds; who knows great enthusiasms, the great devotions; who spends himself in a worthy cause; who at the best knows in the end the triumph of high achievement, and who at the worst, if he fails, at least fails while daring greatly, so that his place shall never be with those cold and timid souls who neither know victory nor defeat.

When we turned to go, we were nearly blinded by a sunrise unlike any I have ever seen. The sky was a normal shade of grayish morning, but the sun, set apart from everything, was a radiant, flaming red ball. It looked like power, if power had a look; it was impervious to everything, contained, and glowing with possibility. It was the perfect visual to accompany Roosevelt's words. It reminded me that perhaps the greatness of the souls surrounding me came not so much from the abundance of talent or intellect (not to discount such gifts) but was perhaps the manifestation of courage itself that catalyzed every other virtue and opportunity—the simple bravery in the willingness to risk the attempt.

That red glow is somewhere inside each of us when we dare to run, to speak the truth, to love, to believe, to raise children, to work hard, to explore and nurture our true selves, to face the things that confuse or intimidate us. The Roosevelt passage reminds me of you, of every single one of us who has the courage to get out there and try.

18 HILLS

I love the hills. I hate the hills.

I can't keep myself from the metaphor, God help me; it's just too good. Maybe that's why I always make myself do the hills, whether it's part of Cassie's weekly boot camp or just some personal torture in my neighborhood on an average, unassuming Tuesday. I want to be fit for hills—in running, in life. They often come, be it in a race or in everyday living, when we least expect them. We think we are giving it everything we have, and then *whoa*, there it is, no way around it except to climb. I want to do these drills, to feel dimensions of this pain, until I have a muscle memory of it—in my legs or in my heart. I want to have practiced enough, done the drills so many times, that when I am suddenly faced with a hill of any proportion, I kick into autopilot. I want to do the right thing and do it well, if for no other reason than that it is what I have been trained to do. In life, there is not time to dwell on assessing the hill. You just climb it because it is blocking your path. Sometimes you even have to be strong enough to carry others with you. Up and over.

You know in races when you are well trained, and you come to a hill notorious for the demise of PRs, and you see people walking, puking, or simply sitting on the curb? And then you just stay steady and git 'er done? It's awesome. It's the difference between *ready* and *not ready*. It's the metamorphosis of pain into power. Sometimes the anticipation and fear alone will inhibit my breathing and jack up my heart rate long before I reach the base. *Oh, God, here it comes,* I think: Dolly Parton Hill (Dallas White Rock), Heartbreak Hill (Boston), the bridge back into Manhattan (New York City), or even Balcones Drive, right in my 'hood. I am not making fun of those who walk these hills. (I have done it myself.) I'm only saying I want to be one of those who don't flinch.

I don't have a goal in mind in my racing schedule per se, and I am not in the midst of personal crisis (of course, it's only noon), but this does not mean that I will not run hills with reverence and consistency and, occasionally, with pleasure. Maybe I just need to know that in a pinch, if the situation requires it of me, I can haul a little ass.

Metaphor girl here loves the hills. I love the way they hurt, the way they refine, the way they challenge, the way they call us forward from fear. I love everything they represent when a parallel is drawn between hills in running and hills in life. They are exactly the same. We cannot fathom or face either one without training for them. We have to prepare in ordinary times for the challenges that lie ahead. And what better way than hills? If we aren't careful, they can steal our oxygen, our confidence, and our morale. But if we are careful, they can transform us, pushing our threshold for pain and our endurance in the face of adversity.

I remember when Jon and I were kids and he would fake-punch me just to see if I would flinch. "Made you blink," he would say. Life can do the same thing; it can throw punches at you, even stopping just short of true injury, to see if you will flinch. Sweethearts, keep practicing hills and you won't flinch, no matter what is thrown in your face. No matter how steep the mother of a hill blocking your path, you can have the confidence and the training to overcome it. Up and over.

Hills separate good from great, viable from victorious. Watch it in your next race; some people hold pace, some accelerate and drop people, and some slide away like they've got banana peels for shoes. You simply cannot become soft or complacent if you seek hills on purpose. You practice something enough times when it doesn't count, you can bet your shapely bottom that you will have what it takes when it does.

A PUSH

Just as I am not one to think about goals only at the new year, growing up only at birthdays, or love only on Valentine's Day, I think gratitude is a virtue worth exploring and honoring all year long. To me, being grateful is not a reflex in response to a kindness or blessing but a default setting worth cultivating. No matter what kind of day I've had, each night I count at least five things I'm thankful for before I fall asleep.

I had an encounter with raw gratitude on Saturday morning and continue to be humbled by it.

Paige and I were running south down Lamar toward the lake. There is a hill between Twelfth Street and the popular intersection at Fifth Street, and we passed a man sitting at the corner of Ninth. "Wonder if he needs some help," Paige said out loud, more to herself than to me. I looked at the man; he was homeless, a large man in a wheelchair with a prosthetic leg. He had his belongings hanging off his chair, including a guitar case. I mumbled something like "I don't know . . . I'm scared." But Paige ignored me, already on a mission.

"Sir, do you need some help getting up that hill?" Paige smiled, her real smile, the one she smiles at me.

He looked startled for a minute. "Oh, um, I'm not sure which way I want to go."

"Well, if you want to go toward Fifth, I can get you there." Still smiling. Meanwhile, I prayed he wasn't crazy and about a pull a knife on my Good Samaritan friend.

"Well, okay, sure. Yes, I want to go that way." He looked at her quizzically, likely wondering how her skinny legs could possibly push him and all his stuff. Or maybe even wondering why she cared.

"Great," she said. And she grabbed the handles behind his chair as easily and comfortably as she reaches for a baby jogger and started up the hill. He must have weighed 200 pounds, give or take, plus his belongings. At first he tried to use his arms to "help" her; he looked very strong from wheeling around town. But after a few minutes of high-speed churning, he gave up trying to hold her pace and accepted the ride for what it was—a gift. It was as if he were weightless, the way she pushed him without effort, chatting and bantering all the way. I ran beside them, making conversation but feeling like a third wheel in the moment, winded by my own lack of initiative, my own fear.

He took over as they crested the hill, his load lightened by kindness and momentum. Perhaps the greatest treat of all is not being overlooked. He thanked her and wheeled off to wherever he was going. Paige and I ran quietly for several paces, very much aware of our legs and what just transpired. I always talk about how important it is to train to be ready, and Paige was trained and ready for that beautiful moment. I will never forget it. She does things more than she talks about the idea of doing them, and that is something I really love about her.

Some might say this is an example of generosity or compassion, but to me, it is an example of gratitude. A grateful life is about seeing, thinking, offering, appreciating, and living beyond self. This is the spirit behind giving thanks.

Sometimes it just takes a push.

FIVE BOXES

We did a grueling hill-repeat workout yesterday at running group. Maybe it was the onset of Halloween, but I swear Cassie gave an evil laugh when she told us the circuit (*mwa ha ha ha!*). I knew I was going to have to dig in, because my mind was someplace else. As we know, it's hard to be successful on the hills without mind and body in unison. *Up . . . and over.*

My family is going through a little "up and over" of our own right now. My parents went to Arizona because my grandmother (95 years old) is in the hospital and it's time to start making some decisions about next steps, such as where she and Grandpa are going to live now that more care is required. My parents and aunts and uncles found a place where Grandma can get the assistance she needs after she's out of the hospital, and she and Grandpa can live together in the same apartment. This was a major blessing, because for a while it seemed like she might have to be in a more medical setting. Today my parents are overseeing the move.

I had an e-mail from my mom yesterday morning, and I could tell she was sad. She was packing up her parents' things and amassed a collection of five boxes. She said, "Isn't it strange? *Five boxes.* That's it, after 68 years of marriage?" Obviously my mom is in the thick of things, dealing simultaneously with logistics and the onslaught of emotion that they represent. Transitions of this magnitude are never easy, and I ache for her, and for myself and my kids, knowing that we all pass through this corridor eventually. The clock is always ticking, but for most of life we don't hear it.

I thought about her, about them, as I willed my legs to churn up the hills and tried to suck air into my lungs. I tried to send some of the power fueling my climb to help Mom with hers and Grandma with hers, and I wondered if something as simple as a run was potent enough to link generations, stretching across all the miles between Austin and Phoenix. I looked at my own watch, thinking about the clock and how I want to spend my time.

On our fourth circuit, a thought came to me about the five boxes. I didn't think it was sad that there were "only" five boxes; I thought it was liberating. Because when I think about my grandparents, I have hundreds of boxes of thoughts and memories in my mind. I can conjure up smells and songs and pictures in my head. In a second I can be 10 years old again, spending the summer at Ottertail Lake in northern Minnesota, chasing fireflies, playing cards with Grandma, watching Grandpa and Dad man the grill, fishing for walleye and eating them for dinner, swimming with Jon while Mom floats on a raft and reads, sleeping in the cabana while rain falls on the tin roof, pulling carrots out of the garden, eating homemade cinnamon bread for breakfast, reading ancient issues of *Reader's Digest* Drama in Real Life stories. Those things, all the sacred things, are way bigger than any box.

We spend so much time amassing things and striving for stuff, yet ironically, none of it matters. When you are 95 years old, you don't give a flip about the stuff. But I love the metaphor of the five boxes. I love it for me, right now, to think about what I'm putting in those boxes today. If I only have five boxes, I am going to pack wisely, making sure that the people, the time, the memories, and the experiences are always first. As for the rest of the stuff, I'm going to spend the rest of my life shedding it—just like my grandparents did. I can't wait to go see them, check out their new digs, and tell them how much they continue to inspire me.

In the meantime, I am going to think about being light on my feet.

THROUGH, NOT TO

Last Wednesday at running group we had our first real hill workout of the year.

We began with a warmup across the park and under the freeway to get to our starting point. We had five repeats ahead, and each hill had two sections: tough and tougher. The stopping point was through (again, our coach Cassie repeated, the end is *through*, not *to*) the stop sign. After our drills and strides, we sipped our water, I stripped off my long sleeves, we set our watches, and we were off. I took the first hill slower than I normally would go out, uncertain of the length or incline ahead. In my book, when in doubt, it's best to conserve something for the end. The second hill was definitely steeper than the first, so when I staggered *through* the stop sign at the top, I wasn't sure I would make four more.

Hills are an interesting challenge. We know we have the strength and the experience to get through the climb, so it isn't a physical thing as much as it is mental. Looking at something hard looming ahead is a daunting exercise in any arena, running or not. I have friends and acquaintances right now who are looking at hills: a move with their family, a cancer diagnosis, an ADD diagnosis, a child with an incurable disease, a job change, a divorce, adjusting to a new baby, longing for a new baby and not having one, and many others. The incline ahead is steep and unyielding. So how do we prepare? Running hills gives us some clues. First, we relax—which is hard to do but essential. We cannot make any assessments in a state of panic. Then we remind ourselves and each other that we have strength for climbing. Then we breathe; ideally, we breathe deeply. Then we begin. We lift our legs and pump our arms and go at our own pace. This is incredibly important. It's so easy to lose heart on a hill when we compare ourselves to those around us. We waste energy by taking our focus off the goal, which is of course going through the finish, not to it. Some people attack a hill; others run steady. Some have a mantra; others need a clear head. It's good to know what kind of climber you are—the middle of a hill is not a good time to mess with definitions or change tactics. When we practice enough by running hills, we develop our own rhythms and strategies. The same with life's hills: The smaller ones make us fit for the biggies, and we can maintain our same rhythm. The more we practice, the fitter we become and the less we fear.

Cassie says to make friends with the hills. Making friends typically means building a relationship, spending time in each other's company, and over time becoming more of our true selves in the context of the friendship. She says if we make friends with the hills, we will look forward to them—as a welcome change of pace, a chance to test our training, a chance to make up some lost time, a chance to witness our own strength, a chance to share our strength with our friends beside us.

I am trying to get to a place where I welcome all the hills in my life in this way—running or not. I am in a perpetual state of preparation, and this gives both pleasure and purpose to my training. I want to be ready. For what? I am not exactly sure.

We finished our last repeat, our times the same as or faster than the first. Cassie was pleased. But Paige had arrived late that day, so she still had one left to do. She took off down the hill toward the starting point. Amy said, "Do you really think she should have to do that by herself?" Amy is a wise woman and a good friend. We shook off our tiredness and headed down the hill after her, and we finished number six as a group.

That's the best way to run hills—strong and together, all the way through.

STRENGTH FOR THE CLIMB

Yesterday I ran the Motive Bison Stampede Half Marathon in Austin.

I didn't want to run it.

The course is notorious for being brutal—a series of hills that would make a car groan. Plus, when I woke up, it was in the upper thirties—a perfect morning to jump back under my down comforter and burrow until further notice. Truth be told, I was intimidated. I went, but only because Paige and Katie were meeting at Paige's house and I said I would be there. Sometimes the only reason I do anything at all is because I said I would.

The start was hectic and teeth-chattering cold. I was uncomfortable with the cold, but mostly I was uncomfortable with myself. I didn't want to push myself. I could deal with the discomfort but not my fear. What if I couldn't hack this course? What if my training was insufficient for this race as well as the upcoming Austin Marathon? What if I let my friends down? It was made clear before we signed up for this race that we were running on pace for a 3:40 marathon goal, and anyone who slid back would be dropped. Paige wanted us to feel race pace and know what it meant to sustain it for 13.1 miles. She has more experience and knowledge than I do, so being the good pupil that I am, I always follow her lead.

I noticed something profound out there on the course yesterday. I started paying attention to the runners around me, which I usually don't do. Many people must have been familiar with the course, because I could perceive a shift in energy right before a particularly grueling section. People got edgy and coltish, and their breathing intensified before the exertion even warranted it. I realized I wasn't alone in my fear. We started breathing harder simply in anticipation of the trial before us.

How often do we do this in life as well? We waste energy and hard-earned training on dread. I want to be the kind of runner and the kind of person who does her work in the workroom of life and trusts in her abilities, her preparation, and her provision when the moment comes. This was a potent lesson for me yesterday.

On this one hill that looked like the side of a building, I had to pull my cap down low, gangsta style, because I couldn't bear to look at the thing. I focused my trudging on the distance between my shoes and the bill of my cap and concentrated on what was before me. I counted in French in my head to divert my thinking and regulate my gasping into something that sounded more like breathing. I thought of Cassie and her mantra: "Up and over." I struggled with the "and over" part. The "and over" in this course amounted to a small respite of mild incline immediately followed by another "up." As I gained ground and my fear of failure didn't materialize, I started to loosen (and look) up. I regained awareness of my form, and my training came to deliberate consciousness. *Relax your shoulders, Kristin. That's it. Pump your arms. Stay light on your feet. Good girl. Open up your chest. Breathe. You got it. Almost there.*

At one point I thought I got dropped but figured if I didn't panic and stayed steady, I might be able to make up some ground and find my friends. It turned out that my gang was just behind me, Paige gathering her chicks like the reliable mother hen that she is.

We finished together, with a sub-8 pace. My biggest cause for celebration was not the time itself but the lesson I learned on the hill. *I will give less energy to dread. I will trust my training. I will do my best not to be afraid.*

19 CLARITY

Our eyes and brains can get so bogged and fogged that all we can see is the partial view from our own limited perspective. We crave clarity. We long for the opportunity to go, and grow, beyond ourselves. We desire understanding. We yearn for those lightbulb moments when we think, *Oh! Now I get it.* We hunger for the ability to see ourselves and each other with clearer lenses and through fewer layers of our own accumulated junk.

What is a more direct path to clarity than a good run? A good run mandates that we travel light. A good run allows us to be alone or with wise friends, to pray, to review our thoughts, to challenge our mind-set, to play devil's advocate, to assess or reassess, to repent, to plan, to see another perspective, to seek understanding and resolution, to reroute back to the high road. A good run, if we're open to it, always reminds us of not only who we are but who we want to be. Maybe there is a correlation between opening our lungs and opening our minds; I am not sure, but when it comes to clarity, we can all use a little fresh air.

SAFE ARRIVAL

My kids are spending spring break with their dad, so my mom and I made an impromptu girls' getaway to the West Coast. It could not have been a nicer trip. The weather was gorgeous, we ate fresh seafood most nights, and my relationship with my mom is warm and unencumbered. It says a lot about two people when their vay-cay juju blends just right. I hope when my kids are grown it feels as delightfully easy with them; I hope we choose each other when our years of mandatory tethering are through. I had enough time to do each of my favorite runs while I was there: a bike path run, a mission view run, a Butterfly Beach run, a trail run, a eucalyptus grove run, and a bluff run. I reveled in each one, knowing how good it was as it was happening, not just later, reflecting back.

The only cloud on our otherwise sunny trip was that my dad called with news that my parents' dog Hogan wasn't doing well—followed by the news you never want: that it was time for him to go. He went to the vet and never came home. Hogan was a 13-year-old Vizsla, with rheumy eyes and a graying face and a heart as big as Texas. He was the kind of dog that made eye contact with the intent to see clear through to your soul; he would stare until he was certain you were okay. He would lean into you and step on your foot to remind you of the importance of being still. His nickname was Velcro, because his close and constant contact reminded everyone to stick together. He patiently shepherded each and every younger dog we added to our clan, trying to teach them something about dignity, manners, and a dog's responsibilities. So far not one of them has been able to fill his paw prints. He was the dog that stood stone still while you slumped and cried on his back, giving comfort during meltdowns at all ages. He made every cross-country road trip without complaint, even when he had to be lifted into the back of the car. No matter what, if his people were going someplace, he was in.

Only this time, he was going someplace without us.

My heart broke for my dad, who had to be there, and for my mom, who wasn't. I did what I always do when I'm broken: I ran. I don't run away from things anymore, mind you; I run through them. So I took my parents' sorrow and added it to my own, compounded by the weight of telling my children when they get home from their trip. I put all this sorrow in my invisible pack and headed to the beach. I took my shoes off so I could feel the sand and frigid ocean under my feet. I felt heavy with my load, punching deep footprints that erased as I went along. I tried to stop thinking and just listen to the ocean, willing myself to remember that it's normal for things to come and go.

Something caught my eye on the sand in front of me. It was my favorite treasure: a piece of sea glass. I am always collecting things when I run at the beach—shells, interesting rocks, sand dollars, cool feathers. I find sea glass sometimes, usually small pieces in hues of green. I guess I love it so much because it reminds me of people, rough edges made smooth over time by the pounding of life. This piece of sea glass was not green, not blue. It was amber, the exact color of young Hogan, many years ago, before he started turning white with age. I stopped abruptly and picked it up. It fit perfectly into the palm of my hand. The edges were round and worn, and I wondered how long it had tumbled before washing up in front of me. I squinted up to the sky, and peace rushed over me like a tide.

It was a safe arrival message. I slid off my unseen pack of sorrows, picked up my pace, and brought the treasure home to Mom.

ANTIVENOM

I started yesterday off on the wrong foot.

My alarm didn't go off—somehow I switched the "a.m." and "p.m." on my phone—so we got up 12 minutes late, and our mornings are timed to precision. The kids were arguing non-stop; Luke wouldn't eat his granola because Isabelle coughed somewhere in the vicinity and it was deemed contaminated; Isabelle ripped out her ponytails twice because she said I made them uneven; my coffee got cold while I was packing lunches and when I reheated it in the microwave it burned my tongue, rendering the remainder of my day tasteless; Isabelle decided now was a good time to change the rabbit cage; Grace was taking a stand against oral hygiene, despite her dragon breath; and Charlie (our Cavalier King Charles puppy) lifted his leg and peed on a corner of the kitchen island.

We made it to school with seconds to spare, and I hate rushing my mornings and parting in a scramble, especially the mornings before the kids have a Daddy weekend. I called the vet and made an appointment for the leg-lifter to get snipped. I took big-dog Mercy for a run, hoping that some hills and her steady company would restore my equilibrium, but I walked back into my house under the same cloud. I tried to write, but my desk was too littered with bills and mail to welcome creative thought, so I wasted the rest of my morning idealess, excavating stacks of paper.

And then, out of nowhere, it hit me: The only way I was going to snap out of my sour mood was with a serious intervention. With sudden clarity, I knew that if I did not flood my poisonous mood with the antivenom, my day and I were going down. For those of you who watch less *Animal Planet* than I do or who did not win the science fair in high school (I really did), let me explain that antivenom is created when a tiny bit of venom is introduced into a subject, triggering an immune response that generates antibodies that fight the venom. These antibodies can be harvested and used on behalf of others. In my particular moody case, the antivenom would consist of the antibodies of kindness, specifically the unspoken kind—the thoughts or gestures we contemplate but don't make time to share. I got quiet with my grumpy self and thought about the previous few days, combing my existence for the things that struck me but were quickly dismissed. I wrote them down. I started to feel a wee bit better. Then I took action.

1. I called the groomer who had taken care of our old dog Boone the day before. Boone is impossible to groom. He's over 12, and many moons ago he fell off our deck in France, so he's a bit off, somewhat contorted and stiff, almost palsied. I told her that when I drove Boone over the previous day, I was close to tears, noticing his old age and overall bad state. But after her tenderness and magic, he looked so much better, even had a newfound bit of spunk that I attributed to his fresh do. I told her that I understood how difficult and time-consuming it must be to work with him, but that I really appreciated her effort and I thought he looked beautiful. She was quiet for a minute before she told me I made her week.

2. I have a dear friend, Dawn, who can't stand being cold. A mother of a cold front is blowing outside my office window as I type, and we all knew it was coming. So yesterday I finished the scarf I had been knitting for her since before Christmas and dropped it on her doorstep with a note telling her to stay warm and I love her.

3. Cassie hates to be sick (we all hate it, but she *hates* it, with narrowed eyes and spite) and has a nasty sinus infection. I thought about this on Wednesday, the way that she summons her energy for her clients and friends, even when she ends up with none left to spare for herself. I left her a message to tell her how much that meant to me. She left word later on my voice mail that I had saved her day.

4. I wrote a note to the librarian who hosted Luke's scout den earlier this week for our monthly meeting. She gave us a tour of her library and made books and reference materials totally interesting to a group of 10-year-old boys. She finished with a scavenger hunt, which was a giant hit, as you can imagine. She has a tremendous gift in her way with children, the kind of gift that makes you stop what you're doing and pay attention. She has probably heard this countless times, but I wanted her to hear it from me, in pen, on my stationery. I mailed that.

And before I realized it had taken place, my day, my mood—and my sense of humor, perspective, and appreciation—had all been restored. I am not sharing this in an "aw, look how sweet I am" kind of way. I'm sharing this in a "holy crap, was I sour" kind of way. I wonder how often we make a swift mental note of something or someone meaningful but it slides into oblivion because we are in such a blasted hurry all the time.

I want to encourage you—no, I flat-out dare you—to try this infusion of light the next time your mood goes dark. It was the fastest road I have ever taken to getting back on track, so from one runner to another, I share the route with you.

TRAIL TRANSLATIONS

I have been marking most of my miles on the dirt lately and learning a lot. The trail culture is so different. Let me explain. It's like practicing golf swings in your backyard without going to the golf course yet thinking you know how to play. Just because I know how to run, as in putting one foot in front of the other, does not mean I know how to go off road. I have a lot to learn as far as technique and terrain go, but there are also information, etiquette, and culture details that I have to understand in order to be proficient.

We had a downhill clinic at our trail-group run last Thursday evening. We did several loops on a rolling course with a repeat every time we reached a big hill. We were supposed to hike up the hill and run down it twice on each loop, ideally with progressively faster times. The coach, Robert, explained the nuances of downhill trail running, things like keeping your foot strike light, easy, and agile; using your elbows for balance; rolling with the rocks; and tracking side to side if you pick up speed too fast and feel out of control. My first pass down the hill, I felt as stiff as an Old Navy mannequin; my limbs were rigid and uncooperative, and nothing felt light and agile about my feet as I scrambled for footing on a moving surface. I have no desire whatsoever to roll with the rocks; in fact, any rolling at all causes my inner panic alarm to whoop and flash like a shoplifter passing through a sensor. Robert flew past me on the trail, literally like he was snowboarding by me, so he could wait for us on that repeat hill and critique our style, or lack thereof.

All this time in nature is heightening my awareness and appreciation for the metaphor. There seem to be a growing number of multilevel applications for the trail lessons as they relate to my life.

Robert gave me one of these lessons running downhill beside me, reminding me to breathe and trust my footing. "You are absolutely going to have to relax," he said with a wise smile. He's like the Zen turtle in the movie *Kung Fu Panda*. I am so lucky to know him. The last loop we did in the dark with flashlights, ripping down the same hill with rolling rocks. My little group was the last to finish, and Robert led us back out to the truck, where everyone was hanging out and having a beer. I realized something halfway through my can of Modelo: I was totally relaxed.

Saturday was my first 20-miler on trails. We started at 7 a.m. and I finished around 11. My sense of time has to change; I am accepting that worthwhile things can take a long time. I wore my new Nathan hydration backpack and felt like a poser at first, until Joyce, a beautiful and far more experienced runner, helped me make some adjustments to the straps, and after about 10 miles of continuous drinking and snacking, my pack was broken in and suited me just fine. In a group trail run, some folks run ahead and others file in at their comfortable pace, and if there is a questionable turn, the group waits and eats and talks until everyone is collected, and we move on together. It's great. I was terrified of being left and lost, but I had nothing to worry about after all.

WHAT YOU SEE IS WHAT YOU GET

Usually I have one run each week that speaks to me on a metaphorical level, telling or teaching me something that I can't seem to get when I read, write, connect with people, or do the things that require doing in the rest of my life.

My metaphor run this week was early Saturday morning. I had a talk to give for the women of Moms in Motion, after their triathlon training (swim and run) at 9:15, so I got up early to run. I wanted to be fully awake and have a clear head, to have something to offer these amazing athletes. I headed out of my house and the morning was misty and foggy, with just enough of a damp chill to make an increased pace seem appealing. I have a run I like to do that winds up behind the Santa Barbara Mission and through the residential streets of an area called the Mesa. The run is essentially uphill for as long as you like, until either you can no longer breathe or you make it to a section where you turn and the view sucker-punches you with beauty and you have to stop and say ahhh. You can't help but smile. I love this route so much that I ration it, allowing myself to do it only once or twice a week, the way a mother apportions M&M's so that the children don't fight over them or end up having a sugar meltdown.

This morning I wanted to treat myself to the view, so I trudged along, thinking about what I wanted to say to these women and focusing on the hill, trying to keep strong and steady in my pace and posture. I was so looking forward to the view, yet with the fog I could see only about half a block in front of me. I kept hoping it would clear around the next bend or when I turned onto the next street. But it just got foggier the higher I climbed. I could see only what was directly in front of me.

I made it all the way up the hill, stopped in my usual eye-candy spot, and saw . . . absolutely nothing. I saw only a haze of thick fog where I usually see the hills, the mountains behind, the boulevard along the ocean, the palm trees, the wharf, the harbor. Nothing. I stopped my watch and stretched for few minutes. Still nothing. The only thing I could see clearly was myself.

And there it was—the metaphor, the message I needed. I came all that way to see the one thing that I needed to see clearly that morning. I felt light and clean, as if my sweat was making me transparent. I smiled and turned back in to the fog and headed downhill. My feet knew the way home.

20 THE WALL

Of course Chapter 20 has to be named "The Wall." Every runner knows that mile marker 20 is legendary. It's where you hit the wall, climb it, or vault it. Some say that mile 20 is where the race ends and the marathon begins. Whatever your theories about mile 20, we can all agree that there definitely is a wall. It can be a stumbling block or an all-out face-plant, but in either case, it cannot be ignored. You can prepare for it all you like, but the challenge of race day is in the unknowing, the factors you cannot control. No runner, from the chafed-thigh beginner to the Olympic-caliber athlete, can escape the wall. That it eventually comes for you is inevitable. But what is negotiable is how you react when you hit it.

And this is where the wall gets interesting to me—because the way you handle bonking on a run is pretty telling about the way you handle bonking in life. Some people acquiesce to their cramping and, once they see their pacer carry their goal and fade into the distance, throw in the towel and walk it on home— slumping their shoulders, sometimes sobbing, totally dejected.

Other people readjust on the fly. The truly remarkable suck it up, pick it up, and chase down that dream. Some calculate a new goal and aim for that with renewed vigor. I have been all of these people, on the race course and in my life. I have been a sideline sobber, I have gotten pissed off and used that as rocket fuel, I have recalibrated and decided that sometimes completion is the greatest accomplishment of all. Regardless of what is revealed about us when we hit the wall, we have an opportunity for growth. Sometimes walls have windows. We can be humbly reminded that running, like life, is hard. It is an effort worthy of respect and gratitude—regardless of performance.

The wall has a lot to teach us, but we have to get close enough to it to be able to learn.

SAME O, SAME O

I did it: I made my break. I escaped the heat. In the nick of time, too, because Wednesday was my last running group of this season, and I don't know that I could have survived another. Regular torture becomes truly masochistic when you crank up the heat and humidity to 100 plus. My face was tomato red for 2 hours after I took a shower. Two hours!

When I stepped off the airplane to cooler California temperatures, I wanted to do a cartwheel. But I was carrying suitcases, my computer, and my dog Boone, so I refrained and cartwheeled on the inside.

I slept past 7 this morning, since I didn't have to run at 5 to survive it. I got up, had coffee, did some work (desperately trying to finish my manuscript before my kiddos come back to me), and went for a run at about 11. In Texas, you would only run at 11 a.m. if you had a death wish or wanted to lose 5 pounds the hard way. I felt sluggish from my flight but happy to be outside and actually enjoying the sunshine instead of running from it in fear. I went to a yoga class afterward, at a new place and with a new teacher, Kelly, who was awesome. She does a move and looks like a dolphin flowing through the water in the poses. I look more like a tadpole, in process of evolution, uncertain whether to hop or swim. But I am starting to like it so much, I do not care. One of the things I really want to work on this summer is being present, truly in the moment. I want to be that way when I run or train, or do yoga, or spend time with my children or family or friends or alone. When I'm working, I want to be working, and when I'm done, I want to be done. It seems so Homer Simpson–*D'oh!* simple, but it's really hard. Yoga forces you to keep coming back to the moment, and because of this I am really starting to see how often I drift off—delving into the past or making forays into the future, both of which are useless and wasteful in the present moment.

Kelly was encouraging us to jump from one pose into another. I almost laughed out loud, because she had no idea that I was stuck until I could worm my way out, so jumping was entirely out of the question. Then, as if she could read my mind, she said, "Do the same thing you have always done and get the same things you have always gotten."

Okay, ouch, ouch, ouch, ouch. Those words were more uncomfortable to me than the pose I was stuck in. I said it over and over to myself so I would carry it with me when I left. And now I'm home and her words are still ricocheting and reverberating in my head. How often do I do the same thing? How often do we all do this?

We parent the same way and expect more from our kids. We put the same old energy into our marriage and expect it to be more fulfilling. Or if we're single, we continue in our same old routine and wonder why we never meet anyone new. We work the same hours doing the same things and thinking the same thoughts and wonder why we aren't promoted. We go to the same places all the time and expect to be inspired. We eat the same things and wonder why we weigh the same and have the same lack of energy. We read, watch, and listen to the same kinds of things and wonder why we don't feel more creative. We do the same activities all the time and wonder why they aren't as fun. We get mad or frustrated by the same stuff and the same people without ever concluding that perhaps we are the common denominator in that equation. We do the same workout and run the same routes and wonder why we are stuck in a fitness and morale plateau. We live and love and give in the same way and wonder why we never grow.

Do you see traces of this in your life? I know I do. If we recognize it, maybe that is the first step toward stepping out and moving beyond the wall. Maybe it's time to change it up.

Do the same thing you have always done and get the same thing you have always gotten.

CHUNKY MONKEY

This weekend was high mileage.

I ran 23 miles on trails on Saturday (5 hours total, with refueling stops) and a 10-mile local road race on Sunday. Combine that training with a (semi) social life and the start of a head cold . . . well, it appeared daunting. I received the same advice from three different sources, so I know it was intended for me. First, my good friend and trail guru Scott Dunlap told me he gets through his ultra races by thinking of them in terms of incremental goals—like the next 5 miles or the next aid station—never the full distance as one goal. Then Roger, the trail coach who was filling in for Robert this weekend, said the same thing when I was questioning him about his 100-mile races. He said sometimes it's all you can do to get to the next aid station, the next mile, or even the next clump of trees—sometimes the only way through it is to break it down into little pieces. Apparently this is even more important from a mental perspective than a physical one.

And again the same lesson from another angle and source: my children. My daughters are learning to read, and one of the first-grade tactics to attempt a word that looks too long and too hard to read is called chunking or, affectionately, chunky monkey. This means taking a word apart into chunks that seem readable or reasonable, working through them, and then putting the pieces together. It reminds me of that old television program for kids called *Electric Company,* where two profiled faces would articulate syllables back and forth to sound out words. Like "Barn." "Yard." "Barnyard!" "Climb." "-ing." "Climbing!" You get my drift.

Saturday morning started out chilly, and my nose would not stop running. The girl in me still resists "farmer blows," so I alternated between soggy tissues and the back of my glove. Very attractive, I know, as was the raw, red skin surrounding my nostrils after my run, stinging from the sweat. Our group had varying distances that day, depending on each person's training program: 9 miles, 23 miles, or 35 miles. We did a 9-mile run first, after which most folks dropped off, then we continued for a 14-mile distance. I ditched my long sleeves, restocked my Kleenex supply at my car, and ate half a peanut butter sandwich after the first 9. It wasn't too hard to motivate to go back out; for some reason, these days 9 miles doesn't seem as long as it used to. My backpack held 2 liters of water, my sandwich remains, some multigrain chips, electrolyte pills, a bar, some pretzels, cookies, my cell phone in case of emergency, my car key, and of course, the tissues.

The next portion of the run seemed long, so my mind started wandering. I tripped a couple of times and wondered if I was getting too tired or too sloppy or was about to bonk. I ate some more and tried to remember to drink even if I was not hot enough to feel thirsty. In Texas it's hard to remember that you are still thirsty if you aren't melting. I wondered if I had 14 more miles in me. And then I remembered *chunky monkey*. I'd already done 9, no problem. I could easily finish these 7. Okay, just 7. It's okay, totally doable. I told myself, *Eat if you are empty, drink, walk if you are tired*. I didn't need to walk, though I always pick my way over steep rocks or roots, not yet able to fly over them like some of the others. We made it to the turnaround point and checked in with Roger. Satisfied that we were doing fine, he helped us refill our water supply; then we ate briefly and took some electrolytes and salt. I stretched and considered the last 7-mile chunk. I ended up running with a guy named Lonnie, and he kept me distracted with conversation and trail-running wisdom—he is an avid runner and reader, interested in all kinds of things. I resisted the urge to ask "Are we there yet?!" about a hundred times. I couldn't very well ask about the end of *my* run when he was tackling 35 miles that day. So I plodded along without any idea of how much was left. Just when I thought I was officially spent, the Hill of Life (a well-known climb in Austin trail lore) appeared like a mirage. We were finished. We hiked up the final stretch, signed out with Roger, and headed to our cars. I took a few moments to take off my shoes and socks, wipe my face, change my shirt—meanwhile, Lonnie restocked and returned to the trailhead. I was glad to go home. It's interesting to me that we seem to have energy only for the task we set out to do and no more.

Chunky monkey got me through the day and through my 10-mile run with Paige on Sunday morning. It's a valuable strategy for approaching long mileage and also for approaching the difficult sections of life. There is no way to sanely consider the magnitude of dealing with a diagnosis, a financial pit, a rocky relationship, a crying newborn, a new job, no job, an addiction, or a challenge of any kind if we look at the distance as a whole. If we can just get to the next mile marker, the next appointment, the next paycheck, the next treatment, the next conversation, the next week, the next day, the next hour, the next 5 minutes, we'll make it.

Wherever we are and wherever we're going, we won't break if we break it down.

THE WALL

Marathoners know the wall.

The wall is typically located someplace between miles 20 and 23, but it can sprout up anywhere. It can even begin as a simple, unassuming speed bump but grow up faster than kudzu in Atlanta. Suddenly you find something massive directly in front of you, blocking the path between right here and the finish line.

The wall is constructed of many bricks: things like fear, pain, loneliness, hopelessness, burdens, doubt, guilt, exhaustion—physical exhaustion, mental exhaustion, emotional exhaustion, spiritual exhaustion. It is a black hole in our psyche, a gap in our fence, a riptide in our reservoir with the potential to carry us away. The wall becomes almost physically tangible to runners, but the same wall exists in other areas whether we choose to recognize it or not.

Maybe part of why I run is to get a good, hard look at that sucker. There is a part of me that likes to know, every once in a while, what I am up against on the inside. If we get up close enough, we might spot some loose bricks, wedge our fingers in, and yank them out, revealing a rectangular shaft of light from the other side. Other times, we get up close enough and spot some handholds, footholds, a way up and over. How much time and mileage do we waste each time we try to go around a wall instead of facing it head-on?

The expression "hitting the wall" has become somewhat clichéd. People use it all the time in a nonrunning context to mean the end of the rope, an empty tank, a point of frustration or of no return, giving up, turning back.

When you reach your limit, your wall, the end of yourself—what happens next? What do you find there? Release? Relief? Grace? Do you have a breakdown or do you break it down? Do you make a plan or an excuse? What gives—the terrain, your goal, or you?

I wonder if it's possible to imagine drawing a new starting line just when we think we can't muster another step. Some experienced runners say the race doesn't even begin until mile 20—until the wall. That's when you find out what you are really up against and, in that same sweet moment, what you are really made of.

21 BALANCE

In the gym my trainer, Cassie, has me work different muscles than the ones I use to run. She helps me with my core strength, my upper-body strength. She has me work my legs in a side-to-side fashion, because running is a linear movement. She is an advocate of yoga, Pilates, rest days, mindful nutrition, and cross-training of all kinds. To Cassie, fitness is a way of life, not an exercise program, and as such it should be enjoyable enough to sustain.

I believe the key to sustaining good habits, in fitness and in life, is balance. We balance trying new things with the comfort of old favorites. We balance seriousness with a healthy splash of silly. We balance hard work with play, motivation with contentment, confidence with humility, effort with rest, wine with water, hunger with abundance, selfishness with sacrifice, alone time with the company of our beloved.

It's easier to know when we are out of balance than to fully understand how we're doing it when we feel total equilibrium. I know that in yoga when I am trying to hold a balance pose,

I cannot look down at myself or I will topple over. I have to pick a point farther ahead and focus on that in order to remain stable. Maybe the lesson for a balanced life is rooted in that example—in looking ahead to whom we want to be or how we want to live—and making choices that hold our course steady in that direction.

DIFFERENT STROKES

Our running group winds down in June for a summer hiatus, when the heat and humidity of the Texas summer oppress us into submission. Yesterday we did a track workout in the blazing heat, and the air was so thick with humidity, it felt like I needed a machete to blaze a path. I'm always glad when we reach our hiatus but also sad to break from my standing weekly appointment with my girls.

But seasons are a good thing, even the hot, sweaty ones, because they force us to regroup and readjust, maybe try some new things. Even aside from the weather, with everyone's kid schedules, camp schedules, work schedules, and summer vacation schedules, we have to take a break. Last summer I discovered trail running; I wonder what's in store for me this summer. To kick off the season, I tried something new earlier this week: stand-up paddle boarding! I loved it.

I met my friend Scott down by Town Lake at a spot where we could launch his two paddle boards. He used the smaller, more agile-looking version and let me borrow the one that he dubbed the aircraft carrier. Apparently he knew I would need a wider ride. He gave me a basic rundown—where to put my feet, how my stance should be (balanced, relaxed, but engaged so I could use my body weight and my core to help turn the board), how to hold the paddle, and how to do some basic strokes—all of this in 3 minutes or less. Scott is a true Aquaman and wanted to get out on the water ASAP. He had me get on my board on my knees first to get a feel for it before I stood up. It was a little shifty but not too scary, so I stood up and we pushed off.

It took a bit of time for me to relax enough to get a rhythm (or semirhythm, not the same as Aquaman), but soon I felt lulled by the peaceful slosh of the water, the occasional jumping fish, the turtles poking their heads up, and the easy conversation with my good friend. Town Lake runs right through downtown, and our main running and biking trail is on either side of it. It was an incredible feeling to be gliding quietly through the water, flanked by the bustle of downtown, the chaos of morning traffic, and the pounding of runners on the trail. It was a perfect illustration, a metaphor for me, for the way I want to spend my summer—or live my life, for that matter. I want to be more centered and more quiet, use my core, and be more intentional about becoming immune to the chaos around me. There is always a more peaceful path that cuts through the middle of all the straining and striving, posturing and progressing, and even if it's harder to find, it's worth it. Trying something new always offers a fresh perspective.

The sun started to poke through the clouds and the heat bade us good morning. We turned our boards and headed back to the shore. I could feel a mild ache in my shoulders and a pleasant burn in my core and in my legs, a different soreness from the kind I get after a hard run. I look forward to working some new muscles this summer, literally and metaphorically. Summer is a season of rest, growth, playfulness, reading, freedom, fun, and adventure.

BALANCING ACT

Balance in life is a slippery, elusive thing. When you have a patch of well-aligned existence with everything humming along nicely, it's smart to stop and notice how you got here, with the hope that maybe you can stay longer. Just like when you finish a great race or training run, it's wise to notice the components of your good performance: What did you eat? How long did you sleep? How did you hydrate? What was your week like? What did you do leading up to that day? What was your state of mind? What shoes were you wearing? What were the weather conditions? Some people write all these things down in a running journal, and I bet it reveals a lot.

I keep a regular journal, and I'm often surprised by the rhythms and patterns in my life, the answers that I missed right in front of me because I was so busy asking the questions. Dieters keep food journals for this reason; I know it would surprise me if I knew the caloric sum of all my handfuls of almonds or stolen bites of the kids' food.

I refer to balance because I seem to be planted steadily right now, and I want to notice why and how I got here. My children are healthy and doing well socially and in school. My running is a pleasant refuge, my sleep is undisturbed, and my health is good. My initial effort at making myself go to yoga once a week has transformed into something that I actually look forward to and rarely miss. I am trying to carry my Zen mind-set beyond the confines of class. My work is productive, my deadlines are being met, and my creative side is not petulant or in hiding, as sometimes happens when I'm out of whack. My relationships are intact, reasonably well-nourished, and peaceful. I want to linger here, somehow, if I can.

I wonder if perhaps the key to my balance right now is tied into contentment. I am okay with who and where I am for the moment—the striving, apologetic part of me has gone on vacation, and I hope she settles into new digs somewhere else.

Last Friday I busted Grace out of school and surprised her with a night alone together while my parents kept my other two kids. I weighted down her lunch box with water bottles so it felt full. But all it contained was a note.

Dear Grace,

I know you probably think I forgot your food, just like you probably think I forgot that it was your turn for some special time together. It has been too long. I packed you no lunch because we are getting lunch on a road trip today. Your teacher already knows and the car is packed. I am hiding in the hallway, waiting for you. Come and hug me if you are ready to go.

I love you,

Mommy

I spied on her in the cafeteria, watching the surprise settle into understanding. She barreled into me with an enormous hug, and we took off together. The hours that followed were priceless. There is something special about being Mom's one and only, once in a while. In return, I got pure, unfettered Grace—in both senses of the word.

Maybe that's why I'm not living in fear of dropping my plate, filled and heavy with heaping helpings of life. (Okay, so it spills sometimes.) I am realizing that when I put my energy into the things I have already designated as priorities (my faith, my family, my friendships, my health and fitness, my work), it seems like everything falls into proper order. Contentment resides in the sweet spot of doing the right things with our best effort and energy available in the moment—and being comfortable with the fact that this changes.

Contentment is an invited guest, inhabiting the rooms and hallways of a well-lived life.

REFILL

In preparation for a speech to a running group, I thought about running, what it means to me right now, at this exact time in my life. I considered talking about how a solid training program helps you meet your race-day goals. But my heart was not intrigued or captivated. I have enough goals, enough responsibilities, enough items on my revolving to-do list, just like everyone else I know. If we think too much about what needs to get done, we can stagger under the weight of it all—not just what we have to do but the people who are depending on us to get it done. We have so many cups to fill that we are like an endlessly pouring pitcher. *Some for you, some for you; here you go, honey, hold it with two hands; that's it . . .*

This is fine—better than fine. I am not complaining; I feel blessed to have cups to fill at all and blessed in the attempt to fill them. But what we must attend to is not so much the importance of filling the cups but of replenishing the pitcher. And this is what finally snagged my heart: the reminder to all of us to stay filled, to remain connected to our source, to refill before we run dry. In an effort to do and be for everyone else, we often put ourselves last by default—thinking we can catch ourselves later, and that as long as everyone else is okay, we'll be okay, too. And so we do this: grab a snack on the go instead of sitting down to a meal, skimp on sleep, forget to have dates with our spouses, stuff an opinion or complaint for "later," run in shoes that lost their cushion last spring. It's not okay. Taking care of ourselves and refilling our tanks is not a luxury. It's just like gas in the car; most of us drive too long with the indicator light flashing, on fumes and a prayer.

Making time to take care of ourselves is essential so that we don't sputter, stall, and come to an inopportune (or even dangerous) halt in the middle of a busy intersection. That's what running is to me, a refill. I check in with myself, notice my levels of fuel (sleep and nutrition levels are hard to ignore on a run), get caught up with my friends, center my spirit, stave off restlessness, and refocus my energy. I can feel my fuel levels going up. After my morning run, I can return to my house, my children, my relationships, and my work and feel replenished and rejuvenated to make my offering to my world. I can do things for others throughout the day, and I don't reach empty because I am starting from a place of fullness.

These words make us nod—we already get it, even if we don't get it right all the time. We know what we need. But what about the people we know—at work, at school, socially, even people in our own families—who don't notice that they are at a dangerous risk for stalling out in the intersection? They might think us a bit odd or decadent in our passion for running, particularly if they misinterpret it as an entitled pursuit of vanity or a luxurious use of personal time. If only they could see that the reason we have the overflow and the awareness to be concerned for them is that we take the time to refill and clear our vision in order to see beyond ourselves.

I want to encourage all of us to make the gift of running more accessible to newbies, to be inclusive and supportive as we share the joy of what we know and how we know it. Even if running doesn't enter the picture at all, any message of health and well-being is best delivered by people whose pitchers are diligently and lovingly filled.

NEW PONY

In keeping with my theme of trying new things this summer, being brave, facing fears, accepting new challenges without shrinking, I did something that for me was unthinkable: I went to a Bikram yoga class.

As a preface, I must confess that I am about as flexible as a steel rod. My Downward Dog looks like a red-faced old woman wearing stilettos bent over at an odd angle in search of an errant contact lens. The only part of regular yoga I like is the quiet lounging that goes on after the instructor dims the lights at the end of class.

If you haven't braved Bikram before, it's the "hot" yoga. The Web site for the class I went to specified that it was "an intense workout designed for endurance athletes." I thought this was a bit of a stretch, but I threw caution (and sense) to the wind and went for it. I wore running clothes and brought a big jug of ice water, a beach towel, a cheap and cheesy yoga mat that I picked up last minute at Longs pharmacy that said "The Firm" on it (I flipped that side over during class so I wouldn't look like a poser—ha!), and the most Zenlike attitude I could muster.

I paid my fee, waited around shyly until I saw people begin to file in, park their flip-flops outside this curtained sliding-glass door, and enter. A pleasant woman took pity on me and encouraged me to try to place my mat near the back door for some hope of a tiny breeze from the crack. I thanked her a little too profusely, as newbies are apt to do, and she raised an eyebrow at me.

I stepped out of my flops and entered the unknown.

It was an assault.

I spent my entire summer escaping the brutality of Texas temperatures, and here I was paying to relive them. That, and there was this rank odor, kind of a combination of curry and feet. I gasped. Someone chuckled, but when I finally stole a look to see who had the nerve to make fun of me under such dire circumstances, everyone was stretched out quietly on their mats. I wedged into a spot near the back door as instructed and did likewise. Within moments I could feel sweat trickling down my armpits.

The instructor entered and I was in awe, having never seen a more perfect female specimen in my life. She was Japanese, in a tiny, tight outfit that showed every cut curve of her ideal figure. I wished I hadn't consumed so much keg beer and late-night pizza in college, likely upping my fat cell count in my more formative years. Now it's all about upkeep and cleanup. She looked like the product of years of tofu discipline. With laser-beam focus she picked me out like the sore thumb I was. She asked me my name—why, I don't know, because she dubbed me New Pony and called me that for the next 2 hours. Often.

We stood, feet planted hip-distance apart, and stretched our arms up. *Okay,* I thought, *I'm a bit dizzy, but I can handle this.* She instructed us to breathe. On cue the whole class, minus New Pony, began a frighteningly loud panting series that sounded like Darth Vader as a Lamaze coach. My eyes popped open—I had to see this. No one else was fighting the giggles.

The instructor spoke in a clipped, staccato Japanese accent, calling out positions, talking nonstop, with all kinds of concurrent reminders ("Shoulders back! Core in! Butt tight! Deep breath! Always breathe!") and then suddenly a loud clap and "CHANGE!" and everyone would snap to the next move with military precision. New Pony was always a few beats behind, trying to spy on other people and copy them while simultaneously swiping the sweat-soaked disobedient layers that escaped my frizzy ponytail. My entire body was sunburn red, and when I bent my head on occasion (in a supposed effort to touch it to my knees), the sweat formed a sheet down my face and dripped collectively off the end of my nose, making a puddle on my already sopping-wet towel. It was about 105 degrees. Perhaps this would be my scientific experiment, a new way to acclimate a California body back to Texas weather, one class at a time.

Then the teacher quipped, "You think you hot? Imagine me, 60 with menopause!" Wait, what? Menopause?! And she's 60?! This body in front of me that looked better than that of any 20-something professional athlete, ever?! I refocused with renewed vigor. There must be something to this.

I may have mentioned before that I do not know my right and left. (Please don't laugh—I was an honors student my entire life, even in physics. It's just a genetic quirk that I hope I have not passed to my children.) So she would call out these instructions, like "Right arm over left, up high, left knee cross over, bend deep, right leg back, left toes out, breathe!" and I kept having to make an L with my left thumb and index finger to confirm; meanwhile she shouted, "Other right, New Pony! *Other* right!" Or she would explain a move and notice that I was shaking with the effort of just the preamble to the move, so she would preface the next instruction with, "Everyone but New Pony . . ." Sometimes to deepen a stretch we were instructed to wrap our fingers around our toes for resistance, upon which my fingers would slip and snap loose because my sweaty hands and feet were as slippery as a hooked fish flopping on the floor of a boat. Ugh. I was exhausted.

Then, blissfully, out of nowhere, she noticed the time. "Ah! I keep you too long! We done!" And the lights dimmed. I collapsed onto my raft and waited for rescue. She told us to tiptoe out so as not to disturb our classmates who needed more time. I grabbed my belongings and slid out, sloshing into my flip-flops.

I was almost out the door when she caught me.

"New Pony, you like?"

I smiled, freezing now, dreaming of cranking the heat in my car and zooming home and straight into the shower, wondering what bacteria were lurking and multiplying on me, wondering if I now smelled like curry and feet.

I was either peaceful or dangerously dehydrated when I replied:

"Yes, I like."

22 LOVE/HATE

In the closest, most intimate relationships, there is always some measure of love/hate. Even the things you love most about your beloved can have a flip side that annoys you more than anything else. "I love how motivated and interesting he is, but I hate how he can never relax with me." "I love how fun and carefree she is, but I hate how she never takes anything seriously and sometimes makes me feel like I'm a drag for being responsible." "I love how gregarious and friendly he is, but I hate how I can never feel like the only person in a room." "I love how creative she is, but I hate how she can't balance our checkbook or pay bills on time." "I love how smart he is, but I hate how condescending he can be in an argument." "I love how fit and beautiful her body is, but I hate how much time she spends working out." "I love what a great mom she is, but I hate how I always feel like second place when it comes to our kids."

Running is no different than any other close relationship. We have our fair share of love/hates. We have our times of passion and our times of plateau. We have times of connectedness and times of parallel lives. We have times of courting and times of commitment. Like all significant relationships, we have to nurture and respect the union if we want it to stand the test of time. Like all significant relationships, it is always worth the effort.

A NEW LINK

My dad sent me an e-mail this week containing this quotation, and it was so good I had to share.

The truth is that we can learn to condition our minds, bodies, and emotions to link pain or pleasure to whatever we choose. By changing what we link pain and pleasure to, we will instantly change our behavior.

—ANTHONY ROBBINS

Naturally this has amazing implications in terms of running. I think of the workout we did at running group yesterday, a torturous twofer combo (as Cassie calls it) with a hill repeat on a street in Austin called Rainbow, followed by a little stretch of recovery, then a tempo run back to start. Suffer and repeat. And repeat it again. Rainbow has no mercy, no warmup ramp of any kind, just step on it—zero to hypoxia in no seconds flat. It would be hard to get a stick-shift car to oblige such a jolting transition, so it was no wonder my poor body was having trouble shifting gears. I talked (wheezed) some smack about how there was no pot of gold at the end of this Rainbow—other than the end of the workout, of course.

Clearly, I link pain with hard effort. I literally say it in my head: *Oh dear, this is going hurt.* Sometimes, when the situation or my mood warrants it, I say something stronger than "Oh dear." I wonder what could happen if I tried a new link and attempted to associate a hard effort with pleasure. And not just the pleasure that comes from accomplishment. I mean pleasure in the moment, the true appreciation of the journey while I'm in the midst of it, regardless of the terrain. Interesting thought.

And then of course I have to back up and broaden my thinking, applying this idea to other areas in my life. What if I choose to link pleasure with things like public speaking, disciplining my children, having uncomfortable but necessary conversations or confrontations, saying "No, thank you" when I've had enough (wine, food, attitude, you name it), working and thinking so hard I get a headache, trying new things—regardless of the outcome, etc. Could I really do that—change my link from pain (or avoidance) to pleasure? Take true delight in uncomfortable things?

Or in reverse, could I link pain to things formerly associated with pleasure? Pain with overspending at Target, eating when I'm not even hungry, having another glass of wine when one is good enough, having the last word, taking the easy route when more is required—things like this?

Imagine how such changes could affect things like our fitness, when we link pleasure to effort. Or generosity, when we link pleasure to what we can give. Or forgiveness, when we link pleasure to letting go. Or courage, when we link pleasure to stepping out of our own shadow. Or authenticity, when we link pleasure to the vulnerability of being real. Or growing up, when we link pleasure to speaking and living our truth regardless of how favorably it is received.

I am not exactly sure how we rewire our linking. But it probably starts with changing our thinking, and this simply takes some training. Luckily, we already know how to train—we practice consistently over time to refine our endurance. So I suppose the same training principles apply to our thoughts; we practice new patterns of thinking until they become natural and usable.

Maybe that is just the pot of gold I was looking for.

EENIE MEENIE

If you're like me, it's hard to tell what to do about running when you're sick. Sometimes it makes me feel better to get out there, and other times it's the kiss of death. I decided to pull some highly scientific data from my running journal to help with this timeless runner's quandary.

GO RUN ANYWAY IF . . .

You can breathe out of only one nostril, or you are emitting strange whistling sounds when you breathe and you wonder if everyone can hear that, or just you.

You really have a hangover, but you are calling it a cold.

You feel like your brain is in a fog. Who knows? It might lift. Turn back for home if the fog gets thicker.

You have someone to watch your kids.

It's just allergies.

Your husband or wife gives you *the look* and says, "Just. Go."

You know all the commercials on TV.

You have taken the old advice to "feed a cold" a bit too far.

Your to-do list and sense of futility increase with every minute at home.

The last *"chrono"* reading on your running watch was for timing cookies.

The last *"chrono"* reading on your running watch was for your child's time-out.

You ache because of lethargy, not effort or illness.

STAY HOME AT ALL COSTS IF . . .

You have a fever or feel lightheaded.

You gave your illness as reason to stay home from work, school, or a party and there is any chance of being seen by a boss, coworker, teacher, fellow student, or the host of the party.

It's icy, sleeting, or slanting rain and cold. You have a perfectly good excuse, so take it.

You bend over to tie your shoes and the contents of your nose pour onto the laces.

Your hack causes your training partners to bristle and suddenly pick up a tempo pace you can't possibly keep.

You breathe deeply and your lungs sound like they are rasping and/or gurgling. Or your cough sounds like a seal bark.

You feel nauseated or have any sign of flu.

Your sinuses are so packed that your face has a noticeable pulse or your ear aches to the point that you lose equilibrium.

You honestly can't remember the last time you slept in.

Maybe these will help.

Remember to take good care of yourself, too, not just those who depend on you. Just like a good racing strategy, a healthy living strategy involves knowing when to hold back and when to push.

Our culture says things like *rush, cram one more thing, play through,* or *RSVP yes* at this time of year. It doesn't mean we have to comply. In fact, my happiest holidays on record have been those when I did less and enjoyed more. I've even gone so far as to literally schedule meetings with *"blank"* on my calendar. It's a code to myself, a call to consciousness, a reminder to be intentional with my time, a sweet surprise, a reason to say no, a time to connect with someone on the periphery of my mind—a phone call or short note, a deliberate pause, a deep breath, a space to fill . . . or not.

It's my time, reclaimed and repurposed, and that is a gift I give myself.

THE TALK

Yesterday I ran for the first time in a week.

It has been weird not running . . . weird like not talking to a close friend or misplacing your cell phone or having road construction on your street and constantly having to follow detour signs. In order to mitigate the various obsessive personalities in our running group, Cassie mandates a week off from running after a marathon. We sometimes laugh over how much power she has over us, though it's not really funny, because once Ellen got busted down at the running trail before her week hiatus was lifted. Cassie just happened to be down there and gave her a proper chewing out.

I don't know that I really mind the break so much. It's like being in a long-term relationship and having your spouse go out of town. You miss him and everything, but there can sometimes be a partial feeling of relief . . . relief to have your own space in your home and in your day and in your head. No one notices if you want to skip shaving for a couple of days or eat Cheerios for dinner leaning against the counter and reading yesterday's newspaper. You have a chance to miss and appreciate him and enjoy reconnecting when he gets home as you share the thoughts and adventures you had in each other's absence. Or you can, *ahem*, skip conversation and get properly reunited in classic Peaches and Herb fashion—because it feels so good.

In my long-term relationship with running, during this time apart, I decided that running and I needed to have "the Talk." It was time to take some time off, maybe even see other people (yoga, Pilates, walking, more time in the gym?). I was tired of always being such a serious couple, contemplating where we were going together and what the future holds. Why can't we just be? I mean, do we need a label?

Really, running, it's not you; it's me. I'm just not sure what I want right now.

Like many long-term relationships, things can get a little stale. We seem to have settled into a groove together; maybe we are too comfortable. You aren't new and exciting anymore. You aren't flashy. You don't raise my heart rate or make me breathe heavy the way you used to. And as long as we're being honest here, you can sometimes be a major pain in my a** (or my hamstrings or my knees . . .).

(Pause.)

But on second thought, we do have it pretty good, you and I. If I were to wake up early on a crisp morning and see our favorite shoes in my closet, I must admit, I would really miss you. If I went on a vacation to a beautiful place and had to explore it without you, I would be lost. If we weren't together and I saw you with someone else, I think I would feel kind of sick.

Maybe just the fact that we *can* take a break is enough for me . . . or maybe I just love that I can express these feelings to you and you won't leave me. Sometimes the greatest comforts of all are the things we are most liable to take for granted. The most beautiful things about a long-term relationship, after all, are the quiet ones—the way the tide of passion ebbs and flows, the way the things unsaid are not without understanding, and the way each other's presence is inexplicably and undeniably enough.

As Cassie says, *loveyameanit.*

A DIFFERENT KIND OF LOVE

Yesterday was a beautiful day to run a half marathon in Austin, Texas. After weeks of cold, gray weather, we were blessed with temperatures in the fifties and sixties and a morning that blossomed into sunshine. If there were ever a day ordained for PRs, it was this one.

It was no secret that Paige and Katie and I were trying to run a strong race, not just out for fun and scenery and free Gatorade, as in some races. My PR in a half marathon is 1:36:26, and I was hoping to bust that, even if only by seconds.

We started strong, Paige ever diligent in setting her pace and recording her split times. I was off from the start and I knew it. My prerace preparation—food, hydration, sleep, red wine avoidance, healthy motivation—all of it was spot-on. But the first mile felt too fast for me (though it was right on track); my heart was racing, and I had trouble catching my breath or finding my stride, even through mile 2. From the start I felt like I was having to work too hard to chase down my friends, and it was really discouraging.

Our friend Annie glided by, and Katie fell in step beside her. Paige hung back to care for her wounded wingman. I encouraged her to go on, all wheezing and dramatic and pathetic: "It's. Okay. Go. Ahead. And. Leave. Me . . ." I had Old Yeller visions of myself, wishing my benevolent owner would take pity on me and shoot me, put me out of my misery. Instead, Paige gave me a raised eyebrow and half of a peanut butter sandwich and we soldiered on.

A couple things occurred to me at this point. One is that Paige has never once abandoned me in any form of misery. She is a mighty friend, loyal to the core, much to my delight and deliverance. Another thing is that I should never let Robert, my trainer, stretch me before any race (as he did on Friday). A nice idea turned out to have miserable consequences. My right hamstring and left hip felt totally out of whack. I should have left well enough alone, even if it meant having hamstrings as tight as cello strings. Once Paige realized that I didn't have the kick to kick it, she eased us back enough to get me home safely and allow enough air for conversation.

Something else entered my mind—as I grunted through the final miles to finish 4 minutes slower than my PR—something somewhere between gratitude and epiphany on the realization scale. I realized that I am out here, most days of every week, pursuing something that does not come naturally or easily to me. And I have been doing this for 5 years. Never in my life, before running, did I ever push hard after something that did not rank high on the list of things that come easily to me. I have always aspired to and excelled at things that I was already good at. This probably stems from fear, pride, laziness, or some perfection compulsion; my priest or therapist would know for sure. But running isn't like that for me. It's hard for me. I struggle. I suffer. I get discouraged. I get mad. I celebrate, sometimes. And when I chase after Paige, Katie, or any other zippy friend, it's not because I suck—it's because they don't. Running is one of Paige's passions, one of her God-given talents, as natural for her as nursing a baby or riding a horse bareback. It isn't one of mine, and that is okay with me (or will be as soon as this epiphany sinks in), because I love it anyway . . . I just love it differently than she does. I love it the way you love a rivalrous sibling, a deep-tissue massage, a session with your therapist, childbirth, or a big fight with someone you love. It doesn't always feel good in the moment, but ultimately you are a better person for it.

So I may not always run the way I want to run or race the way I imagine myself racing, and my performance outside may only rarely reflect the runner on the inside, but there is a certain endurance rush reserved for those of us who have to work extra hard just to stand on the start line and dream.

There is a unique beauty to pursuing the glow that resides just beyond our reach.

23 RACE DAY

Paige loves race day. She is giddy, enthusiastic, childlike in her exuberance. I am moody, fearful, stressed, sarcastic, and overly anxious. I can never sleep, alternating between worries about bonking and not hearing my alarm go off. If I am in a hotel, I am bothered by the wrong kinds of pillows or the sound of the elevator. If I am at home, one of my dogs snores too loudly, or one of my children wakes up and crawls in my bed and proceeds to kick and flail the rest of the night.

I love training—most of the time, anyway. I love the time with my friends and the deliberate process of preparation. I guess what I don't like about race day (which is, ironically, what Paige loves) is the notion of being put to the test. Race day is when all your time and energy spent in preparation either yield the result you were aiming for—or they don't. Perhaps it's a matter of personality, Paige being much more competitive than I am and therefore more likely to enjoy the challenge. Or perhaps it's a matter of maturity as a runner. Paige has experienced maybe a hundred more race days than I have, so maybe she is more likely to take them in stride, so to speak. If it is a matter of maturity, I want to grow into a more peaceful acceptance of the challenge. I don't want to dread the test; I want to embrace it. I want to be curious about my potential, respectful toward my body, and grateful for my results—no matter what.

I want to be more willing and joyful about putting myself on the line.

TRANSITION ZONES

Sunday morning I had the pleasure of watching all three of my children do a triathlon. It was Bella's second triathlon, and Luke's and Grace's inaugural event. They each formed relay teams with their friends. Bella's team was the B-Rileys, with her friends Riley A. and Riley C. Bella was the cyclist. Grace did the running portion, and her team was called the Lizards. Luke rode his bike for the Extreme Three. It was chaotic trying to sign in three children, write entrant numbers on arms and legs and heat numbers on hands, and get bikes checked in and everyone stationed in the appropriate transition zones. Of course, everyone promptly left their transition zones to go find a snack, explore the playscape, look at a baby bird in a nest, and make trips to the bathroom.

The type A in me, fueled by the latte Paige brought me, was wondering how on earth these kids were going to be in the right place at the right time and find their teammates. After initial check-in, parents are not allowed in the transition areas, and it's probably a blessing, because we are so annoying. Besides, I reminded myself, it's not my race. It's their race, their experience, their day—and it's up to them, not me. After almost an entire school year of hustling around and getting people to the right place at the right time, it was bliss to simply let go and be a spectator, knowing nothing was up to me.

I love how the velocity of a child increases in relation to the volume of their fans. There must be an equation for this phenomenon:

$$V_{final} = V_{original} + ATC \text{ (acceleration} \times \text{time} \times \text{cheering)}$$

Picture me, teary-eyed and camera in hand, zooming back and forth along the fence line (holding the fence posts and hopping madly when one of our beloved passed by, likely looking like I should be in a cage), trying to see everyone and shout everyone's names at once. In rapid succession, Luke's buddy Zachary swam like a torpedo and was first out of the water in his heat, handing off to Luke, who launched into the woods on his bike with a fierce and focused look on his face that was vintage Armstrong. I ran to check if Riley A. was in the water (not yet), then ran back and nearly missed Grace coming across the finish line like a seasoned champ, her stride steady and sure, her pink face all smiles for the cameras. She shot into my arms with her medal flying, for a full arms-and-legs-spin-around hug. (Her official postrace statement: "I want to do it again!") Luke passed off to their runner, Keaton, who proudly finished off the Extreme Three's valiant effort. Swimmer Riley, goggles flying, slapped hands with a pensive and powerful Bella, who shot into the woods like a deer pursued, her tiny bottom in padded shorts high in the air above her seat. Finally we could remain in one spot, the final transition zone, when Bella skidded into sight, hopped off her bike mid-motion like a lady riding sidesaddle in a Western, and slapped hands with Riley C., who brought Team B-Rileys swiftly across the finish line, where all three teams were dousing themselves (and each other) in water, mugging for cameras, OD'ing on Gatorade, inspecting their medals, talking smack, and strutting their stuff.

I took my sweaty champions out for lunch, followed by ice cream at a place that charges by weight, letting you squirt your own portions into gluttonous tub-size bowls and add enough toppings to sink a ship. They ate themselves ill while they talked on the phone to Dad, who was more excited about their day than about finishing the Giro d'Italia. "No one passed me, Dad," said Luke through a mouthful of cookies 'n' cream with additional Oreo topping.

"Someone passed you," I said, after he had hung up the phone.

"Nuh-uh."

"Yep. You. You passed yourself, buddy. Way to go."

He smiled that certain smile, the one that is usually accompanied with oversize teeth and averted eyes, the bold-shy smile of a boy who is big one minute and a child the next. If I could, I would freeze him right now, just like this, in a transition zone, so to speak, and hold him close until Mom was ready to move on.

SURROUNDED

Last Sunday was a cold morning in Austin; a foggy, damp chill was in the air at the start of the 3M Half Marathon. Paige and I did a warmup to try to knock the frost from our legs, then tucked into the mass at the start, huddled up next to some friends. It is always so much warmer in the mosh pit of the start line, with all the bodies compressed, hopping and breathing in one place.

A short-lived coziness, then the gun fired and we were off. Paige is pace girl; always has been, always will be. She can keep us right on track with some kind of inborn internal Garmin. It's different from having a watch. I mean, we can all push a button and record our splits. She instinctively feels speed and can adjust accordingly.

We ran steady and strong, and the miles ticked off without much complaint from legs or lungs. Compared to last week's workout, this was easier. Paige got us to about mile 10 or 11 and then tried to suggest that I "take off" without her. She is so cute. I guess she thought I was holding back some secret reserve, like a jetpack fueled and ready to go. Not so much, but I was thankful to feel steady and strong.

I pushed myself, and as I closed in on mile 12, I was on my own. I saw Cassie on the sidelines like a mirage, an oasis in the desert. She casually appeared by my side, her curly brown ponytail swishing, her stride smooth and effortless. "Mind if I run with you?" she said without fanfare. "That . . . would . . . be . . . nice," I wheezed gratefully. She said nothing, did nothing, just ran with me, slightly ahead but not so much that I felt the discouragement of chasing her.

It was precisely that—her steadiness and her silence—that refocused me. I paid attention to my body and recommitted myself to the last mile. She said one thing: "One more curve, then straight home. Go on, now." I hunkered down and crossed the line happy and breathless at 1:39.

Isn't it great how certain people can elicit our improvement simply with their presence? It's similar to the way we drive better and are careful about our speed when we see a police car on the side of the road. Or how we double-check our spelling and our grammar when we hold the recipient of our letter in high regard. Or how we stand up straighter when we talk to our yoga instructor. Or how we choose our language more carefully when we know our children are listening. Or the way new love generates an excess of thoughtfulness. When Cassie has her eyes on me, I think about my form, about keeping my shoulders back and staying focused on the effort before me.

This phenomenon heightens my awareness of the people I spend my time with. It encourages me to gravitate toward people whose standards inspire me subconsciously to raise my own, just as the company of a particularly honest person elicits integrity, or a highly motivated person adds momentum, or a particularly funny person piques my sense of joy. Not only do I want to seek and nurture these kinds of relationships, but also I am inspired to offer my gifts and perspectives more freely, knowing how much I cherish the effect other people have on me.

Right now is a perfect time to consider the people who lift us up and to make a conscious decision to spend more time in their good company. We can also consider how we might use our gifts more effectively and abundantly to be that kind of person to others.

OUR OWN RACE

Sometimes I have a spell of weeks when I feel content with "good enough." It is enough that I get the kids to school on time with lunches packed and homework done. It is enough that their nails are trimmed before they start looking like a French manicure with white tips. It is enough that a balanced diet is balanced out over the course of the week. It is enough that I make all my writing deadlines with work that means something to me. It is enough that I get out there and try, over and over again, every day, 7 days a week, 52 weeks a year.

Some weeks, good enough is pretty darn good.

And then it happens: A wave of doubt leaves me sputtering and gasping for air, and suddenly "good enough" is up for debate. Suddenly I wish I made a more concerted effort to steam and puree vegetables to "hide" in my children's food. I wish I set aside specific time to tutor my children individually in their key areas of interest. I wish I had "international nights" when we ate cuisine from another culture and no one complained that they really wanted grilled cheese. I wish I were brave enough to sell the television on eBay. I wish we went to help in soup kitchens more often than only around the holidays. I wish I spoke to my children in French or Spanish so regularly that they were bilingual by now. I wish I were so finely attuned to each child's inner motivation that I no longer needed to harp on homework.

I am a practical woman. I know that wishing is for stars and that change comes to those who pursue it. It's just that the sheerly overwhelming nature of parenting can make my head spin. Suddenly all the things I'm not doing eclipse everything that I am doing well. We had parent-teacher conferences yesterday, and even in the midst of all the positives, I fixated on what I should and could be doing better. Nothing motivates me like the three little people who captivate my heart.

I have a ceramic sign that hangs in my office: "Run your own race." This mantra is huge to me, in my running life and in every other aspect of life as well. So many things can be compared to the analogy of the race—parenting, career, deadlines, relationships, etc. When we look around at what or how other people are doing rather than at what our own race holds, we waste time and energy.

Think about the first mile of a race. It's crowded with all kinds of people of every ability level, every pace, every strategy, and every conceivable objective. They have different backgrounds, different training regimens, different bodies, and different levels of experience. The horn blares and all the runners take off in a mad pack. I have had races when I have been so focused on the people around me that I have blown my first mile by wasting precious energy on the panic of the start, taking off like a skittish animal, adding mileage by weaving around people, and trying futilely to get ahead. I know better! I need to stick to my own pace, not look at what anyone else is doing, and ease into my miles according to plan. Competition is best utilized on the inside. I need to run my own race.

And I need to apply this tactic to other areas of life. In those moments when "good enough" no longer feels like enough, I need to stop and breathe. I need to figure out if the voice that is criticizing me is the voice of truth, calling me in earnest to step it up, or if it is the voice of doubt, the sole purpose of which is to undermine my core. I need to respond to the truth. I need to turn up my iPod on doubt.

This applies to my faith, my parenting, my work, my relationships, and my running. In all the races that matter to me, I need to remember to start steady in order to finish strong. Once again, my children have taught me a lesson that I intended to teach them.

Contentment and improvement are not mutually exclusive. It is indeed possible to be good enough in the midst of getting better.

FACING MY GIANT

The day after a marathon, I always feels like the victim of a Mafia street hit: run over by a car that then reversed and ran back over me again, just to be certain. Yet in the midst of this brokenness of body, my spirit feels oddly rejuvenated. Maybe it's the afterglow of survival; I am not sure. But I'm glad to be done.

The weather yesterday would be considered unbelievably beautiful by anyone's standards, but after the training conditions we endured, the beauty was nearly explosive in contrast. The start was chilly, in the thirties, and the sunrise was glorious. By race end we were in the sunny fifties, and the day ended (at a poolside party with a margarita machine, mind you) around 65 or 70 degrees. This alone was something to be thankful for (that and the margaritas).

I never imagined that our group of seven, which later grew to nine, would stay together. But we did, for the most part, until the very end. I have never run a race with a group of more than three. We traveled like a pack, and there is something to the idea of safety in numbers. Regardless of my changes in morale or circumstances, I knew that staying in the confines of my group was my best chance for survival. So I did. Paige was our leader, and as we passed each mile marker, she shouted out the chosen scripture verse for that mile. "Can you hear me?! Colossians 1:29, people! 'To this end I labor, struggling with all his energy, which so powerfully works in me!'" She wore so many homemade verse bands that it looked like her arm was in a cast. As we traveled along, I noticed that strangers running near us were unpopping one iPod earbud at the mile markers, waiting for her new lifeline. She also entertained us with a recap of the movie *Facing the Giants*. She naturally interspersed segments of the film into our race from start to finish at times when the road grew long in front of us and the easy banter of conversation stilled into trudging silence. It helped pass time and served as motivation when it seemed like time was standing still.

The message that remains with me, lingering from her recap and from its relevance to my situation at that moment, is this: Prepare for rain. Of course, that was funny because we trained primarily in rainstorms this winter. But the message was bigger than that. In the movie, the coach learns this profound lesson from a farmer who prepares his field for rain even in the midst of drought. He expects a yield, and his faith is rewarded. Training for a marathon is much the same thing. My own talents and reserves often feel like a drought, insufficient for the harvest. And yet somehow God carries me beyond my expected yield.

He did this for me yesterday. This course was much harder than I expected. I ran portions of it in preparation, of course, but never the entire thing. They changed the course, which in prior years was flat and designed for speed, to be more representative of Austin's topography and scenery. And that, to use my daughter Grace's word, was *owie*.

There was a hill at mile 20 that was so demoralizing it made me want to cry. I saw Cassie at the bottom of it, and I quickly squeezed her hand as I slogged past her. I was trying to collect enough of her energy to get me through. What I got was her now vintage holler, "UPANDOVERLADIES!" She did tell me that when I made it to the top, to the right I would see my parents and my brother. This actually did make me cry. Somehow in my life, they always show up right when I'm on the edge of losing my resolve. I made it up—and over.

At mile 24, Katie looked at me and said in clenched-jaw, don't-mess vernacular, "Do. Not. Leave. Me." I promised. Then at mile 25/almost 26, there was another subtle hill that felt about as subtle as a stranger pinching your bottom as a greeting. I started to seriously lose it here. Perhaps I was overcome by temporary Tourette's, because I said some things that I wouldn't normally utter. One of them was something to the effect of "BLEEP. Where's my bleeping downhill?!" It was not pretty, but neither was my situation. I was starting to falter. I wanted to walk—but then I saw Gilbert.

Gilbert Tuhabonye is a local celebrity and running coach with a story that will make you want to stand up straighter and try a little harder. He is a transplant to Austin from Burundi who survived a tribal massacre at his boarding school, escaped a burning school building, and ran to safety. I saw him and I had to suck it up.

We rounded the state capitol building, and I finally got my bleeping downhill. Paige, Katie, and I finished the race the way we started our training: steady and together.

Steady and together in 3:35:44!!!

ON YOUR LEFT

Where to begin? You know how it feels to sit down to your favorite meal and not know what bite you want to sample first?

That's how I feel when I think about sharing the tale of my first ultramarathon (50-K). I guess I should start with "thank you," because that is where I like to start, and because I felt the prayers and energy of all runners with me as I had the best race of my life.

When I was a kid and I'd jump into the car after school and start blabbering 20 different thoughts at once, trying to recap my day for my mom, she'd always say, "Whoa, honey, start at the beginning and tell me everything." So, I begin.

Every day my "Mom's Journal" calendar has a quotation. For Saturday it said "Adopt the pace of nature. Her Secret is patience." —Ralph Waldo Emerson. Okay, duly noted, thank you.

We left late morning on Friday, in my friends Jon and Nancy's pickup truck, towing their trailer (our abode for the night). I packed like I was going on a 3-week European adventure: three duffel bags and one enormous bag of food. I baked a cobbler, a spinach-and-egg dish for morning, and some pumpkin bread; I brought enough snacks to be snack mom for a month. I figured Jon and Nancy would have less opportunity to regret their invitation if I came with good food. I was so nervous before I left that I started my 1-cup coffee maker and went to the sink holding my cup in my hand as coffee brewed all over my countertop.

It took forever to get to Huntsville, going trailer pace with prerace-hydration pee stops and a diversion into Houston to pick up our race packets. Huntsville State Park is beautiful, piney, and lush and smells like Christmas. I felt like a kid as we got the trailer parked and leveled out and took a brisk walk to check out the start/finish area. It was freezing—I wore two fleeces, a jacket, gloves, scarf, and hat. I prayed it wouldn't be that cold in the morning. The evening passed too quickly, with lots of food, laughs, a bad movie, a Shiner Bock beer, and the preparation of my drop bag. Jon and Nancy laughed at my neophyte nerves; I had anally packed everything in plastic bags and labeled them with index cards, so the contents were both "visible and easily accessible," I explained. They had another beer.

I slept in a nook of a bed, with at least six pillows (two I brought from home, in case) and a thick comforter. I love small spaces, so I was in heaven, total "Princess and the Pea." I slept 9 hours in pure bliss. I have never had a prerace night of sleep when I didn't wake up at least three times. Not even for a 5-K. What a gift.

Most race entrants stayed at the race hotel in Houston and were up at 4:45 to catch the race bus to the start. Nope, not us. We watched TV, brewed coffee, ate breakfast, got dressed, and arrived for the 7:45 start at about 7:25. Talk about a dream come true. I never had time to get cold. I had two big bags slung over my shoulders: my drop bag and my finish bag. I chose a home base for myself and set my things down under the Rogue Running tent (my training group); got a hug from my coach, Robert; and headed over. We started. There was no fuss or fanfare, no anxious folks hopping from side to side and stressing over watches and eyeing competitors. It was very chill.

I heeded the advice I received in an e-mail from ultra endurance icon Dean Karnazes: "Start out slow, and when you think you are going too slow, slow down." Jon had other goals in mind, so he took off, and Nancy and I ran together. Our first 6.7-mile loop passed by easily and without incident, other than the sad sight of an Austin friend sprawled out on the course with an injured ankle. Bummer. After that lap we passed by the start area again and made our first stop at an aid station. (We skipped the aid stations on the first loop because it was early and we were full.) For those who are used to typical road-race water stops where the selections include water, Gatorade, and possibly Gu if you are late in a marathon, or maybe some orange slices if you have some grassroots volunteers, this is going to blow your mind. Here were some of my selections: cut oranges, cut bananas (some topped with peanut butter), Doritos, M&M's, jelly beans, pretzels, boiled and salted potato slices, vanilla wafers topped with peanut butter and a banana slice, sandwiches, peanuts, water, Pepsi, Gatorade, Hammer products, Oreos . . . the list goes on. I'm not kidding. Remind me to schedule my next trail race to coincide with PMS. I ate often, hydrated well enough that I had to use the facilities several times during the race, and took my salt and electrolyte pills according to plan.

After the second loop, which was 12.15 miles (I ignored miles during the race, simply instructing myself that I had three things to do today, that's all), I felt a hot spot on the callus of my right foot. I stopped at the tent and had to problem-solve on the fly, and I decided on some Bodyglide and a fresh pair of socks. It did the trick. Nancy stopped to stretch a problem area on her back. We refueled and headed out for loop number three—the last 12.15 miles.

The weather could not have been nicer: a chilly start and a cool and sunny afternoon. Huntsville is in a very odd ecosystem for Texas, with oaks, pines, sand on the ground, an occasional low palm tree. (Huh?) The sun filtered through the trees, making everything appear to glow. It was gorgeous. We hiked the steep sections, ate when we felt like it, and kept steady forward progress. Running with Nancy is easy, both the conversation and the silence. I could not believe it when we got to the last aid station. I didn't want to know about mileage during the race because I figured I wouldn't be able to fret about passing my 26.2-mile so-called limit if I ignored the so-called limit. It worked. I popped a handful of jelly beans, and we headed for the finish.

It was either the sugar or the euphoria or both, because I felt amazing. I worried about getting tired and tripping over roots (lots of them on this course), but my feet obeyed and my legs were responsive. I was glad for all the training I had done on more technical trails and in the dark, because these trails were easier and I was more than ready for them. Thank you, Robert. I felt us picking up speed. Fear left me and I was elated, flying on the inside. And suddenly I said something I never, ever thought I would say, least of all at a moment like this.

"On your left."

We were passing people! I don't mean that I like the idea of beating someone; trail running has nothing to do with passing anyone because people are going different distances, and everyone walks different sections. But for me it was something huge, because *I had something left to give at the end* and I couldn't believe it.

We raced toward the finish line, huge smiles on our faces. Robert was cheering for us. My parents were there, and seeing their faces was truly a homecoming. No one knows quite how far you've come like your family. Nancy's husband, Jon, was waiting. (He ran at an incredible pace, finishing in 5 hours to our 6:13.) I felt stronger, fitter, better, more satisfied than ever. I smiled nonstop for the remainder of the day.

We got medals and finisher jackets, posed for pictures, and went to soak our legs in the mossy lake. I showered up and bade farewell to the cozy trailer and my friends. My parents had the backseat set up for a queen, with pillows, blankets, snacks, water, wine, and movies (selected by my brother, Jon, cinematic guru). We went straight out for a Mexican dinner, and I didn't care that I was dressed in the equivalent of pajamas on a Saturday night.

I woke up on Sunday, still smiling. I got out of bed, put the dogs out, fixed coffee, and noticed the most bizarre and wondrous thing. I almost wanted to go back to bed and get up again just to be sure it was real.

I wasn't sore! I am not kidding around.

It's Monday now. I am still not sore and I am still smiling.

24 PACE

By mile 24 of a marathon, you pretty much know whether you are on pace or not. You know whether you have what it takes to complete the race and meet your goal, or you know if you have deviated from your pace so much that there is no way on God's green earth that you can earn it back. Pace is elusive to me. I don't wear a Garmin (yet, but maybe I should), and I have no idea what a specific pace feels like; they all fall somewhere between *ahhh* and *ouch,* and even this changes from one day to the next. I gauge my pace by where I am positioned in the pack with my friends. If a coach asked me what my pace was, I would probably answer, "Definitely behind Paige, Karen, and Sara. Somewhere around Katie, Amy, Ellen, and Jena?" If that coach was anyone other than Cassie, he or she would look at me like I was completely nuts.

Pace is essential, in running and in life. We have to know when to pick it up and when to conserve. It is the most strategic component of running a good race, and as such it requires the greatest amount of maturity. It is a worthwhile study and one that never ends, because our abilities and our goals are always in a state of flux. But if you know your ideal pace, you know yourself. From moment to moment, I want to be able to adjust so I can handle what is required of me. I want to have what it takes to push it when I need to be there for myself or someone I care about. I want to be comfortable with rest when it's time to recover. Often for runners, it is a greater challenge to be still than to press on. We need to be equally adept at both, knowing that they serve us well.

BECAUSE I CAN

This week marked my reinitiation into speed work. It was my first time back to running group after the Austin Marathon. I would have gone last week, but I was the lucky reading mommy in Bella's class (so I got to slide another week). I have not had any lingering postmarathon aches and pains, just an overall feeling of tiredness and malaise. Maybe it's the fact that the marathon is behind me and I don't have a looming goal staring me down. Or maybe I am just in a phase of not being particularly motivated to hurt. Maybe I'm resting. Maybe I'm lazy.

I feel content, and yet I wonder if contentment can breed a sense of complacency. I thought about this very thing as Coach Cassie explained the combination hill-repeat and fartlek workout on Wednesday morning: four intense continuous circuits, beginning with a steep climb, leveling into a relatively even stretch, catching your breath on the downhill, then running a tempo loop around the park. Because of our varying levels of experience, Cassie gives orders plainly, using terms of exertion levels instead of pace times. (Some folks don't know their pace; others, like me, are rebellious and don't wear a watch. I like to feel my pain, not quantify it. Either that or I can never figure the damn thing out in time to make it worthwhile.) So the hill, on a scale of 1 to 10, is supposed to be a 7, and the tempo loop is supposed to be an 8. That sounded pretty grim to me. "Continuous means no water, and tempo means no air to chat," said Cass, with her usual no-nonsense charm. She has ways of translating her raw athleticism into terminology we can't avoid understanding.

Work like this is easier for me when I have a marathon I want to survive, a heartache I want to numb, unsaid things I want to scream, a problem I need to untangle, or anger I want to unleash. Imagine a petulant artist who can create only when she is miserable, so she wears only black and lots of eyeliner, chain-smokes, and creates obscene levels of drama in all her relationships to insure proper levels of toxicity needed for inspiration. For me it's strange; it's as if I only want to hurt like that when I'm trying to displace pain from someplace else. Otherwise I am happiest when I am comfortably running along. I wish I could borrow some of Paige's innate competitiveness, because I just don't work that way. She can fly out of the gates like a whipped horse just because it's Wednesday.

This workout was far from comfortable, and there was no way to just "run along." So it was here, on my third lap of that blasted hill, that I started to wonder about the dangers of complacency. When we work this hard to get in the kind of shape that yields 26.2 miles, it's complacent to let that fitness slide just because it's uncomfortable to keep it up. As you know, I am all for respectful rest for the body and spirit, but I think there is a difference between rest and regression. I fought my natural impulse to plug along, and I tried harder. Cassie yelled at me to hold my shoulders back, pump my arms—my body listens to her even when I ignore her, even when she only talks to me in my own head.

Running hard only because I'm being chased is not good enough. I need to run hard because I can, because I should. Not all the time, of course, but often enough that I don't forget what it feels like to burn. I can apply the same concept intellectually, spiritually, emotionally . . . where ordinary times of life are the workroom, the classroom, the track. We need to practice our work here. We need to study, learn, run the drills over and over again so that when the moment of crisis comes (and it always does), we do what needs to be done automatically. In the moment of crisis it's too late to train.

I tried to catch my breath on the downhill, but it was eluding me. My brain was full of all these thoughts. I decided that I need to train my motivation the same way I train my legs and lungs, guiding it, informing it, refining it, and cajoling it from one level to another. Complacency is not okay. Contentment is. They are different.

I ran the last tempo loop harder and faster than my first, my breath rasping and my shoes kicking up gravel beneath me.

SPOT-ON, BERTHA

People keep asking me about my next marathon like I must have a next marathon. It's valid, though, to wonder why someone would go on 1½- to 2-plus-hour runs on weekends without a plan or goal in mind. I wonder the same thing myself sometimes, when my alarm clock goes off at 5 a.m. on a Saturday and I grab Gatorade, snacks, and dollar bills on my way out the door, keys in my teeth, pulling my cap down low, rubbing the sleep out of my eyes, and hopping on one leg to get my shoe on. Or when I pop an ibuprofen in the afternoon, achy and tired after my morning exploits in the oppressive heat.

"Why?" one might ask. "What's the point?"

I don't exactly know how to articulate the answer, even though articulating things is my specialty. (I hope my editor isn't reading this.) I know I always feel better after my run, even if I'm depleted in my body—my soul is full. I know I need that time with my friends. But as far as a goal . . .? A method to my madness and my miles . . .?

One morning this week I read a devotional before my run and had one of those *Ahh-HA!* moments when I can picture the cartoon lightbulb in a bubble over my head. The devotional theme was a reflection on the importance of preparedness.

It began by saying, "Bless me and make me a blessing." Then it went on to explain that the biggest way we can help those we love is by having already helped ourselves. This means we are supposed to deal with our own stuff, tidy up our own lives and our own hearts. We are supposed to work at our fitness (of course this is my word, not the author's) in all capacities (spiritual, mental, emotional, physical), and not simply because it is an end in itself but because we are in a constant state of being made ready. If we are fit, in every sense of that word, then when someone we love needs us, we can make a difference for her. In that way and in many others, every hill is a metaphor. We trudge up it knowing that we may be called upon to carry someone else up it the next time. In this manner and for this reason, we work hard to be stronger, fitter, faster, more agile. Fitness has a purpose far beyond vanity, beyond even good health, when a person is trained to think of it in these terms.

The author of this particular devotional is a woman named Bertha Munro. She had one line in there that buckled my knees, a line that summed up everything about fitness to me: "You cannot always do something to help your friends, but you can always be something to help them . . ."

Okay, that's it. That's why I train, right there. Thanks, Bertha. I don't train because I want to be able to *do* things (run a faster 5-K, beat my marathon PR, make someone eat my dust on a trail, though those things aren't bad). I train because I want to *be* someone better than I would be if I didn't train. If someone I love is faltering, I want to be the kind of woman who can haul some ass; I want to be first on the scene. I want to be strong enough to carry some of his or her burden along with my own. I want to have a clear head and a clear heart so if I am asked for advice, I can offer wisdom instead of mere opinion. If my big opportunity arises to serve, I want to be ready. If it takes more out of me than I anticipated, I want to know something about endurance. If the terrain suddenly changes, I want to be steady. If someone I love looks at me with eyes full of fear, terrified that she won't be able to finish whatever happens to lie ahead of her, I want to look at her, wordless, with unblinking eyes that assure her that there is no way that she won't.

That right there is why I run. In case you were wondering.

A WOMAN WHO RUNS

I am the odd man out. Don't get me wrong, I'm happy as can be to be in California for a chunk of time this summer. There is only one flaw: My training buddies have started marathon training without me, in Texas. God knows they must be melting, but that will only make them tougher. They have also done something we have never done before: They have joined a marathon training group—Gilbert's Gazelles, which meets several times a week. Gulp. I thought of starting my own group out west—Kristin's Koalas, maybe? Somehow it hasn't gained momentum. I sometimes run with friends out here, but often it's just me and the sea.

Without my friends, I have no concept of time, distance, directions, or pace. This shows just how much I rely on them, very likely to my detriment. Somehow I have to be ready to fit back into my pack when I return. I'm trying to think about what to do. I could join a training group here. I could invest in a Garmin and finally learn about pace. I could get an online training program from Cassie and follow instructions, being the diligent student I am. I could have my friends e-mail me whatever they did in Texas time and copy them in Pacific time; the 2-hour time difference might work out just fine.

More than anything, I am feeling uneasy about the level of seriousness they have taken on in my absence. Especially since I feel more like running for pleasure and enjoying my vay-cay with my children. Without being obsessive, I usually get in better shape when I'm here. I have a gym I like, a weekly 5-K to measure my progress, trails to run, mountains to climb, bluffs to explore, routes I have timed, and fast friends and energetic children to keep up with. I should be fine, but part of me is nervous I won't have what it takes upon return. Maybe a part of me feels like they are going to leave me behind.

It occurred to me this morning, as I forced myself to haul ass up a giant hill, that instead of being whiny and fearful and having my feelings hurt, I need to buck up and suck it up. They are just doing their thing, and I need to do mine. I need to face my training with intent and confidence, all on my own. I need to get my brain and my body on the same page and figure it out. I know that running comes more easily and naturally to them than it does to me, but that just means I need to work twice as hard.

As I made the final curve after the giant hill, gulping great lungfuls of foggy morning air, I crossed the sign where I stop and time myself. Typically at the end of a hard-training summer, a perfect ascent for me on this hill is 30 minutes on the nose. I hit it on the nose this morning, *at the beginning of summer.* "YES!" I squealed, scaring a man out getting his newspaper in his robe.

It's time for this runner girl to start acting like a woman who runs.

25 ROADBLOCKS

There is nothing that has more potent potential to take us off course than a roadblock. We're running along at a nice clip, our route specifically mapped out, and then, out of nowhere, totally unexpected, there it is—the orange sign in big block letters: ROAD CLOSED. Now what?

Whether we are sidelined with an illness or injury, fall short of our goals to set a PR or qualify for Boston, get passed over for a promotion at work, get a bad report from our doctor or our child's teacher, or go through a rough patch with our spouse or a child or a dear friend, having to regroup and reroute is no small ordeal. Some of our roadblocks are circumstantial, some of them are relational, and many of them come from within—and are often rooted in fear or resistance.

When we encounter a ROAD CLOSED sign, in traffic or in life, the next logical thing to look for is a DETOUR sign. As runners we know the benefit of being light on our feet; we have to be able to adapt quickly to climate changes, terrain changes, pace changes, and course changes. No matter what we come up against, there is always a detour. And sometimes, when we're really lucky, the detour leads us to a more scenic route. Roadblocks always have something to teach us. Maybe it's a lesson in patience or perseverance. Maybe it's an opportunity to rethink the direction we chose in the first place. Maybe it's an essential tutorial about life. Maybe it's a profound examination of self.

Whatever we learn, we can be almost certain that we would not have learned it any other way. And that is the most direct route from frustration to gratitude, no matter where the detour takes us.

RESISTANCE

Today is day 2 or 3 of Austin posing as Seattle: gray and rainy. The constant pitter-pat of rain on my bedroom window kept me sound asleep through my normal 5 a.m. wake-up for an early morning run with my friends. The morning wore on and the rain picked up, so I opted for yoga instead. I got to the studio early enough that I could sprawl out on my mat in the heated 80-something-degree room and close my eyes for a bit. I pretended I was on a raft someplace tropical. Just as I was about to order my first cocktail, our teacher entered and started class, turning my raft back into a mat.

We began in Child's Pose, with our foreheads smashed into the ground. I like this because I prefer to begin anything, especially yoga, in a posture of humility. This particular teacher always begins class with a reading from some yoga-guru book she has. And just as I used to comb the newspaper for my horoscope and then freak out when it seemed written just for me, every time I have ever gone to her class, her reading may as well begin, "Dear Kristin . . ." It's so cool that it's borderline eerie.

Today was no different.

She began with the question "What are you resisting today?" She went on to read about the fact that the very thing that we resist is the thing we must be compelled to investigate or address. The place to begin is to recognize, and then properly name, the point of resistance. Once we properly name it, we can begin to approach it and dismantle it. The author stated that the point of resistance is nearly always something from within us, not something from outside. And the lesson we need most is embedded in our resistance—the thing we won't look at, the issue we won't address, the thing we won't try, the transgression we will not forgive, the conversation we won't have, the dream we refuse to realize.

The lesson of the day is always further intensified as it plays out in our practice. When we were in a particularly difficult pose, the kind that for me creates muscle shaking so intense it might register on the Richter scale, our teacher asked quietly, "Why are you resisting instead of breathing?" A very good question, indeed. And again when she gave the choice between staying in a certain position or extending it even further into an inversion, like a handstand, she stated to all of those who held back (me), "It isn't as hard as you think. But you have to overcome your resistance to try." Part of my holding back has to do with the legitimate period of hard work required to raise my strength and my confidence to matching levels sufficient for the task at hand. But the other part is, I will never know if I'm there if I never have the nerve to test myself.

I have serious resistance to pushing my quaking body upward and somehow balancing on my meager arms, without toppling directly over the top and cracking my enormous front teeth (phobia?) on the ground. I don't have any trust in myself in this regard. And my body knows this. I am just like a good horse on a jumping circuit with a mediocre rider; the horse can sense the rider's fear and reluctance and abruptly stops short of the jump or goes around it entirely—even when the horse could have easily cleared the jump. Without mutual trust and cooperation between horse and rider, neither party catches any air. I think my body is like that horse. It senses that I don't believe in it sometimes, and so it holds back or holds out on me. I get that sometimes when I run: "Uh-oh, it's getting hard to breathe" or "Mayday, Mayday, this hurts. Reel her in." And I let my resistance dictate my performance instead of letting my horse run.

I wonder if the reading today is true, that if we can name our point of resistance, we can begin to overcome it.

My point of resistance is consistently called *fear* (fear of pain, fear of failure, fear of wandering too far outside my comfort zones and getting lost or hurt, fear of the implications of success, fear of opening up my heart unwisely, fear of saying the wrong thing—or perhaps worse, saying nothing at all—fear of doing irreparable damage, fear of missing my cue, fear of mislabeling adventure as foolishness, fear of missing the point or missing the person, fear of wasting precious time).

I know this resistance affects my ability to do inversions in yoga, to break PRs in my running, to invest more deeply in my relationships, and to take more risks in my personal and professional life. I have to consider what might happen now that I've named it: *Take that, fear. I know who you are. I know where you live. Now, scram.*

TAPPING IN

I taped a segment for a television program the other day, and the makeup artist and I got into a conversation about running. As she attempted to slick down the humid-weather frizzies in my hair and camouflage the shadows under my eyes, she shared with me that she was lacking motivation these days when it came to running.

"I don't understand it," she said. "Several years ago I was training for a marathon; I couldn't wait to get out there and push myself. Now I can't seem to get going, and I feel out of shape, but even that isn't motivating me. I don't know what's going on."

She tried to matte down the glare of my skin with powder as she spoke, and I wondered if it had been a bad idea to try to fit in that hot yoga class an hour earlier. I thought about what she was saying, reflecting on times in my life when I felt exceptionally motivated, on a mission when it came to running. I asked her, "Were you happy when you were training like that?"

She got quiet for a minute, then, "I was happy when I was running, but no, other than that, my life was miserable at the time."

Ahhh.

I have run like that before. I have used running as my therapy, a way to literally hurt in order to work out other hurts. A purging feeling like that is hard to replicate any other way, so it's easy to stay motivated because we are seeking release and relief. We are often "sad-skinny" and attempt to control our pain because we feel like we want to control something, anything. But what happens when that painful season passes? I asked her how her life felt today. "Oh," she said, "I'm really happy. I'm at peace." It made me smile to think of how much runners share, how easy it is for us to find common ground.

So when she's happy and peaceful, she doesn't feel as much like running because she associates success in running with working something out, overcoming. When she has nothing to work through, she starts losing her motivation to work. Maybe some of you can relate? I told her I understood completely. I thought what she needed was a way to redefine her idea of success and come up with a new association for running. Maybe she needed to begin to associate running with things like *fun, celebration,* and *peace.* Maybe if she took away the theme of *striving* from her running, she would feel more compelled to go out and play.

Just as we sometimes need a girls' or guys' weekend to revisit our friendships with fresh eyes, or a date with our spouse or significant other to renew our connection, our relationship with running needs maintenance, too. If it always feels like work, we are missing the joy. And as author John Eldredge says so beautifully, "You have to be intentional about the joy."

BLINKERS

In the introduction portion of a speech I gave last week, I talked about being stricken with the fraud complex. I described how easy it is to feel out of our element, outside our comfort zone, beyond our capabilities, posing as an expert on the outside but feeling sorely insufficient on the inside. It's not a fun feeling. Without warning, at any given moment, I can feel like a maternal fraud, a relational fraud, a professional fraud, an athletic fraud, a spiritual fraud—any of these or a combination of them, especially when crippled by fatigue, malaise, or PMS.

Just this week, I have experienced an amalgam of various fraud complexes. Yesterday morning I lost my patience with Bella and her outfit selection process before school—and spent the rest of the day wishing I could have a morning do-over to eradicate maternal fraud. Later I went to running group and felt like I had a ball and chain attached to each ankle, slogging up the hills watching my springy-stepped friends, feeling every bit the athletic fraud. I had a big burst of a book idea last week, got really excited, and e-mailed a well-connected person about it. This week I got the reply, and it's sitting in my in-box; the professional fraud is concerned that the follow-through won't be as interesting as the idea. I prayed with a friend that she would be able to accept grace, only to be chided by the spiritual fraud complex, reminding me of all the times I deny myself the same peace.

I am getting better about naming the fraud complexes so I can acknowledge them and let them go. When I view them with a sense of perspective and (perhaps more importantly) a sense of humor, I am more quickly able to stop thinking about how I might miss the mark, and I start focusing on my target. My friend Leticia says, "Honey, far better to fall forward than backslide." She's right.

A measure of clarity came to me on this subject as I was driving home from Grace's acting class in evening traffic. I was sitting at a red light with my blinker on. It occurred to me that a turn signal is clear and common, an accepted and universal point of understanding. I put on my blinker and all the cars around me know I'm planning to make a left. At some point, in the near future, when the timing is right and the coast is clear, I'm going to make my move, and everyone knows it. We don't forget to put the blinker on. We trust other people to follow through on their blinkers. And we all get where we're going in one piece, with some measure of order. It works.

So I'm putting my blinker on. I'm heading in the direction of being a better mom, a better friend, a better daughter, granddaughter, sister; a better writer, a better speaker, a better thinker, a better runner, and maybe someday a better wife. Even if you can't tell a difference right now, even if it appears that I am stuck in traffic, that's where I'm going. I'm in the turn lane.

BUTTERFLY GIRL

Saturday afternoon we worked on a project for Luke's second-grade class—the construction of a caterpillar. I covered the kitchen countertop with materials and watched Luke go to town. The body was Styrofoam balls, cut in half and toothpicked together to make the mandatory 13 segments. Glue-gunned Cheerios became the spiracles so the critter could breathe, pipe cleaners became antennae, and penne pasta topped with an Apple Jack became the prolegs.

"What are prolegs?" I wanted to know.

Luke, the budding, almost-8-year-old entomologist, replied, "The prolegs have suction cups on them so they stick; these disappear. The true legs are the legs that stay with the butterfly."

Well, I'll be. The message wasn't lost on me Saturday afternoon, as I was already anxiety-ridden about a marathon relay on Sunday morning. My running lately has been a little blocked (I guess this is like writer's block, but for sport?), and it occurred to me that I was using my prolegs—getting suctioned down, stuck in old patters of fear and in uncomfortable comfort zones. I want to start using my true legs.

As added motivation, the group was racing to try to raise funds for Cassie, so she can work less and devote more time to training before the Olympic marathon trial in April.

I tried to get the kids to bed early so I could be well rested for Sunday morning. But sleep did not come easily for me. I woke up in a foul mood.

The marathon relay was split into a 12-K (Paige), a 10-K (me), another 10-K (Katie), a 5-K (Katie's Adam), and a final 5-K (Paige's Jamil). My heart was clogging my throat as I listened for our team number at the transition point and nervously scanned the crowds, watching for Paige to come flying in so I could take the wristband. I really had to pee, but I waited too long and the portapotties were too far away, and then I worried she would arrive and I would be nowhere in sight.

I saw her approach in classic Paige fashion, red-faced and utterly spent, giving every last ounce to push toward the line. She handed me the wadded-up wristband and said something that I couldn't hear over my pulse slamming against my inner ear. It was a primal fight-or-flight moment for me, and I'm happy to report I chose flight. The race was hot and difficult.

There was a stretch along Cesar Chavez Street that looked like an endless pilgrimage marked into oblivion by orange cones. I nearly had a meltdown, a total face-off with futility, when I could not see the turnaround point. Either God spoke to me or I had a multipersonality moment: "Run to the end of your hat, that's all." So I did that. I stopped looking ahead into the distance, tried to even out my ragged terror-breathing, and focused on the steps ahead of me, chasing the brim of my hat.

Every so often I looked down at my hand, where I had put a fake tattoo (from my daughter Grace's collection) of a butterfly. When I made the turn onto Congress Avenue and finally had the end in sight, I kept looking at the butterfly and repeating "true legs" to myself until I crossed the line, red-faced and spent and very happy to see Katie.

There is something powerful about sharing the burden of the marathon distance with people you know and love. Together we ran a 3:23 marathon, 12 precious minutes faster than my own PR. The passing of the baton (or wristband, in our case) reminded me of something I read about an ancient Olympic race. I looked it up; it's called the *lampadedromia,* which is Greek for "torch relay." The goal is not only to complete the distance but to keep the torch lit for the duration.

That pretty much sums it up for me right now, where I am with this sport we love so much. Fear, prolegs, runner's block, and all, I refuse to let the torch go out.

26 GRATITUDE

I believe that gratitude is one of the most powerful forces in the universe. It is underrated and underutilized, yet it has the power to transform people and perspectives. Maybe that's why I saved it for mile marker 26. When you hit mile 26 in a marathon, the final 0.2 can seem like a pilgrimage. Your body might be aching or shutting down. You might be pulling over to stretch—or retch. You might be in tears. You might be ready to quit. You might be saying words you never utter in any other circumstance. I have done all of these things. And I can tell you, each time, in that moment, that it was not my training, not my endurance, not my "mind over matter" mentality, not my friends (okay, maybe a little bit), and not my determination that got me through the final stretch. It was the power of gratitude.

When things get really miserable in my life, when I can't think about one tiny thing that feels redeeming, at the precise point when I am fading to black—I remember gratitude. I start to think about all the things I am thankful for, and I begin to recount them one at a time. And when I do this, something overtakes me that eclipses both my mood and my meagerness. With every thankful statement I make, power pours into me and carries doubt and weakness away with its current. I have seen this work so profoundly in major life moments that I am committed to pursuing it in my everyday life.

I'll start by saying that I'm thankful to share this chapter with you.

I GET TO

Isn't it awesome how the slightest shift in attitude or terminology can create an entirely new perspective?

I had a meeting on Wednesday that I had to be showered and presentable for, which meant that my usual running group time, immediately before my Bible study, was not going to work. I explained my schedule to Cassie, and she sent me an e-mail outlining this week's workout. Of course, she made me swear to secrecy, because naturally, if people know about our torture in advance, our numbers are far fewer.

I didn't tell anyone about the workout and showed up to the specified park location just after school drop-off. I had a water bottle, my watch, a printout of the e-mail telling me what to do, and my trepidation about being able to do a workout like this all by myself. Being a good schoolgirl by nature, I followed instructions. I did a 10-minute warmup on the trails, drills (much to the amusement of the homeless people in the park, who looked at me like I was crazy, a lonely lady doing high-knees and butt-kickers), two eternal hill repeats, two fartlek loops around the park (1 minute on, 1 off), two more eternal hill repeats, two more fartlek loops around the park (30 seconds on, 30 off), then a cooldown. It was humid and hard, and it felt strange to push myself using my watch instead of my position in the running hierarchy of my friends. It was a workout for my body, sure, but it also stretched some new muscles in my morale.

I started to hear the voices in my head: *I have to get up this hill . . . I have to complete this loop. I have to, I have to . . .*

All this in the context of other news I learned this week: that my friend and training buddy from my trail group last year has recently been diagnosed with ALS (Lou Gehrig's disease). Odd to think that just a year ago I was doing 20-mile runs with this crazy, fun-loving, fit, healthy, ultramarathon-running guy, and now his life has turned upside down. I e-mailed with him this week, checking on him and sending some love his way, and I was happy to hear the same sense of humor, irony, and perspective as always. He even joked that he has become an administrative assistant to the disease and his new "boss" can be quite demanding. Meanwhile, the news has continued to weigh heavily on my heart.

He even changed my perspective when I was pushing up that hill and thinking of him and everything he's facing right now. *I have to . . .* No, I *don't* have to. *I want to. I get to.*

I get to charge up this hill. I get to wake up early and run. I get to hit the gym after work. I get to work on a new writing project. I get to make dinner for my children. I get to clean my house. I get to pack lunches. I get to help with homework. I get to take Luke to football, Grace to drama, Bella to choir. I get to pick them up from school. I get to go to the grocery store. I get to run an errand/do a favor for my husband/wife. I get to call my mom/dad/grandparents today. I get to help my neighbors while they are out of town. I get to make healthy choices for my next meal. I get to stand up for myself or someone I love. I get to train for this marathon, triathlon, half marathon, 10-K, 5-K . . .

The more I thought about what I get to do, the less I realized I had to do. It was just a shift, just a new perspective, just a new and more grateful method for labeling the things in my life. Think about it—if you stopped yourself every single time you were about to say *I have to* and changed it to *I get to,* it might change your entire experience. It might also have a profound effect on the people you are speaking to. Try it.

GRUNIONS

My day today began with a sleepy-eyed, barefoot stumble to the curb with coffee cup in one hand and trail shoes in the other, water bottle and banana tucked under my arm. My friend Terra wheeled up at 6:30 and we were off to Romero Trail. It's best to be half asleep because the base of this trail is rather jolting otherwise, a steep and seemingly endless ascent, merciless and totally oxygen-depriving without a proper warmup. By the time I am fully conscious, we have gained enough ground that the endless ascent is broken up by brief sections of lesser grade. I am typically more conversational at this point, which is good because Terra brought up something interesting: the idea of letting your inner child come out to play and the idea of how often we resist it. My kids talk about the "kid inside" sometimes, and they usually make a comment when they catch a glimpse of the kid in me.

They see her sometimes on the trampoline at Dad's house, when I kick off my shoes, climb inside the protective netting, and "popcorn" them or jump in a circle with them, holding hands and giggling uncontrollably, my hair flying madly above my head. They see her when we hike and stop and take the time to make forts out of branches or find lizards. I see her dusty and scampering down a trail, or pensive in front of the blank canvas on my easel, or wearing huge sunglasses and a floppy beach hat in the Beetle filled with kids and sandy boogie boards, listening to Bob Marley on the way to the beach.

The kid in all of us came out one night this week, when my parents, my brother, and I piled the kids in the car way after bedtime to drive to the beach in hopes of seeing the grunions. Grunions, supposedly—we never did see them—are fish that come up on the shore to lay eggs—thousands of fish glowing silver in the moonlight and covering the beach. This appealed to the kid in me, the scientist in the basement of my being, abandoned back in high school sometime after honors chemistry or physics. We bundled up and waited. I never go to the beach late at night, and it's fantastic. The beach is like your most interesting friend (or your spouse, if you are really lucky), always surprising and yet still somehow a comfort at the same time. It's a place that looks and feels different at every time of day, depending on tides, weather, and light.

At night it's magical. Luke and Grace ran along the shore playing flashlight tag, actively on the lookout for any signs of silver in the water. Bella started to get sleepy, so I sat cross-legged on the cool sand and held her hooded little body across my lap. I watched the way the light from the full moon splayed across the waves. The rhythmic sound against the shore lulled me into that cozy pocket of consciousness just between sleep and wakefulness, where a placid sense of well-being overtakes any thought. Bella's breathing deepened and became regular as she melted into my lap, fully asleep. The fish never showed while we were there, and though normally I would have been disappointed or labeled it a failed mission, I considered it one of the finer memories of summer so far. So now *grunion* is a new term for me, something much larger, deeper, and more poignant than any silver fish.

> **grunion** *n*: anything we seek that eludes us, but in place of which we are mysteriously blessed with something sweeter than what we set out after in the first place

That moment on the beach at night with Bella in my arms was a grunion. My love life these days is a grunion. PRs in my current running results are grunions (as fitness and fun are becoming blissfully indistinguishable).

My shore is covered with them, glinting and hopeful, now that I've finally learn how to look.

GRATITUDE

I love Thanksgiving, a mellow, easy holiday when the only expectation is to gift each other with the preparation and sharing of a meal. It is a day that runs counter to the striving and acquiring mode of our society and offers respite—a day spent in restful, grateful acknowledgment of what is already there.

Wherever I spend Thanksgiving, whether in Austin or away, I like to start the morning by running the local turkey trot. This year, just after 5 a.m., I heard a small voice next to my ear, the telltale scream-whisper of a child. (Bella, in this case.)

"*Mommy!*" she breathed.

Startled, groggy: "Yes? What is it?"

"I want to run the turkey race!"

Suppressing a smile: "Okay, honey, you can. But it doesn't start for 4 hours, so can we sleep some more?" I lifted the corner of the down comforter as the universal signal of invitation and she jumped in, wedging her tiny body in exact conformation to mine, pressing cold toes into my warm legs, and soon we were both asleep.

Later, I extricated myself from our tangle to make coffee and begin peeling potatoes so I could make headway on the preparations before ducking out to run. The day before Thanksgiving there was a long, slow downpour, so walking outside in the morning was almost surreal. The day was so clean and bright and hopeful that it sparkled. Bella and I took our old Beetle convertible to meet up with our good friends the Allisons. Michael has a stress fracture in his foot, so he watched their youngest (Sammi) while Jamie and I ran with Bella and Kate. As we were registering, we met up with another of our best friends, Scott Dunlap, and made our way to the start. The little girls took off at breakneck speed, the idea of pacing utterly foreign and a waste of exuberance.

We covered 4 four miles in childlike patterns of sprints, jogging, and walking. Bella found a flyer for a lost dog, so we spent about a mile hunting for the wayward pooch (to no avail). At one point Bella took off on the dirt path next to us, announcing, "Look! I'm *trail running!*" Scott, being a trail ultramarathoner, was pleased at the protégé potential. I couldn't stop smiling; the freedom of a child is contagious. It was a beautiful morning to catch up with friends and enjoy some special time with my daughter. Anyone with more than one child knows the rare sweetness of a little one-on-one.

We crossed the finish line en masse and dove into the postrace spread of muffins, Goldfish crackers, and powdered doughnuts. Bella and I stopped on the way home to put the top down on the car, and we reentered the family fray energized and giddy, the scent of outdoors in our hair.

Thanksgiving should serve as a reminder, not an exception. What if gratitude could become our default? There is nothing as potent as gratitude when it comes to quelling a longing, calming restlessness, quieting anxious thoughts, filling emptiness, overcoming doubt, or celebrating abundance. It is a force we can tap into at will, one with the ability to change our perspective and fuel our potential.

When our starting point is a place of gratitude, we have already won before we begin.

SUSPICIOUS PACKAGING

On a run recently (when I always do my purest thinking), I had a mindbender of a thought about gratitude. What if (and this is a big *if*) I could wrap my head around being thankful for things that don't normally fall into the blessings category? Bear with me. I mean being specifically thankful for the things that seemingly did not go right at all.

For example, an idea or a relationship that "failed." A goal that was not met. An injury. An illness. Loneliness. Delays. Reversals. Embarrassments. Struggles. Weaknesses. Addictions. Temptations. Depression. Setbacks of every kind and every degree.

These types of things do not typically make it onto my gratitude radar. These things are total flops! Why should we think about them gratefully? Why should we consider them at all?

My mindbender came along these lines, at about mile 10, and it had to do with opening my mind (and my heart) to consider that every no makes room for an unexpected yes. Every delay fortifies our patience and allows for time to prepare and mature. Every physical setback forces us to rest and recover, building strength in other ways. Every weakness and temptation heightens our awareness of our need for others and for God. Every bout of loneliness or depression reminds us to love lavishly when we are able. Every embarrassment keeps our sense of humor intact. Every gaping hole of loss could be a window.

Perhaps every failure is not really a failure at all but a blessing in suspicious packaging.

So for all these things, the obviously good and the not so obvious, I am going to try to be thankful this week. I'm going to slow down and think. I'm going to appreciate the little things— the gestures, sentiments, and details often overlooked. I'm going to savor what I eat and the people I am eating with. I am going to run and center myself in gratitude, thankful for blessings of every kind.

A GRATITUDE ATTITUDE

The desire and ability to run is indeed something to be thankful for. When fellow runners are sidelined by injuries, I ache for them because I know what it means to have something precious taken away. When I can't run, I feel like I have lost my release valve. Suddenly any race plans or personal goals turn to mist, and the only thing that matters is that I can't put my running shoes on, go outside, and put one foot in front of the other at any pace until my head and heart are clear. Running and gratitude are intimately related in my book.

When Paige and I ran the Boston Marathon, our pace bands were free of split times, listing only "gratitude miles." Each mile represented something we are thankful for. This is my running mentality quite often, not just on marathon day. I may not be a great runner in terms of talent, but as far as attitude goes, I am always happy to be here.

I learned something about gratitude when I was going through my divorce (which is incidental; you can put any tough time to fill in the blank). I realized the power I had over my own thoughts. I could have a good or bad day simply by being more conscientious about choosing my mood. Gratitude is like fiber. Fill up on that and it takes up so much room that other things (like negative thinking, resentment, or pity) are crowded out. We are satiated. By focusing on what is, we forget to think about what is not. Even by being thankful for not having things that we don't want, we are replete.

Sometimes the only choice to make in a moment is the choice to have a grateful heart. I can now look something daunting straight in the eye and thank God for the challenge and the way out even before I panic or formulate a strategy. (Okay, I still panic sometimes, but less often.) By choosing to be thankful, we can change the entire energy flow of a situation. Try it. In a moment when you feel low or frustrated with someone, find something to be thankful for and speak it: *Thank you for being patient with me. Thank you for doing what you could. Thank you for being here.*

I hope you can get outside soon, put one foot in front of the other, work up a clean sweat, feel your breath, and take some quiet time to reflect on your blessings.

> Gratitude unlocks the fullness of life. It turns what
> we have into enough, and more. It turns denial into
> acceptance, chaos into order, confusion to clarity
> . . . Gratitude makes sense of our past, brings peace
> for today, and creates a vision for tomorrow.
>
> —MELODY BEATTIE

26.2 Epilogue

I remember my final moments of the New York City Marathon, after my meltdowns and calf cramps had either decided to have mercy on me or left me for dead. I felt surreal, like I suddenly had earplugs in and was moving through a movie montage in my own life. I can tell you, even today, how the crowds lining Central Park looked, cheering and soundless in my mind's eye. I can tell you the way the light fell, dappled and golden through the trees overhead. I remember the way Nancy was smiling; the way Cassie's curly ponytail slapped against her shoulders ahead of me. The moment sparkles for me. You know how people say their life passes before their eyes when they think they are about to die? Well, I can tell you that on my death bed, those moments in Central Park will be a scene that does not end up on the cutting room floor. And I have others like them. The moment I crossed the line of my first ultramarathon, I was *elated*. I felt utterly shocked to find myself in my own skin on the other side of the finish line. I couldn't figure out whether to laugh or cry, so I did both at the same time.

.2 is about completion. .2 is about having what it takes. .2 is about mastering pain. .2 is about getting it done. .2 is the "and over" of "up and over." .2 is about strength. .2 is about commitment. .2 is about growth. .2 is about experience. .2 is about life.

If you have experienced .2, then you will never be the kind of person who does something "almost" or "half-assed." You will never hastily approve something that isn't done right. You will never take a shortcut on effort just because no one is watching.

You will never say, "Eh, it doesn't matter." Because it does matter. If you have slogged or sprinted through the final .2 of a marathon, then you know intimately the difference between 26 and 26.2. And it's not as simple as 200 meters.

.2 is the metaphorical distance between you and any finish line in your life, anything you have ever dreamed of doing or becoming. It's what's separating you from your truest, most authentic self and your most actualized life. It's what's worth thinking about, strategizing about, planning for, training for, and going for.

.2 is simultaneously the end and the beginning. Because when we cross one finish line, we arrive at the next start line, carrying with us everything we learned from prior distance. Hopefully, we manage to drop a few unnecessary things that weigh us down along the way, making our journey lighter as we go along. .2 also marks the final pages of this book. But you and I are just getting started. I cannot tell you how I look forward to sharing the miles ahead.

Godspeed,

Kristin

Acknowledgments

The completion of a book is a glorious and humbling thing. It's a combination of "Hooray, I did it!" and "I sure as heck did not get here on my own."

I have had key people, in decisive moments in my life, who have believed in me. The power of that belief translated into courage, and courage lifted my voice and my perspective out of my head and onto the page. My family and certain teachers come to mind when I think of my childhood.

As a grown-up, or aspiring grown-up, other people also come to mind.

Paige and KT, my friends who believed I could finish my first marathon and were my wingmen across the finish line. That experience changed me, and I will never forget that gift. They later told me my words were good, and I believed them enough to write and submit my first article for *Runner's World* magazine.

David Willey, editor in chief of *Runner's World,* who gave me a blessed opportunity—he gave my words, and me, my very first chance.

Katie Neitz, my *Runner's World* editor, who always challenges me to think harder and go deeper. I love writing, knowing she is shepherding my words and ideas.

Mark Remy, my *Runner's World* online editor, for keeping me real and appreciating my humor.

John Atwood, from Rodale Inc., who believed this book was a worthwhile pursuit.

Stephanie Knapp and Shannon Welch my Rodale editors, and all the talented people who had a hand in the editing and design of *Mile Markers;* who entered into the personal pages of my life with wisdom and tenderness.

To all the readers who follow my work in print and online, thank you. I hope to honor you with words that validate, liberate, and inspire.

Luke, Grace, and Isabelle Armstrong, for reminding me that it's always worthwhile to do what you love, and that you can make a living while making a life.

About the Author

KRISTIN ARMSTRONG is a mother, a writer. and a runner. She has written five previous books: a children's book called *Lance Armstrong: The Race of His Life; Happily Ever After; Strength for the Climb; Work in Progress: An Unfinished Woman's Guide to Grace,* and *Heart of My Heart.* Her work has appeared in *USA Today, Glamour, O, the Oprah Magazine, Parenting,* the *Austin American-Statesman,* and she writes a regular column for *Tribeza* magazine. She is a contributing editor for *Runner's World* magazine and keeps a weekly blog, Mile Markers, on www.runnersworld.com. Kristin has run seven marathons and one ultramarathon. She lives in Austin, Texas, and Santa Barbara, California, with her three children, Luke, Grace, and Isabelle.